Believing on Upside Down Country

The Changing Faith-scape of Bendigo

Believing on Upside Down Country

The Changing Faith-scape of Bendigo

Jennifer Jones, Timothy W Jones, Nadia Rhook and Charles Fahey

with Elizabeth Offer
and Natasha Joyce

ANU PRESS

ANU PRESS

Published by ANU Press
The Australian National University
Canberra ACT 2600, Australia
Email: anupress@anu.edu.au

Available to download for free at press.anu.edu.au

ISBN (paperback): 9781760467272
ISBN (online): 9781760467289

WorldCat (paperback): 1572989740
WorldCat (online): 1572989765

DOI: 10.22459/BUDC.2026

Cover design and layout by ANU Press. Cover photograph copyright Donna Bailey.

This book is published under the aegis of the Humanities and Creative Arts editorial board of ANU Press.

Text copyright © Jennifer Jones, Timothy W Jones, Nadia Rhook and Charles Fahey, 2026
Design and typography copyright © ANU Press, 2026

Contents

List of illustrations vii

Acknowledgments ix

About the authors xi

Introduction 1

1. Religion and social cohesion on the goldfields 13
2. Djaara resilience amid disruption: The impact of settler actions on Aboriginal connections to Country 27
3. Common law and religious difference in Bendigo courtrooms: 'The Chinese Oath' 59

Popout One: Giving as cohesion: 'Hospital Sundays', religion, and medical philanthropy in fin-de-siècle Bendigo 73

4. Jewish, British, middle-class: A history of Jewish adjustment on the Central Victorian Goldfields 81

Popout Two: Spatial organisation and hierarchies of prejudice in Central Victorian goldrush cemeteries 103

5. Divine intention and family misfortune on the Central Victorian Goldfields: How 'Providence orders all things well' 111
6. Building an Irish-Roman Catholic Church on the goldfields and Northern Victoria, 1852–1914 131

Popout Three: Interfaith marriage and Jewish familial identity on the Central Victorian Goldfields: The Herman family experience 155

7. Militant Protestant sectarianism in a religiously plural community: Why Bendigo failed to become a 'Protestant city' 161
8. Faith after the gold rush: Demographic and religious change 179

Popout Four: Completing the Sacred Heart Cathedral: Craft and tradition in Bendigo's faith-scape 203

Popout Five: Emu Point Joss House: The spirit and architecture of faith 211

Popout Six: Transforming 'Old Sandhurst Town' into the Great Stupa of Universal Compassion 217

9. Navigating faith and cultural diversity: The Bendigo Mosque controversy 223

10. Conclusion: Womin-dji-ka (welcome) to Bendigo, a city of flourishing diversity? 243

Glossary 249

Index 251

List of illustrations

Figures

Figure 2.1: Interactions with Aboriginal men per quarter 37

Figure 2.2: Documented interactions between Tragowel and Aboriginal people, by station affiliation 42

Figure 2.3: Stock movement in mobs per quarter, August 1856 – December 1861 42

Figure 4.1: Ballarat synagogue 87

Figure 4.2: Saturday night market in Ballarat, 1868 92

Figure P.1: View from the upper section of White Hills Cemetery looking south east, downslope toward the Chinese and Jewish sections on the creek flat 104

Figure 6.1: Marriages, baptisms and burials conducted at St Kilian's parish, 1852–1880 137

Figure 8.1: Major Christian religions in Bendigo, 1871–1921 180

Figure P.2: Paul Copock on the roof of Sacred Heart Cathedral, 1973 204

Figure P.3: Postcard of Chinese Joss House 212

Figure P.4: People circumambulating the Great Stupa of Universal Compassion, Bendigo, 2022 218

Figure 9.1: Bendigo Mosque 226

Maps

Map 0.1: Victoria, Australia, map 6

Map 0.2: Regional Bendigo map 6

Map 0.3: Bendigo CBD map 7

Tables

Table 2.1: Stations of the Upper Loddon plains, 1847–1884 31

Table 2.2: Named Aboriginal workers engaging with Tragowel, 1856–1861 38

Table 2.3: Unauthorised stock movement across station boundaries prior to fencing, 1857–1861 45

Table 2.4: Progress towards boundary fencing, 1857–1861 46

Table 2.5: Development of local weirs and dams, 1857–1860 48

Table 2.6: Graded contribution to Loddon dam expenses, 1858 50

Table 2.7: The rise of settler infrastructure in the Upper Loddon, 1857–1861 54

Table 2.8: Efforts to create settler infrastructure, 1857–1861 54

Table 5.1: Antipodean deaths in the Hamilton-Hoey families, 1859–1869 117

Acknowledgments

This project was initiated by our Industry Partner, the Aspire Foundation, a cultural and charitable auspice of the Catholic Diocese of Sandhurst. Aspire was concerned by a secularised and monocultural civic identity in Bendigo that had somehow obscured a longer history of religious coexistence and diversity. With funding from the Australian Research Council, and in partnership with Aspire and the City of Greater Bendigo, we aimed to rediscover the processes by which Bendigo had negotiated its religious and cultural diversity over time, as the gold rush transitioned to a gold industry and became today's city. The lead Chief Investigator of our team was Associate Professor Jennifer Jones. The Chief Investigators were Professor Timothy W Jones, Dr Nadia Rhook and Associate Professor Charles Fahey. Our Partner Investigator, archivist at the Sandhurst Diocese, was Dr Donna Bailey. Funding provided by the Australian Research Council, Industry Partners and La Trobe University supported two Higher Degree Researchers, Dr Elizabeth Offer and Ms Natasha Joyce. Our project was supported by expert research assistance from Dr Brian Rhule, who worked as Project Officer and assisted with the research and writing of Chapter Seven 'Militant Protestant sectarianism in a religiously plural community: Why Bendigo failed to become a "Protestant City"'. Dr Rachel Goldlust provided research assistance for Chapter Eight 'Faith after the gold rush: Demographic and religious change' and the research and writing in Popout Four 'Completing the Sacred Heart Cathedral: Craft and tradition in Bendigo's faith-scape'. Thanks also to Susan Poole, who made a vital contribution via statistical data and analysis in Chapter Two. Research assistance and expert guidance are important to our outputs, and we gratefully acknowledge these collaborations. We are especially grateful for the oversight of the Aspire Foundation staff and Traditional Owners represented by the Djaara Clans Traditional Owner Group, who both reviewed relevant sections of the manuscript.

The research and writing were undertaken on Djaara, Wiradjuri, Dhudhuroa and Wurundjeri lands, and on Whadjuk Noongar boodja. We acknowledge the Traditional Owners of these unceded lands and pay respect to their Elders, past and present.

About the authors

Our research team brought together scholars from different backgrounds with different personal histories and relationships to the Bendigo region and to faith, spirituality, and cultural difference. We are all white settlers, some the first generation in our family to be born in Australia, and others whose ancestors were early settlers and farmers. Some of us grew up in Bendigo, some have lived there for short and long periods of time and others have only visited. Between us, we are people of faith, people who once had faith and people who have never had affiliation with religion. As detailed below, we each led the research and writing for different aspects of the project and book. We hope that our multifaceted perspectives bring a richness to this book and to understandings of faith, spirituality, social cohesion and belonging.

Jennifer Jones is a national award-winning educator whose reparative, place-based pedagogy assists students to recognise rural and Indigenous diversity. Her research interests include Indigenous Australian history, rural and religious history, and histories of childhood and education. Jennifer led the research and writing for the Introduction; Chapter Two, 'Djaara resilience amid disruption: The impact of settler actions on Aboriginal connections to Country'; Chapter Five, 'Divine intention and family misfortune on the Central Victorian Goldfields: How "Providence orders all things well"'; Chapter Seven, 'Militant Protestant sectarianism in a religiously plural community: Why Bendigo failed to become a "Protestant city"'; Popout Four, 'Completing the Sacred Heart Cathedral: Craft and tradition in Bendigo's faith-scape'; Popout Six, 'Transforming "Old Sandhurst Town" into the Great Stupa of Universal Compassion'; and Chapter Ten, 'Conclusion: Womin-dji-ka (welcome) to Bendigo, a city of flourishing diversity?'.

Timothy W Jones is a historian and social researcher whose work has focused on equality and wellbeing in various contexts related to religion, gender and sexuality. Tim led the research and writing for Chapter One, 'Religion and social cohesion on the goldfields'; Chapter Nine, 'Navigating faith and cultural diversity: The Bendigo Mosque controversy' and he collaborated with Charles Fahey to research and write Chapter Eight, 'Faith after the gold rush: Demographic and religious change'.

Nadia Rhook is a non-Indigenous writer and educator who is interested in the histories and geographies of colonisation, language and belonging. Nadia is a published poet. Her research and writing forms the basis of Chapter Three, 'Common law and religious difference in Bendigo courtrooms: "The Chinese Oath"'; Popout One, 'Giving as cohesion: "Hospital Sundays", religion and medical philanthropy in fin-de-siècle Bendigo'; Popout Five, 'Emu Point Joss House: The spirit and architecture of faith' and Chapter Ten, 'Conclusion: Womin-dji-ka (welcome) to Bendigo, a city of flourishing diversity?'.

Charles Fahey taught history at La Trobe University from 1990 until his retirement in 2018. He is renowned for research exploring Australian labour, rural and mining history. Charles led the research and writing for Chapter Six, 'Building an Irish-Roman Catholic Church on the goldfields and Northern Victoria, 1852–1914' and Chapter Eight, 'Faith after the gold rush: Demographic and religious change'.

Elizabeth Offer is a professional historian and Heritage Consultant. She also works as a Research Officer at La Trobe University and is Vice President of the Professional Historians Association (Victoria and Tasmania). Awarded a Doctor of Philosophy by La Trobe University in 2021, her thesis examined the connection between an emerging British identity and the shifting religious practices of the Hebrew Congregations that formed in Bendigo and Ballarat between 1851 and 1900. Elizabeth led the research and writing for Chapter Four, 'Jewish, British, middle-class: A history of Jewish adjustment on the Central Victorian Goldfields' and Popout Three, 'Interfaith marriage and Jewish familial identity on the Central Victorian Goldfields: The Herman family experience'.

Natasha Joyce is a Higher Degree Research student at La Trobe University. Her thesis is titled, 'No place for children: accidental childhood fatality on Victoria's goldfields, 1852–1893'. Natasha led the research and writing for Popout Two, 'Spatial organisation and hierarchies of prejudice in Central Victorian goldrush cemeteries'.

Introduction

Since its inception in 1871, the Bendigo Easter Fair has used ritual procession and displays of lavish regalia to cultivate a festive spirit. Drawing upon British cultural traditions attached to the most important holiday in the Christian calendar, the early fairs combined processions with other forms of money-raising carnival entertainment, including bazaar stalls, charity auctions, theatre productions and band performances. The organisers hoped to promote enjoyment and relaxation through the increased consumption of food, drink and entertainment while encouraging generosity for the benefit of the Bendigo Benevolent Asylum and Hospital. Indeed, it was said in 1876 that of all public events throughout the year, none created such a 'unanimous feeling' or met 'heartier support' than the Easter Fair:

> The importance attached to the holding of this fair is undoubtedly because it has for its main object that which is noblest and most admirable in human nature—the securing and support of the sacred cause of charity. It is in the furtherance of this sublime cause that the distinctions and differences of creed, caste, and character are forgotten ... It is one of the grandest things, and resounds greatly to the credit of Old Bendigo, that no matter what degree of prosperity its citizens enjoy, they always are most ready to stand forward nobly to help those to whom providence is not a gracious smiling deity.[1]

By framing altruistic giving as a 'sacred' duty, the writer draws upon the capacity of ethical frameworks to unite disparate people by providing strangers with a point of connection and nurturing a sense of belonging. Spirituality and religion can be important sources of meaning-making in the world, and associated ideas can assist people to encounter others outside their own community. On the goldfield in 1876, says this writer, the 'distinctions and differences of creed, caste, and character' were 'forgotten' in pursuit of shared fundraising goals.

1 'The Easter Fair of 1876,' *Bendigo Advertiser*, April 18, 1876, p. 2, col. 6, para. 1, nla.gov.au/nla.news-article88255623.

Diggers rushing to the valley of Bendigo in the 1850s brought with them a multitude of faith traditions, and most British citizens expected to practice or abstain from these customs without obstruction. The newly formed colony of Victoria was founded on the principle of religious freedom and equality, and the mass display of Friendly Society regalia at early Easter processions illustrates this liberty of association. Misfortune on the goldfields encouraged the importation of British fraternities and lodges whose principles of 'discipline, conviviality and benevolence' aided members and encouraged proud affiliation.[2] But other performances at the Easter Fair reveal the struggle and difficulty that negotiating religious and racial difference involved. People on the early goldfields were physically proximate but not always connected. Respectful engagement can overcome social distance and promote peacemaking and community cohesion, even where religious and spiritual traditions are viewed as incommensurable. The changing participation of Mr H Marks at the Bendigo Easter Fair illustrates this challenge.

Crowds at the Bendigo Easter Fair were dazzled by regal and exotic displays that drew upon familiar British carnival themes. In Bendigo, these included the mayor parading in his robes of office, members of the mining board acknowledging the crowd from a fine carriage, various fire brigades and minstrel exhibits, boxing contestants and uniformed lady cricketers marching 'with their bats'.[3] But some costumes and performances amused the crowd at the expense of others. In 1875, Mr H Marks, a local auctioneer and later mayor, was among several notable lodge members who were 'done up in splendid style' to ridicule local minority groups through racist and dehumanising blackface stereotypes.[4]

Perhaps because spiritual and faith communities draw upon powerful forces of belonging, differences in culture and religion can be hard to navigate. Significant divisions and world conflicts have involved geographically proximate but socially distant groups. Intolerance of difference has structured how their relations have been understood, so disrespect and misunderstanding are often emphasised in public writing and communication explaining conflict. Faith-based forces for improved relations, cooperation and peacebuilding usually don't get as much attention. But the humble acts

2 Dan Weinbren and Bob James, 'Getting a Grip: The Roles of Friendly Societies in Australia and Britain Reappraised,' *Labour History*, no. 88 (2005): 87, www.jstor.org/stable/27516038.

3 'The Easter Fair', *Bendigo Advertiser*, March 30, 1875, p. 2, col. 7, para. 3, trove.nla.gov.au/newspaper/article/88257785/9116265.

4 Ibid.

of engagement by the Chinese community and figures like Mr Harry Marks at the Bendigo Easter Fair bring the transformative power of neighbourliness into view. 'Neighbourliness' provides a useful frame to examine relations between people who live together and whose actions 'affect one another'.[5] It considers people's understandings of their moral responsibilities and how these ideas shape behaviour towards others. In 1879, the viability of the Easter Fair was jeopardised by the piqued withdrawal of several friendly societies who had been stalwarts of the parade. But timely and generous efforts by a local Chinese resident saved the event and ensured its longevity.[6] The Bendigo Chinese community 'made themselves indispensable to the success of the Fair' by capitalising on precedents set at Beechworth and especially Ballarat in 1879, where Chinese 'processions and entertainments' attracted 8,000 spectators and garnered £400 in profit (despite 'wretched weather').[7] Harry Marks' 'unceasing interest' supported Chinese sponsorship of the event and expressed the shared desire for ongoing positive relationships between the organisers and this key stakeholder group.[8] These dynamics resulted in splendid annual processions. Amanda Rasmussen suggests that the constructive connections between the Bendigo Easter Fair organisers and the Chinese community were established 'just as anti-Chinese agitation was at a peak level' among white Australians elsewhere.[9] Chinese residents of Bendigo and its districts presented an illuminated address to Mr Marks in 1896 to express their gratitude for this rare degree of cross-cultural harmony. Represented by James Lamsey, a herbalist and powerful white–Chinese community mediator; O'Koey; James Ni Gan; Wing Chung Sing; Sin Tip Waugh, a Bridge Street storekeeper; Sin Ah Goon; Sin Cum Tien, another Bridge Street storekeeper; Tommy Ah Toon; Ka Joe; Lee Goon Lie; Ten Soney and James Ah Poo, a court interpreter, local Chinese people expressed their 'very best thanks for the very great patience, courtesy and

5 Noah Walker-Crawford, 'Climate Change in the Courtroom: An Anthropology of Neighborly Relations,' *Anthropological Theory* 23, no. 1 (2023): 81.

6 'Easter Fair Committee,' *Bendigo Advertiser*, March 12, 1879, p. 3, col. 2, nla.gov.au/nla.news-article 88224286.

7 Amanda Rasmussen, 'Networks and Negotiations: Bendigo's Chinese and the Easter Fair,' *Journal of Australian Colonial History* 6 (2004): 82.

8 As Rasmussen notes, Marks had 'been involved with the Fair since its inception, was Chinese marshal in 1885 and 1886, and Easter Fair secretary from 1891–1908, and in 1914'. 'Networks and Negotiations,' 88–89.

9 Rasmussen, 'Networks and Negotiations,' 88.

kindness you have at all times extended to them'.[10] Mr Marks, in turn, attested that 'his associations with his Chinese friends [were] always of the most pleasant nature'.[11] Chinese participation became a hallmark of the Bendigo Easter Fair, now recognised as a rare space where difference is mobilised to demonstrate commonality.

We cite this episode to introduce our project because it illustrates how religious and cultural differences have, at times, been better managed by individuals and communities than by institutions and government bodies. This research set out to investigate the history of religious and spiritual difference on Djaara Country since European settlement and to expand understanding of the importance of religious literacy. By examining the changing relationships between diverse people who came to the region seeking gold, seeking a new home and seeking refuge, we have found other evidence of 'patience, courtesy and kindness' that supported neighbours to cohere. We bridge historic and contemporary experience as we investigate historic links between belief and community relations, focusing on three research themes and questions:

1. Gold mining and transformation: Aboriginal land-based cultural practice has been impacted by the destructive extraction of gold that has been encapsulated by the 'casualties of colonial dispossession' narrative. Can a new focus on the resilience and love of Country transcend this narrative?
2. Faith as a layer of social history: What value did faith hold in peoples' lives, and how did it guide actions? How were different religious beliefs expressed through the customs, rituals, beliefs and lifestyles of their adherents?
3. Material faith and the built environment: How are the beliefs of established, disappeared or emergent faith communities expressed in Bendigo's material culture? How does evidence of religion outside traditional religious spaces (down the mine, at the cemetery, in the court room) inform us about the function of religion in everyday life? What does this tell us about faith as a driver of social cohesion or conflict?

10 'The Chinese and the Easter Fair,' *Bendigo Advertiser*, April 28, 1896, p. 2, col. 6, nla.gov.au/nla.news-article88896020. Leigh McKinnon, Research Officer at the Golden Dragon Museum, Bendigo, notes that the spelling likely reflects the language of the unnamed source informant; Sei Yap dialect versions of names are usually given more standard Cantonese transliteration. Sin Cum Tien was probably the Bridge Street storekeeper known as Sun Kum Cheung, and Sin Tip Waugh of another Bridge Street store was usually known as Sun Tip Wor. Sin Ah Goon might be Sun Ack Goon. This newspaper article was published at a time when two main dialect groups were present in the Bendigo Chinese community. The article also suggests ad hoc romanisation systems.

11 'The Chinese and the Easter Fair,' *Bendigo Advertiser*, April 28, 1896, p. 2, col. 6. nla.gov.au/nla.news-article88896020.

We address these questions through traditional examination of documentary historical sources, as well as oral sources and the objects and spaces of the material culture of religion. The research findings are presented in nine chapters of customary length, augmented by six shorter 'popouts'. Together, these sources help to elucidate the relationship between past and present meanings of faith as a lived dimension of experience. The Catholic Diocese of Sandhurst and the City of Greater Bendigo have supported this research as part of their mission to build a community whose members are engaged in constructive dialogue and where faith commitment and diversity is understood and respected.

Situating Bendigo and this research

Present-day Bendigo is on Djandak, meaning 'Country' in Dja Dja Wurrung, the language of the Djaara people. Located in the geographic centre of Victoria, approximately 150 kilometres northwest of the capital Melbourne, Djandak was violently seized and re-coded as a 'goldfield', a term that implies property. This area in Central Victoria is perceived and described by Djaara people today as 'upside down Country', where the sacred earth has been rotated and removed by mining.[12] Under Djaara governance, the resources of this dry valley were managed holistically. 'Dja Dja Wurrung value quartz', writes Clare Needham, 'it's a great material for knapping and creating tools, historically we had no use for the soft material of gold. Yet quartz and gold come hand in hand … this has had a catastrophic impact on my People'.[13] When pastoralists seized Djaara land in the late 1830s, they assumed a level of fertility and abundance that proved ephemeral under their management. The pastures of native grasses disappeared and the sustaining chain-of-ponds systems in the creek beds became cracked and dried. In late 1851, newcomers discovered rich gold deposits underneath these new sheep pastures, and by June 1852, multitudes of diggers arrived each week to exploit the finds. The rush for gold turned this district into a 'goldfield' and normalised the overturning of Djaara land and lifeways.

12 Clare Needham, 'Undercurrent: The History Beneath the Image,' *Bendigo Art Gallery* (blog), July 24, 2020, para. 12, www.bendigoregion.com.au/bendigo-art-gallery/blogs/undercurrent-the-history-beneath-the-image; on the significance of re-coding Country, see Robert Nichols, 'Theft is Property! The Recursive Logic of Dispossession,' *Political Theory* 46, no. 1 (2018): 5, doi.org/10.1177/0090591717701709.
13 Needham, 'Undercurrent,' para. 12.

Map 0.1: Victoria, Australia, map

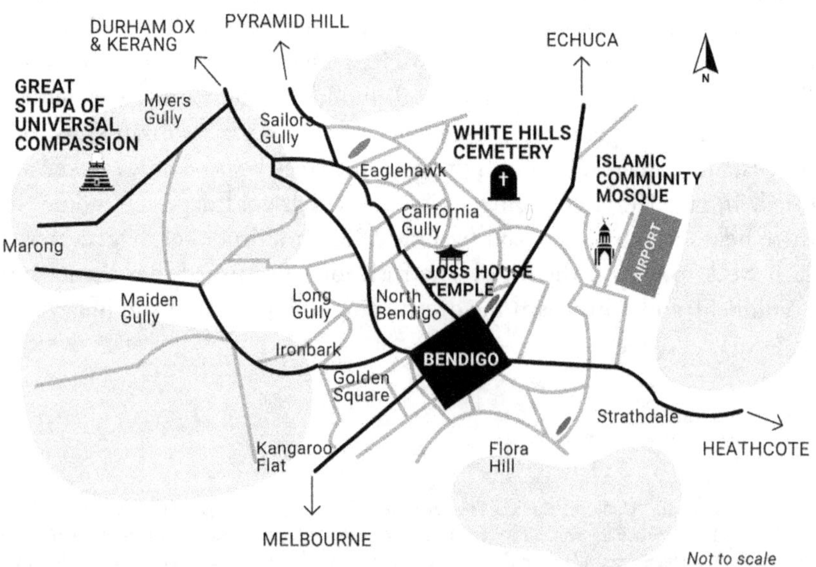

Map 0.2: Regional Bendigo map

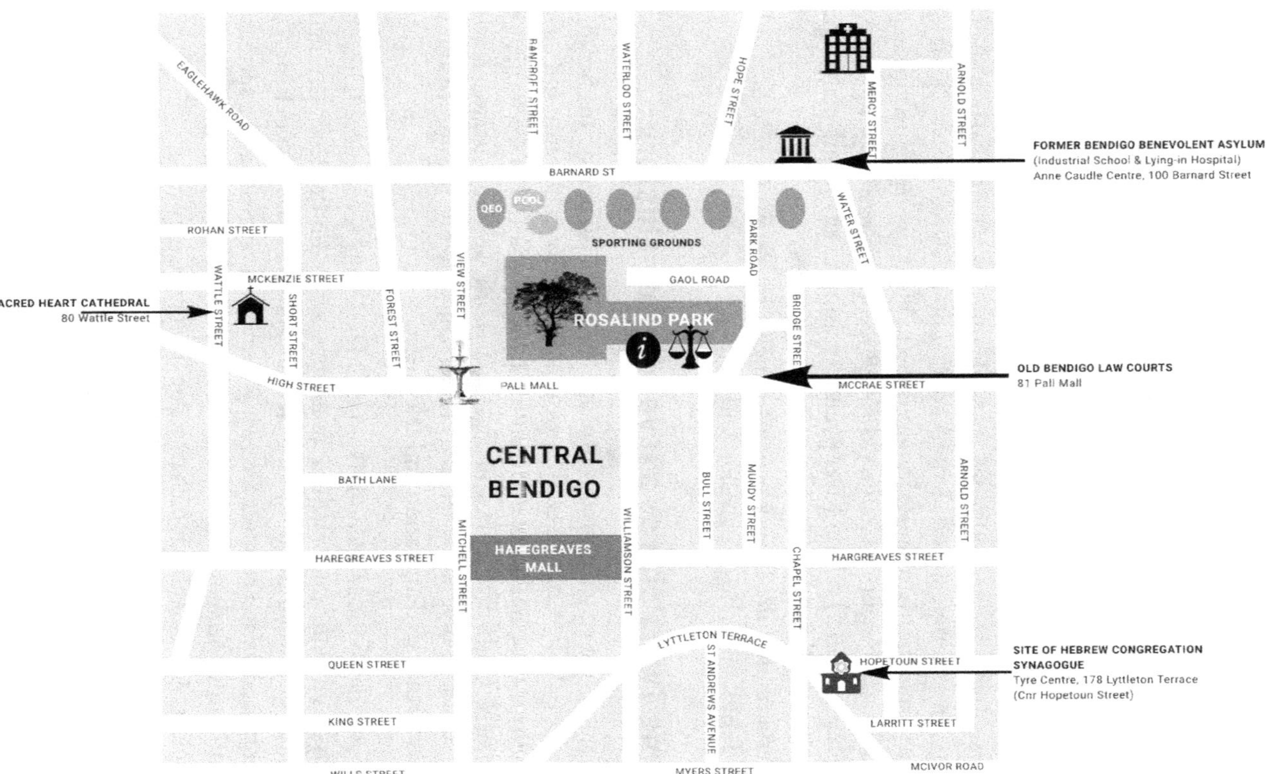

Map 0.3: Bendigo CBD map

A reparative approach to these sensitive topics, we hope, will support genuine transformation that recognises the full impacts and legacies of gold digging, including how any focus on spirituality, faith and religious difference must recognise the Djaara meanings of and connections with Country.

Theme One: Gold mining and transformation

In Chapter One, 'Religion and social cohesion on the goldfields', we introduce our methodology, the theoretical underpinning of this research and the themes that truthfully identify the legacies of this foundation, identifying hope and provide a conduit for healing.

Chapter Two, 'Djaara resilience amid disruption: The impact of settler actions on Aboriginal connections to Country', develops our focus on Djaara responses to upheaval and conflict. Here, we trace the tenacity of Djaara attachment to Country through records of pastoral employment in the Laanecoorie/Loddon River plains. By using an environmental history approach and following the life story of apical ancestor Emma Kerr, the chapter amplifies the Djaara people's struggle to sustain their loving links to land through strategic cohesion with settlers.

Theme Two: Faith as a layer of social history

In Chapter Three, 'Common law and religious difference in Bendigo courtrooms: "The Chinese Oath"', we examine religious plurality and racial inequality in the latter nineteenth century Bendigo courtroom. Performances of Chinese Oath ceremonies in legal spaces, as we demonstrate, render non-Christian polytheistic faiths as understandable but incommensurable and susceptible to denigration and relegation.

Our first brief 'popout' section, Popout One 'Giving as cohesion: 'Hospital Sundays', religion, and medical philanthropy in fin-de-siècle Bendigo', examines the social use of outdoor recreation and entertainment in Bendigo's fine public parks as a conduit for giving to medical charities and a spectacle of multi-faith belonging. This section also marks the closing of the era when compulsory Christianity and charity donation were entwined.

Chapter Four, 'Jewish, British, middle-class: A history of Jewish adjustment on the Central Victorian Goldfields', provides an overview of Jewish history in the region. Tracing early worship through to contemporary identifications reveals how individual adherents and congregations both maintained fidelity to tradition and pursued reform that was cogent with their middle-class British and contemporary Australian identities.

Chapter Five develops our focus on bereavement to consider how lived religion provided meaning and solace to women who were separated from family support. In 'Divine intention and family misfortune on the Central Victorian Goldfields: How "Providence orders all things well"', letters sent from and to Bendigo in the 1860s provide rare evidence of women's experience on the diggings. This includes insight into environmental realities and how they shaped the corporeal practice of breastfeeding, and how faith informed child-rearing decisions.

Chapter Six, 'Building an Irish-Roman Catholic Church on the goldfields and Northern Victoria, 1852–1914', shifts our focus from Protestantism to Catholicism in Bendigo and surrounding regions. By contrasting the religious and secular legacies of an influential but atypical cleric with that of the first Bishop of Sandhurst and his successors, we identify why Bendigo's strong Catholic community drew upon the Irish devotional practices of Bishop Crane rather than German spiritual traditions of the founding priest, Father Backhaus.

Shifting to an intimate setting, we continue this examination of religious tradition and change in our third 'popout' section. 'Interfaith marriage and Jewish familial identity on the Central Victorian Goldfields: The Herman family experience' looks beyond the ubiquity of love marriage in the mid-nineteenth century to identify the impact interfaith unions had upon religious belonging and family identity. This popout follows the story of Solomon Herman and Elizabeth Oxlade, who negotiated non-Jewish status and institutional decrees to form a family religiosity of their choosing.

We then chart the views and behaviours of Bendigo's civic and religious leaders and contrast them with those of individuals in their congregations and wider community. Chapter Seven, 'Militant Protestant sectarianism in a religiously plural community: Why Bendigo failed to become a "Protestant city"', examines how increasingly secular working families and their neighbours responded to militant Protestantism prior to the First World War. This chapter provides insight into the pressures of industrial illness and how sad individual circumstance became a unifying force in Bendigo.

Chapter Eight follows the trajectory of secularisation further into the twentieth century. 'Faith after the gold rush: Demographic and religious change' suggests that the capacity to adjust to de-industrialisation and associated population shifts had a greater influence on the waning Protestant character of Bendigo than apparent traditionalism did. With case studies drawn from Bendigo's Church of England/Anglican and the Uniting Church of Australia/Methodist congregations, and from the Catholic Diocese of Sandhurst, we posit that the decline of institutional religion was experienced differently. Charting demographic change and the rise of nonreligious identities, we argue that this shift can be understood outside the limiting success–failure dichotomy.

Theme Three: Material faith and the built environment

Popout Two, 'Spatial organisation and hierarchies of prejudice in central Victorian goldrush cemeteries', furthers our material religion theme. Examining the physical organisation of graves at the White Hills Cemetery enables us to determine why the early practice of collective burial in the early goldrush period later made way for the entrenchment of religious difference and the reification of marginal social status in death.

The next three 'popout' sections all focus on Bendigo's built environment, and we use material heritage as an axis to understand how faith was translated into community values and belonging. Popout Four 'Completing the Sacred Heart Cathedral: Craft and tradition in Bendigo's faith-scape' tells the personal story of carpenter Paul Copock and his father. Their dedication to craftwork and oversight of the Sacred Heart Cathedral project, 1953–1977, provided employment for specialist workers from different ethnic backgrounds and grounds for cross-cultural mateship and intergenerational continuity. Executing fine work on the landmark also provided existential meaning for Paul, who, like many of his generation, had relinquished his personal faith practice by the 1970s.

In Popout Five, we consider the infrastructure of non-Christian worship traditions in Bendigo from 1871 to today. By attending to temporal and spatial parameters of religious change in 'Emu Point Joss House: The spirit and architecture of faith', we identify how processes of sacralising space in a new home are negotiated between existing residents and newcomers.

In 'Transforming 'Old Sandhurst Town' into the Great Stupa of Universal Compassion', Popout Six, we extend this investigation into sacred space by considering how the slow transformation of a beloved tourist facility generated both revenue and 'religious capital' for the Buddhist community on the outskirts of Bendigo.

We complete the chapters that investigate stories of faith through tangible and intangible heritage assets in Chapter Nine, 'Navigating faith and cultural diversity: The Bendigo Mosque controversy'. This chapter examines how urgent contemporary problems are driven by the contradictory processes of secularisation and de-secularisation. It examines how a proposed major asset was made controversial by intolerance and misinformation, as monocultural white communities feared that non-Christian worship traditions would be disruptive of social harmony. By considering the subsequent failure to engage with the concerns of the mosque opponents, we draw attention to the challenges of religious illiteracy among citizens who increasingly identify as nonreligious.

Our 'Conclusion: Womindjika (welcome) to Bendigo, a city of flourishing diversity?' returns to the iconic Easter Fair and its evolution since 2016, when Djaara people began to head the procession. We ask whether this deliberate reversal of traditional hierarchy, which represented the organisers prioritising diversity and multicultural cohesion over the usual displays of civic power, achieved the aim of promoting reconciliation through public displays of recognition.

We hope that in the pages that follow, readers will encounter aspects of regional life that have not previously been brought into historical focus: the changing 'faith-scape' of Bendigo. While Bendigo may not have always been a site of interracial harmony, interfaith and value-driven collaboration have often undergirded improvements in interracial acceptance and appreciation. Each chapter and popout has a nuanced story to tell about the influence of faith on people and place, revealing historic links between belief and community relations. We demonstrate that the physical disruption of mining did not sever the Djaara people's spiritual connection to their sacred lands. We also demonstrate that faith forms an important layer of social history: it holds a valued place in peoples' lives, guides their actions and finds expression through lifestyles, customs and rituals. By paying attention to material religion and space, we rediscover how faith-based assets in the built environment helped people from disparate backgrounds to form new communities. By discussing the impact of faith, we illustrate how communities can use histories of belief, spirituality and religious practice to foster social cohesion and good neighbourliness.

1

Religion and social cohesion on the goldfields

Loud and competing voices warning of religious danger have challenged peaceful relations and social connections in many societies and communities. They have also introduced dramatic inequalities between how different religious groups are understood and treated in social policy. Although classic secularisation theory predicted a fatal decline of religion in modern societies, in the twenty-first century, religious difference has come to dominate both international geopolitics and local cultural politics. Militant Islamist actions in New York, Bali and London were the catalyst for a two-decade international war on terror. It also sparked a new political narrative about the threat of Islam that presented all members of a major world religion as potential terrorists and enemies of liberal democratic societies. Simultaneously, conservative Christians, who were alarmed by advancing civil rights for women and lesbian, gay, bisexual and transgender people, have campaigned strongly for their own religious freedom and for the maintenance or extension of their religious privileges in the law. Interestingly, social researchers note that the character of Australian religious and spiritual practice has been neither secularised nor radicalised. The Australia's Generation Z Study has shown high levels of faith, belief and spiritual practice among today's youth.[1] This reveals a disjunction between

1 Anna Halafoff, Heather Shipley, Pamela D. Young, Andrew Singleton, Mary Lou Rasmussen, and Gary Bouma, 'Complex, Critical and Caring: Young People's Diverse Religious, Spiritual and Non-Religious Worldviews in Australia and Canada,' *Religions* 11, no. 4 (2020): 166, doi.org/10.3390/rel11040166.

what is in the headlines and what is in the hearts of ordinary young people. We suggest that attending to what people do, and have done, rather than what the loudest voices say, might light a more hopeful path.

Concerns about social harmony have been an enduring theme of historical and social research. Responding to social conflict, numerous scholars have sought to understand and theorise ways for neighbours to live well together. From the mid-1990s, increasing inequality and cultural differences have made it difficult for many communities in Australia (and globally) to maintain harmonious relations. Indeed, the latest Scanlan report shows declining social cohesion in Australia.[2] These challenges led policy-makers to begin paying particular interest to theories and programs that promoted and improved social cohesion.[3] At its core, social cohesion describes the quality of engagement between people brought together in common purpose that requires a high degree of generalised trust. In this context, trust means that strangers can be accepted as part of a 'moral community' and share an underlying commonality of values.[4] A key element and measure of social cohesion is, thus, a 'community's acceptance of people from diverse racial, ethnic, or cultural groups'.[5] Some leading Australian sociologists of religion have noted that agents of social cohesion, such as policies that promote multiculturalism, have often been used in policy contexts as a tool to maintain the status quo.[6] Increased religious and cultural diversity, they observe, may be experienced as disruptive to existing traditions, cultural practices and social structures. They argue that this disruption can be productive, but for this to be the case, an ethic of respectful engagement in the spirit of deep religious and cultural equality is required.[7] In this book,

2 James O'Donnell and Qing Guan, *Mapping Social Cohesion* (Scanlon Foundation Research Institute, 2024). scanloninstitute.org.au/wp-content/uploads/Mapping-Social-Cohesion-2024-Report.pdf.

3 Xavier Fonseca, Stephan Lukosch, and Frances Brazier, 'Social Cohesion Revisited: A New Definition and How to Characterize It,' *Innovation: The European Journal of Social Science Research* 32, no. 2 (2019): 231–53, doi.org/10.1080/13511610.2018.1497480; Andrew Markus, *Mapping Social Cohesion* (Scanlon Foundation, 2021), scanloninstitute.org.au/wp-content/uploads/Mapping_Social_Cohesion_2021_Report_0.pdf; Andrew Markus and Ludmila Kirpitchenko, 'Conceptualising Social Cohesion', in *Social Cohesion in Australia*, ed. James Jupp, John Nieuwenhuysen, and Emma Dawson, (Cambridge University Press, 2007).

4 Eric Uslaner, *The Moral Foundations of Trust*, (Cambridge University Press, 2002), 1.

5 Eric Uslaner, *The Historical Roots of Well-Being and Social Cohesion*, (2019 UNDP Human Development Report, Background Paper No. 1, 2019), 3. hdr.undp.org/content/historical-roots-well-being-and-social-cohesion.

6 Douglas Ezzy, Gary Bouma, Greg Barton et al., 'Religious Diversity in Australia: Rethinking Social Cohesion,' *Religions* 11, no. 2 (2020): 92, 1–15, doi.org/10.3390/rel11020092; Ghassan Hage, *The Racial Politics of Australian Multiculturalism: White Nation, Against Paranoid Nationalism & Later Writings* (Sweatshop, 2023).

7 Lori Beaman, *Deep Equality in an Era of Religious Diversity* (Oxford University Press, 2017).

we use social cohesion as a useful historical category of analysis, concurring with the prevailing caution regarding its use in policy contexts (see especially Chapter Nine).

Key determinants of social cohesion include education and societal equality, as they promote understanding and contact between social groups. But because levels of education and inequality do not change much over time, as political scientist Eric Uslaner has demonstrated, a community's history is a key predictor of social cohesion in the present.[8] Uslaner describes these factors as being 'sticky'. Common values, ideals and practices can also produce and maintain social cohesion. Such common qualities are often understood in religious terms, which has been explored in the Victorian goldfields in the context of communal searches for lost children and weekly communal days of rest: the 'goldfields Sabbath'.[9] Attention to histories of social cohesion is, thus, important for understanding and influencing social cohesion in the present.

This book investigates a history of social cohesion with reparative intent. Histories of religious difference and social conflict often merely document how things have gone wrong, or they tell how one religious community survived 'against the odds'. We have approached this history of a community navigating difference with the aim of learning how neighbours lived with difference peacefully. Our hope is that the histories in this volume will assist the maintenance and repair of social cohesion and support the development of deep equality across religious differences in the future. Specifically, the book explores how the Central Victorian Goldfields community around Bendigo worked to maintain social cohesion in the context of changing religious and cultural diversity from the gold rush to today. We primarily concentrate on Djaara Country, where Bendigo is situated. Djaara Country includes the water catchment areas of the Loddon and Avoca rivers and is bordered by the Campaspe River to the east and the Avon River to the west. We also include border areas belonging to the Barapa Barapa people around Pyramid Hill to the north and Wadawurrung Country, where Ballarat is situated, to the south. We recognise significant historical connections

8 Uslaner, *The Historical Roots of Well-Being and Social Cohesion.*

9 Tim Calabria and Tash Joyce, 'Bush-Lost Children's Place in New "Moral Communities": The Emergence of a Cultural Rite in Colonial Victoria (and Across Australia), 1850s–1890s,' *Rural History* 33, no. 2 (2022): 179–94, doi.org/10.1017/S0956793322000012; Timothy Willem Jones and Clare Wright, 'The Goldfields' Sabbath: A Postsecular Analysis of Social Cohesion and Social Control on the Ballarat Goldfields, 1854,' *Journal of Religious History* 43, no.4 (2019): 447–59, doi.org/10.1111/1467-9809.12626.

between neighbouring First Nations and the social flow between Bendigo and Ballarat mining communities. This chapter traces the story of changing religious populations in these regions. It explains how a focus on the built heritage and materiality of religious culture provides a tangible link and ongoing resource for understanding how communities can use history to nourish and maintain social cohesion.

Faith(s) on the goldfields

The Djaara lived and cared for Djandak, or Country, for many thousands of years before Europeans and other migrants moved into the area we now know as Central Victoria in the early nineteenth century. The Djaara describe Djandak as 'a living entity which holds the stories of creation and histories that cannot be erased'.[10] Aboriginal law, culture and spirituality was, and remains, intimately related to the lands and waters, its rhythms and seasons and the care for and maintenance of the land. The Djaara believe that their great ancestral beings 'formed the land, created all species, and laid the foundations for their culture'.[11] Bunjil, the eaglehawk, is the creator, and Mindi, the giant serpent, enforces and implements Bunjil's laws and ceremonies 'that ensure the continuation of life'.[12] Despite the profound disruption of Aboriginal lifeways and alteration of landscapes caused by colonisation, knowledge of Djaara traditional culture and spirituality has survived.

Europeans moved into Djaara Country seeking land, first for pastoralism and then pursuing gold and precious minerals. The tragic consequences of European-introduced diseases, violent dispossession and destructive land use for Aboriginal people and Country are well known and documented. Aboriginal culture and spirituality, however, were maintained and preserved through this period through both determined and fortuitous means. Whether they continued to live on Djandak or moved to other First Nations' lands, Djaara sought to hold onto Culture and their connection to Country and maintain their kinship obligations and relations. They also shared cultural knowledge with selected Europeans, such as William Thomas and

10 'Giyakiki | Our Story,' Dja Dja Wurrung Clans Aboriginal Corporation, accessed June 10, 2022, para. 2, djadjawurrung.com.au/giyakiki-our-story/.

11 Bain Attwood, *The Good Country: The Djadja Wurrung, the Settlers and the Protectors* (Monash University Publishing, 2017), chap. 1.

12 *Dhelkunya Dja: Dja Dja Wurrung Country Plan 2014-2034* (Dja Dja Wurrung Clans Aboriginal Corporation, 2017). www.centralgoldfields.vic.gov.au/About-Us/Governance-and-Strategy/Council-Plans/Dhelkunya-Dja-Dja-Dja-Wurrung-Country-Plan-2014-2034.

Edward Stone Parker. Appointed by colonial administrators as 'protectors', these men recorded traditional Aboriginal ceremonies and some of the ways that Aboriginal peoples understood their encounter with European people, animals and diseases, including in theological or spiritual terms. The Djaara, for example, told of a large serpent that had unleashed the devastating diseases that may have reduced Aboriginal populations in the district by three quarters.[13] Some Aboriginal people identified the invading squatters as resuscitated relatives – amydeet or ngamadjidj – which enabled them to incorporate newcomers into their kinship structures.[14]

Aboriginal people also engaged with and responded to the Europeans and their religion in numerous ways, while remaining 'determined to hold onto Culture'.[15] They incorporated European monetary practices and objects into traditional rituals and arts. They engaged with introduced religion in thoughtful and self-protective 'syncretic' ways, guarding knowledge of traditional spirituality from most white settlers.[16] Many Aboriginal people transformed, added, adapted and adopted Christian spirituality.[17] Some Djaara became Christian and farmed the land in the European fashion.[18] Robert Kenny's nuanced account of Nathaniel Pepper's engagement with Christianity may give insight into the experiences and understandings of Djaara, such as Kolain, Yerrebulluk and Beernmarmin (Tommy Farmer), who adopted Christian beliefs and ways of life.[19]

The Christianities that arrived in Central Victoria with the European pastoralists and gold seekers were varied. At the start of the gold rush, 48 per cent of the population belonged to the Church of England, 23 per cent to the Roman Catholic Church, 16 per cent were Presbyterian, and the remainder were mostly other nonconformist Protestant Christians.[20] These different versions of nineteenth-century Christianity were vastly different

13 Edward S. Parker, 'Aborigines of Australia,' in *The Good Country: The Djadja Wurrung, the Settlers and the Protectors* (Monash University Publishing, 2017), 18.

14 Ian D. Clark and David A. Cahir, 'Understanding 'Ngamadjidj': Aboriginal Perceptions of Europeans in Nineteenth Century Western Victoria,' *Journal of Australian Colonial History* 13 (2011): 105–24; Attwood, *The Good Country*, chap. 1.

15 'Giyakiki | Our Story,' para. 7, djadjawurrung.com.au/giyakiki-our-story/.

16 Fred Cahir, Rani Kerin, and Kylie Rippon, 'The Aboriginal Adjustment Movement in Colonial Victoria,' *Journal of Religious History* 43, no. 4 (2019): 478–494, doi.org/10.1111/1467-9809.12630.

17 Cahir et al., 'The Aboriginal Adjustment Movement'.

18 Attwood, *The Good Country*, chap. 5.

19 Robert Kenny, *The Lamb Enters the Dreaming: Nathanael Pepper and the Ruptured World* (Scribe, 2007); Attwood, *The Good Country*, chap. 6.

20 Geoffrey Serle, *Golden Age: A History of the Colony of Victoria, 1851–1861* (Melbourne University Press, 1977), 336.

from Djaara spirituality, law and ceremony, which focuses on external and material practices, including how humans should relate to each other in the present and care for the land and waters. Nineteenth century Christianity had an internal and otherworldly focus on the salvation of human souls from eternal punishment in the afterlife. For Catholics, salvation is found through participation in the sacraments, the rituals of the church such as baptism, confession and Holy Communion. For Protestants (Church of England, Presbyterian, Methodist, etc.), especially since the eighteenth century evangelical revivals, salvation comes primarily through an experience of personal faith in Jesus Christ and fidelity to the authority of scripture. Christian differences also overlaid ethnic and class differences, with Irish Catholicism and British Protestantism forming a long-lasting, sometimes bitter and extremely fragile social divide.[21]

Numbers of Jewish people arrived and settled with the British in Australia. They were among both the convicts and free settlers who arrived from 1788 and those who came seeking gold in the 1850s. Judaism is ethnoreligious, without a particular missionary focus. It is concerned with the relationship between the Hebrew God and the Jewish people, as described in their history and regulated in traditions of law and scholarship. While Jewish community life was established in the colonies, religious observance prior to World War Two 'had become increasingly attenuated', as Rodney Gouttman writes. Gouttman argues that colonial Jewry 'prided themselves on their loyalty to Empire, King and Country'.[22] In Chapter Four, we outline the origins and shape of the Jewish community that formed in the goldfields in the 1850s. They negotiated complex multiple identities as British, European and Jewish, seeking to maintain their community, law and rituals and providing sites for explicit interfaith dialogue and exchange.

The gold rush also attracted significant populations of Chinese people. In the two decades after the settlers discovered gold, 60,000 Chinese people left China for Australia, with as many as 42,000 travelling to Victoria. Up to 20 per cent of the population of male settlers on the Victorian goldfields were Chinese.[23] The Chinese people who arrived on the goldfields had

21 Patrick O'Farrell, 'Double Jeopardy: Catholic and Irish,' *Humanities Research* 12, no. 1 (2005): 7–12, doi.org/10.22459/HR.XII.01.2005.

22 Rodney Gouttman, 'Was it Ever So? Anti-Semitism in Australia, 1860-1950?' *Humanities Research* 12, no. 1 (2005): 56, doi.org/10.22459/HR.XII.01.2005.

23 Fei Sheng, 'Environmental Experiences of Chinese People in the Mid-Nineteenth Century Australian Gold Rushes,' *Global Environment* 4 (2011): 98–117, doi.org/10.3197/ge.2011.040705; Serle, *Golden Age*, 320.

diverse religious practices: Buddhism, Taoism, Confucianism and ancestor veneration. Chinese religious beliefs and practices tended to be plural and syncretic, as opposed to the singular and purist tendencies of Christianity.[24] As such, the assemblage of rituals and beliefs held by traditional Chinese people fits uneasily in European categories of religion, and also perhaps in Aboriginal understandings of law and spirituality. Chinese 'religion' is often equally described as philosophy, with a monist metaphysics that points to the oneness of all things. It is directed towards achieving a state of harmony and the transcendence of suffering. On the goldfields, Chinese people built temples or 'joss houses', which became familiar features of the landscape. Christian missionaries attempted to convert Chinese people with mixed success. While some Chinese Christian congregations were established, their vastly different metaphysics and approach to religion often confused Christian missionaries. Some Chinese people may have been happy to incorporate new Christian beliefs and practices into their existing religiosity. Benjamin Penny observes, however, that Chinese religion was beyond the understanding of many Christian settlers, who framed it in terms of biblical idolatry.[25]

While Muslims have a longer history of encounter and exchange with First Nations peoples in Australia than European Christians, their part in the history of the goldfields societies has not featured prominently until recently. Islam is a religion of orthopraxy, following religious law and ritual. Muslims from Central and South Asia, today's Pakistan, Afghanistan and India, played a key role in the goldfields as merchants and hawkers. While little physical heritage of their nineteenth or twentieth century presence in the community remains, Chapter Nine discusses the record of their religious practice and relative cohesion in late nineteenth- and early twentieth century goldfields society. Local historians have noted that many of the South Asian Muslims in Bendigo served with British forces in imperial conflicts in Afghanistan. As imperial subjects, Muslim men had the franchise and identified actively with the imperial project. This history of belonging is being deployed actively by contemporary Muslim communities in the design of mosques, as they seek to secure belonging in a community that has struggled to find acceptance.

24 Yu Tao and Theo Stapleton, 'Religious Affiliations of the Chinese Community in Australia: Findings from 2016 Census Data,' *Religions* 9, no. 93 (2018): 93, doi.org/10.3390/rel9040093.

25 Benjamin Penny, 'Taking away Joss: Chinese Religion and the Wesleyan Mission in Castlemaine, 1868,' *Humanities Research* 12, no. 1 (2005): 116, doi.org/10.22459/HR.XII.01.2005.

A vast diversity of faith, religious practice and ethnic and cultural traditions were brought together in goldfields communities over time. Managing this religious difference and maintaining social cohesion was never easy. The majority population of settlers from Britain carried with them a fraught history of religious privilege and prejudice. Religious differences between Protestants and Catholics had been the source of much conflict between and within the societies of Western Europe since the sixteenth century Reformation. The Australian state sought novel solutions to this conflict, becoming what Patrick O'Farrell described as 'the first secular, state-controlled society in modern times'.[26] While the Church of England and its members had special privileges in Britain as the established church, the colony of Victoria had no established state church or religion. This meant that, theoretically at least, all faiths should be free and equal. Similarly, the Australian Constitution established a formally secular political system when the settler colonies federated in 1901. Section 116 of the Constitution states that:

> The Commonwealth shall not make any law for establishing any religion, or for imposing any religious observance, or for prohibiting the free exercise of any religion, and no religious test shall be required as a qualification for any office or public trust under the Commonwealth.[27]

Australian politics was designed to be secular, in that no one religion was established or politically privileged over the others; the Australian government was secular in that it was non-sectarian.[28] Nonetheless, for the Protestant majority, 'Irish Catholics were a standing menace to the majority assumption that British Protestant values and outlook would prevail harmoniously in a racially homogenous Australian society'.[29] As we note across this book, especially Chapter Seven, the ferocity of sectarianism as expressed in the loudest public voices contrasts strongly with how sectarian difference was expressed and experienced among neighbours.

It was not until the latter twentieth century that these Christian sectarian divides began to fade, and other cultural differences began to seem more important. Since the 1960s, Australia has also had globally low and

26 O'Farrell, 'Double Jeopardy,' 8.

27 *Australian Constitution* s 116.

28 Stephen A. Chavura, John Gascoigne, and Ian Tregenza, *Reason, Religion, and the Australian Polity: A Secular State?* (Routledge, 2019), 255.

29 O'Farrell, 'Double Jeopardy,' 10.

declining religious adherence and practice, making it relatively secularised in terms of traditional sociological measures of religious belief and practice. The empirical data on trends in Australian religiosity are unambiguous. Census and other survey data demonstrate that the largest and fastest-growing category of religious identity is 'no-religion'. In 1901, 96.1 per cent of Australians identified as Christian in the census. By 1966, this had declined slightly to 88 per cent. In the most recent data from 2021, however, only 43.9 per cent of Australians nominally identified with one form of Christianity, the largest single faith community being Roman Catholics at 20.0 per cent.[30] Active participation in religion is even lower. A 2017 report on faith and belief in Australia showed that only 20 per cent of Australians across all faiths are actively practicing their religion or worshipping as part of a group at least monthly.[31] This is significantly lower than the 38.9 per cent of Australians who identified with no religion in the 2021 census. Nominal religious identification has unambiguously declined, and purposeful identification with 'no-religion' is significantly greater than active participation in traditional forms of religion.[32] This is even more pronounced in Bendigo, where 47.0 per cent of people identified with no religion in 2021.[33]

This secularisation – the decline in traditional religious identification and practice in Australia – is historically recent and unconnected to (and even at odds with) Australia's political secularity. Indeed, the dominant political meaning of 'secular' in Australia until the 1960s did not connote an absence of religion; it assumed widespread religiosity. Sectarian conflict, especially between Protestants and Roman Catholics, was an ongoing problem in European societies and empires. Non-sectarian, secular government was developed in the Australian colonies in response to that problem. But this attempt to keep inter-Christian religious conflict out of politics as much as

30 '2021 Census Shows Changes in Australia's Religious Diversity,' Australian Bureau of Statistics, released June 28, 2022, www.abs.gov.au/media-centre/media-releases/2021-census-shows-changes-australias-religious-diversity.

31 *Faith and Belief in Australia: A National Study on Religion, Spirituality and Worldview Trends* (McCrindle Research, 2017), mccrindle.com.au/app/uploads/2018/04/Faith-and-Belief-in-Australia-Report_McCrindle_2017.pdf.

32 As Rory Shiner astutely explains, social research and measures have so far been inadequate to determine whether this nominal decline corresponds to a significant shift in rates of substantive religious belief and practice, or whether large numbers of people who were always only nominal in their belief are newly comfortable identifying more accurately with 'no religion'. Rory Shiner, 'What Happens After the Last Christian? Australia, Secularisation and God', *Eternity* (blog), September 9, 2019, www.eternitynews.com.au/opinion/what-happens-after-the-last-christian-australia-secularisation-and-god/.

33 Discussed in more detail in Chapter 8 of this volume.

possible has not proved especially successful in dealing with other forms of religious difference. In the context of increased religious pluralism associated with multiculturalism and migration, and new religious differences associated with increased secularisation, new strategies for navigating religious difference peaceably are required.

Australian religious history has been dominated by these two elements: secularisation and sectarian conflict. The dual lenses of ecclesiastical and secular history have provided a view of Australian spiritual life that is coloured by bitter sectarian rivalry, restless secularisms and uncomfortable religious pluralism. A history of the functioning of different religious groups in the social, public and private life of the Central Victorian Goldfields presents a different story. This story provides a model for the re-visioning of religion and social cohesion in Australia more broadly. The turbulent conditions of the Victorian gold rush presented opportunities for the reinvention of ancient religious traditions and practices, for cooperation in spiritual endeavours and for the negotiation and management of religious difference in emerging civic spaces. The story of faith on the goldfields can be retold as a story of efforts to build social cohesion and negotiate religious difference. It is a story that holds hope for present (and future) religious troubles.

Faith, heritage and material culture

For a book about spiritual diversity, this book has a (perhaps unusual) focus on physical things: buildings, monuments and the spaces in which religious oaths, prayers, rituals and ceremonies were made. We look at places of worship, such as the Sacred Heart Cathedral, the Great Stupa of Universal Compassion and Bendigo's first mosque. We explore spaces that were temporarily made sacred through ceremony, from Rosalind Park to the Bendigo courtrooms. This focus on the materiality of religious history is useful in several ways. It provides a lens through which to view different faith traditions on similar terms. It enables readers to imagine how religious difference was organised and managed. And, it speaks to how religious heritage and meaning is maintained and understood by present-day communities.

A material approach to religion treats different religious traditions more equally in historical and conceptual terms. As Lucinda Matthews-Jones and Timothy Willem Jones have observed elsewhere, understandings of religion in European-derived modern societies came to be associated with the written word through a series of historical processes.[34] The Reformation doctrine of *sola scriptura*, or scripture alone, meant that spoken and heard expressions of faith such as hymns, sermons and prayers came to dominance in the Protestant tradition.[35] This hierarchy of value influenced nineteenth and early twentieth century theorists of religious study, from Marx to Durkheim, who replicated this Protestant binary between the spiritual and physical.[36] Physical and visual practices became associated with superstition and primitive and pre-modern religion. 'Modern' religion was characterised as a matter of the mind and soul. Catholic religious practices and the material practices of other faiths were dismissed as idolatry. But, of course, Protestants too practiced their faith with physical objects in physical spaces. Attending to the common materiality of devotion in time and space goes some way to combatting the inherited hierarchies of religious difference that shape contemporary understandings of faith and belief.

An attention to the physical arrangement of different faith traditions in the goldfields is also useful in comprehending how a culture worked to maintain social cohesion. Mutual understanding is a key step in the management and peaceful coexistence of diverse religious, ethnic and cultural groups. Yet, modern societies have been characterised by social distance and have become societies of strangers.[37] As Gary Bouma and Philip Hughes observed, in modern Australia, many people have little contact with their neighbours. There are limited contexts in which they are exposed to people of other religions.[38] Except when it is specifically sought out, cultural difference is usually only encountered in shared facilities, such as schools, shopping centres and public transport. This lack of familiarity with difference in contemporary society has been used to explain why major issues have arisen over particular buildings that signify religious difference. The conditions of the gold rush saw people of many faiths and cultures seeking mineral wealth side by side. A town emerged rapidly, in-between and around valued ore deposits, disrupting the typical separation and social distance

34 Lucinda Matthews-Jones and Timothy Willem Jones, 'Introduction: Materiality and Religious History,' in *Material Religion in Modern Britain: The Spirit of Things*, ed. Timothy Willem Jones and Lucinda Matthews-Jones (Palgrave MacMillan, 2015).

35 Robert A. Orsi, 'Belief,' *Material Religion* 7, no. 1 (2011): 13, doi.org/10.2752/175183411X12968355481773.

36 Grace M. Jantzen, 'On Changing the Imaginary' in *The Blackwell Companion to Postmodern Theology*, ed. Graham Ward (Blackwell, 2007), 280–92.

37 James Vernon, *Distant Strangers: How Britain Became Modern* (University of California Press, 2014).

38 Gary D. Bouma and Philip J. Hughes, 'Using Census Data in the Management of Religious Diversity: An Australian Case Study,' *Religion* 44, no. 3 (2014): 442, doi.org/10.1080/0048721X.2014.903639.

between different social groups. This history of faith on the goldfields is a story of unusual religious proximity. Though not without tension and conflict, that physical proximity enabled an uncommon level of knowledge about religious and cultural difference. This knowledge was lost when the quest for gold declined, and policies that promoted a monocultural society triumphed. Fifty years of proximal diversity was succeeded by a hundred years of relative sameness. The push for cultural homogeneity produced by the White Australia Policy[39] deprived white settlers in the historic goldfields community of the resources, tools and knowledge to manage the rise in religious and cultural diversity that arrived in the twenty-first century.

The way that a society maintains and interprets its physical heritage reveals much about its relationship with history. In the places, spaces and objects that are set aside, registered and valued as 'heritage', a community institutes practices of both remembering and forgetting. While a written history tends to tell a singular story, places inevitably hold multiple histories and significances. And as E. Frances King reminds us, places and objects are not just things to look at.[40] Interacting with them is an embodied experience involving touch, smell, hearing and even sometimes tasting the thing and its past. When using material heritage to engage with the religious past, this experience invites the participant to reflect on how religion(s) functioned in an embodied way in particular times and places, rather than why particular faiths emerged or declined. It also makes more obvious those people and faiths whose stories have been built up and those who are no longer given space.

Approaching a history of religious difference through objects, place and space, thus, provides a path for the navigation of multiple stories and a means of holding together difficult and contradictory histories and experiences. Rosalind Park, for example, is listed on the Victorian Heritage Register for its historic, archaeological, aesthetic, botanical and architectural significance.[41] The tangible heritage cited in its statement of significance tells the story of the government's management of the goldfields. The plantings, art and architecture triumph white settler achievements funded by the gold excavated from this and nearby sites. But reflecting on the transformation of the creek into a stone-lined channel associated with gold

39 Known formally as the *Immigration Restriction Act 1901* (Cth).

40 E. Frances King, *Material Religion and Popular Culture* (Routledge, 2010).

41 'Rosalind Park,' Victorian Heritage Database, H1866, vhd.heritage.vic.gov.au/local/result_detail/1774?page=1&type=user.

mining and the importation of European trees recalls the transformation of sacred Djaara Country into recreational space for European settlers. The Yi Yuan Chinese Gardens reflect the historic significance of East Asian gold seekers and community members and their philosophies. Less tangibly registered (or remembered), the gardens at Rosalind Park were also the site of Muslim public prayers and feasts at the start of the twentieth century. A century later, they hosted protests against the building of the community's first mosque and picnics in solidarity with the contemporary Muslim community. The physical space can hold all these stories and reflect the multiplicity of faiths and beliefs that have been honoured on this site.

2

Djaara resilience amid disruption: The impact of settler actions on Aboriginal connections to Country

When early pastoralists took possession of Aboriginal lands in the Loddon River plains, they imagined future adaptation that would increase their personal wealth and support new settler communities. This held consequences for Djaara people, who knew this river as Laanecoorie.[1] The spiritual traditions of Aboriginal peoples acknowledge human kinship with places, plants and creatures. Instead of practicing extraction, they manage relationships of 'reciprocity, balance and plurality' with Country.[2] By contrast, European landholders in the Loddon River plains 'read' the landscape; they compared it to forms and functions they had known in Europe.[3] They saw the opportunity to exploit their proximity to Victoria's goldfields by supplying mining communities with meat. In this early stage of invasion and settlement, the landscape of the Laanecoorie/Loddon, thus, became 'a product of and repository for shared cultural experiences and

1 Jennifer E. Cain, *Laanecoorie: Hub of the Universe* (J.E. Cain, 1990).

2 Kirsten Anker, 'The Truth in Painting: Cultural Artefacts as Proof of Native Title', *Law Text Culture* 9, no. 1 (2005): 93, doi.org/10.14453/ltc.540; Irene Watson, 'Re-Centring First Nations Knowledge and Places in a Terra Nullius Space', *Alternative: An International Journal Of Indigenous Peoples* 10 no. 5 (2014): 512, doi.org/10.1177/117718011401000506; Irene Watson, 'Aboriginal Laws and the Sovereignty of Terra Nullius', *Borderlands* 1 no. 2 (2002), para. 14.

3 Tiffany Kaewen Dang, 'Decolonizing Landscape,' *Landscape Research* 46, no. 7 (2021): 1006, doi.org/10.1080/01426397.2021.1935820.

histories' for both colonised and colonising peoples.[4] To understand these shared but contrasting connections to Country, this chapter adopts a novel approach to religious history. We analyse pastoral records and Djaara life stories to determine how Aboriginal spirituality, measured through relations to Country, was impacted by settler land management.

We examine the causal impacts of the gold rush using the tools of environmental history, including a comprehensive quantitative analysis of the 'Tragowel' Station journal authored by Abraham and Hannah Booth. This daily log, documenting activity on the 120,820 acres that the Booth's ran with partner John Holloway in the Laanecoorie/Loddon district from 1856 to 1861, provides key insights into Aboriginal and settler social patterns (see Table 2.1). Station and farm diaries are important sources for rural historians and, as we show, provide new insights for religious history. Everett Edwards noted, in the US context, that station and farm diaries represent 'a sort of catch-all depository for information which the farmer sought to preserve [functioning as] account book and diary under one cover'.[5] Australian station and farm journals (similar to their counterparts in other [former] British colonies) record daily routines that make it possible to trace larger shifts over long periods, which provides insight into the interactions of land holders with 'the forces in the Nation'. This includes the forces of colonisation and settlement that shaped 'land policies, systems of landholding and labour'.[6] Because station journals detail 'the accepted code of manners, customs and morals' in their communities, they also reveal patterns in the social lives of Aboriginal and settler communities. The explicit capitalist and colonialist purposes of the pastoralists necessarily shaped the interactions with the Djaara people and the diary record because they are at odds with Djaara connections to Country and free movement within it. Our examination aims to disrupt the naturalised status of rural development by questioning the belief that Aboriginal connection to land was terminally altered.

4 Dang, 'Decolonizing Landscape,' 1005.

5 Everett E. Edwards, 'Agricultural Records; Their Nature and Value for Research,' *Agricultural History* 13, no. 1 (1939): 1. www.jstor.org/stable/3739387.

6 Ibid., 5.

By exploring Djaara engagement as workers on pastoral stations in Upper Loddon, this chapter examines their responses to settlement. We analyse the relationship between Aboriginal employment and stockwork tracking sheep and cattle movements at Tragowel Station. We also briefly adopt an environmental history perspective, noting the squatter efforts to achieve water security and profit. We then overview the rise of religious infrastructure and Christianity's impact on the district and First Peoples. Finally, we trace Emma Kerr's (or Curr) experience from 1852 to 1870, as she is an important ancestor for a contemporary Djaara clan. We highlight her life to underscore the importance of kinship with land in Aboriginal cultural practices. Custodial obligations that stem from this kinship 'bind future generations' to their homeland.[7] As Irene Watson notes, connections to the past are 'lived in the present and to be recreated in the future'.[8] These links motivated Djaara resistance to settlement. Importantly, relocation to state-controlled reserves in Victoria may have 'intensified [Aboriginal] exclusion and disadvantage', but it also enabled clans 'to preserve their oral traditions and identity'.[9] Settler overthrow transformed the land and forced the removal of its people but could not extinguish their loving links to each other.

Historical background: Djaara people, pastoralism, the gold rush and Emma Kerr's story

In recent decades, scholars have examined how Western cultural concepts of land motivated and justified the conquering mentality of settlers.[10] This 'work of the mind' categorises some places as special and worthy of protection and others as exploitable assets. When pastoralists rushed to seize territory in the Port Phillip District between 1839 and 1840, few paused to 'see' the distinctive Djaara cultural signature on the landscape or to understand their

7 Irene Watson, *Aboriginal Peoples, Colonialism and International Law: Raw Law* (Routledge, 2014), 14, doi.org/10.4324/9781315858999.

8 Ibid.

9 Janet McCalman and Len Smith, 'Family and Country: Accounting for Fractured Connections under Colonisation in Victoria, Australia,' *Journal of Population Research* 33, no. 1 (2016): 64, doi.org/10.1007/s12546-016-9160-5.

10 Simon Schama, *Landscape and Memory* (HarperCollins, 1995), 6–7.

world view. Settlers mostly ignored the basic courtesies Aboriginal cultures expect of international visitors.[11] Rather, newcomers overcame their fear of 'wild' Australia by subjugating the land and its inhabitants.[12]

Following Major Mitchell's expedition across 'Australia Felix' in 1836, the Port Phillip District was settled as a pastoral outpost by well-connected and well-resourced squatters. The publication of Mitchell's findings, which recounted 'open, grassy plains, beautifully variegated with serpentine lines of wood', encouraged these men to seize enormous stations (see Table 2.1).[13] To protect their possessions, which included millions of sheep and cattle, the squatters styled themselves as 'moral but embattled' settlers whose violence against Aboriginal people was unfortunate but justified.[14] Archibald Macarthur Campbell, who occupied the 'Gannawarra' run of over 103,680 acres on the Murray River (between present-day Koondrook and Cohuna) from October 1844, recounts his cultivation of 'a friendly feeling with the natives', whom he found 'inoffensive and obedient'.[15] He nevertheless encountered numerous duplicitous threats against his person and reported neighbours experiencing (and initiating) murderous attacks. The complex local circumstances that enabled Campbell to cultivate trust while others were embroiled in cycles of violence is beyond the scope of this chapter.[16] But such upheaval and suffering on the frontier led officials to establish a protectorate and assume responsibility for Aboriginal welfare four years after British settlement in 1839.

11 Alan Lester, 'Indigenous Engagements with Humanitarian Governance: The Port Phillip Protectorate of Aborigines and "Humanitarian Space"', in *Indigenous Networks: Mobility, Connections and Exchange*, eds. Jane Lydon and Jane Carey (Taylor and Francis, 2014): 55; 'border crossing' traditions expected visitors to herald their arrival in advance, to establish credentials and eligibility, and to communicate intentions and respect for the integrity of the host nation. As Irene Watson asserts, these protocols have 'been seriously breached since the time of Cook' and are still 'deemed by the state to not even exist'. Irene Watson, 'Aboriginal Laws and the Sovereignty of Terra Nullius', *Borderlands* 1, no. 2 (2002), para. 16.

12 Alan Lester and Fae Dussart, 'Trajectories of Protection: Protectorates of Aborigines in Early 19th Century Australia and Aotearoa New Zealand,' *New Zealand Geographer* 64, no. 3 (2008): 205–220, doi.org/10.1111/j.1745-7939.2008.00146.x.

13 Major T. L. Mitchell, *Three Expeditions into the Interior of Eastern Australia, with Descriptions of the Recently Explored Region of Australia Felix, and of the Present Colony of New South Wales*, 2nd ed., vol. 2 (T. & W. Boone, 1839; repr., Adelaide: Library Board of Australia, 1965), 155.

14 Angela Woollacott, *Settler Society in the Australian Colonies: Self-Government and Imperial Culture*, 1st ed. (Oxford University Press, 2015), 153.

15 Thomas Francis Bride, ed., *Letters from Victorian Pioneers: Being a Series of Papers on the Early Occupation of the Colony, the Aborigines, Etc. Addressed by Victorian Pioneers to His Excellency Charles Joseph La Trobe, Esq., Lieutenant-Governor of the Colony of Victoria* (Robt. S. Brain, Government Printer, 1898), 143–44.

16 Philip Dwyer and Lyndall Ryan, 'Reflections on Genocide and Settler-Colonial Violence,' *History Australia* 13, no. 3 (2016): 335–50, doi.org/10.1080/14490854.2016.1202336.

Table 2.1: Stations of the Upper Loddon plains, 1847–1884

Station name	Acres	Pastoralist	Years of occupation
Gannawarra	103,680	AM Campbell	1848–1855
		AM Campbell & AR Cruikshank	1855–1858
		James Magarey	1858–1860
		JB Hughes	1860–1863
		National Bank of Australia	1863–1866
		Henry Miller	1866–1870
		Benjamin Rochfort	Apr–Jun 1870
		WJT Clarke	1870–1873
		Charles Brown Fisher	1873
Tragowel	120,820	Graham	1848–Feb 1860
		Booth and Holloway	1860–1873
		Abraham Booth	1873–1877
		Edward Holloway	1877–
Leaghur	28,800	Alexander McMillan	1847
		Alexander McMillan & John Boyd McDonald	1848–1863
Duck Swamp	115,000	Booth & Argyle	1847–1853
		Edward Argyle	1853–1863
		Trust & Agency Co	1863–1873
		Edward Argyle & Salathiel Booth	1873–1876
		John & George Holloway	1876–1880
		R Goldsbrough & DM Parker	1880–
Mount Hope (Mount Pyramid)	97,280	A McCallum	Oct 1847 – Aug 1848
		William Campbell	1848–1857
		CJ Griffith & Molesworth Greene	1857–1883
Boort	64,000	Bear & Godfrey	1846–1848
		Henry Godfrey	1848–1857
		Henry & Frederick R Godfrey	1857–1864
		Henry Godfrey	1864–1871
		Robert Farie	1871–1875
		Thomas Armstrong	1875–1876
		WG Laidlaw & R Gibson	1876–1884
		George Holloway	1884–

Station name	Acres	Pastoralist	Years of occupation
Edgars Plains or Fernyhurst	89,000	Abel Thorpe	1847–1851
		John Hunter Kerr & Robert S Neill	1851–1855
		Richard Grice &TJ Sumner	1855–1859
		EH Alfrey & RG MacPherson	1869
		Robert Alfrey	1869–1874
		H Cunningham & JK Smyth	1874–1876
		EH Alfrey	1876–
Serpentine	90,000	John Bear	1847–1857
		Edward William Jeffreys	1857–1861
		Carmichael & Russell	1861–1869
		John Matheson	1869–
Terrick Terrick	51,200	AE Wheatley	1847–1855
		John Pearson Rowe	1855–1868
		Austin Mack	1877–1882
		Alfred Featherston Kelly	1882–

Source: Compiled by the authors.

Djaara survivors of frontier violence and disease were relocated to the local Aboriginal protectorate called 'Larrnebarramul' at Franklinford in 1841. Here they found protection from attack and management that satisfied their expectation of 'proper maintenance' through reciprocity.[17] This protectorate, however, was crippled by settler criticism and budget cuts that undermined Djaara confidence in the station as a permanent refuge. Using the protectorate as a point of replenishment, they resumed traditional patterns of mobility to the extent possible. Djaara clans moved 'as far North and East as they could' in 1848 to the Yung baluk and Tanne baluk clan areas north of present-day Bendigo.[18] This movement was aided by work on settler stations, which became more important after the protectorate was

17 For an explanation of 'right behaviour' in a later Victorian context, see Richard Broome, '"There Were Vegetables Every Year Mr Green Was Here" Right Behaviour and the Struggle for Autonomy at Coranderrk Aboriginal Reserve,' *History Australia* 3, no. 2 (2006): 43.1–43.16, doi.org/10.2104/ha060043.

18 Most abandoned the station for eight months in 1847–8 in response to recent deaths. Alan Lester and Fae Dussart, *Colonization and the Origins of Humanitarian Governance: Protecting Aborigines Across the Nineteenth-Century British Empire* (Cambridge University Press, 2014), 149; Bain Attwood, *The Good Country: The Djadja Wurrung, the Settlers and the Protectors* (Monash University Publishing, 2017), 138.

abolished in 1849 and after gold was discovered in 1852.[19] Significantly, this work also enabled the intergenerational maintenance of spiritual connections to land.

A small group of Djaara people who had converted to Christianity, fifteen per cent of the population, stayed at Franklinford to farm the former protectorate. Historian Bain Attwood notes that this group had few or no ties with traditional land and kin groups.[20] In 1864, Reverend John Green advised moving this cohort to Coranderrk.[21] Meanwhile, those who moved north adapted their traditional practices to new circumstances, working on pastoral stations to maintain access to their land-based spirituality and culture. Increasing settlement led to similar experiences in both southern and northern lands, as seen in the life of Djaara ancestor Emma Kerr and traces left by Aboriginal workers. During this period, Victoria's population grew rapidly. Djaara land was significantly impacted by gold mining and the exploitation of surrounding lands to support the settlers. Despite this, the Djaara people adapted.

To survive and remain on their land, Djaara people became stock workers, shepherds, hut keepers and domestic servants. They 'outsourced' their labour by washing sheep, stripping bark, chopping wood and carrying water.[22] Richard Broome has examined Aboriginal pastoral employment in the Port Phillip District and identified general trends among the Kulin Confederation, but scholars are yet to localise the extent or duration of employment by clan or language group.[23] Our purpose is to accrue detailed knowledge of local employment that supported access to Country and Culture, both fundamental to Djaara spiritual wellbeing. To do so, we now turn to the life story of Emma Kerr and the pastoral industry that both severed and enabled Djaara connections to Country.

19 When white workers abandoned their posts for the diggings. Lester and Dussart, *Colonization*, 153.

20 Attwood, *The Good Country*, 144.

21 The capacity of the enterprise was reduced by lack of adequate support and the poor health of Djaara family members, which ravaged their numbers. Attwood, *The Good Country*, 88.

22 Ian Clark, *Scars in the Landscape: A Register of Massacre Sites in Western Victoria, 1803–1859* (Aboriginal Studies Press, 1995), 87; Attwood, *The Good Country*, 150.

23 Richard Broome, 'Aboriginal Workers on South-Eastern Frontiers,' *Australian Historical Studies* 26, no. 103 (1994): 202–20, doi.org/10.1080/10314619408595960.

Emma Kerr is an apical ancestor for contemporary Djaara people, and her life story reflects Djaara contact experience and their struggle to survive. Emma was born at 'Kelly's Station, on the Bendigo Creek', in about 1853.[24] 'Kelly's Station' neighboured 'Terrick Terrick', where Bendigo Creek merges with Mount Hope Creek.[25] Little is known about Emma's early life, including her mother's identity. Haw and Munro suggest that Emma Kerr's father was the 'squatter Jamie Kerr', referring to John Hunter Kerr, co-owner of Fernyhurst Station (also known as Edgars Plain) from 1851 to 1855. This aligns with Emma's birth date.[26] By age sixteen, Emma was living at nearby Mount Hope Station on Barapa Barapa land. Here she received rations once a week from pastoralist and local 'Guardian of Aborigines', Molesworth Greene, who owned the lease to Mount Hope and Pyramid Hill stations.[27] Seven Aboriginal people were then permanently resident on the station:

> Four men and three women and their children lived and worked on the station, go[ing] away perhaps for a few days fishing, but they were, to all intents and purposes, resident; and other members of their tribe used to come occasionally.[28]

Emma Kerr and the other two women apparently cohabited with white station workers on Mt Hope, relationships that Greene publicly condemned.[29] Aboriginal women's agency in these relationships is difficult to determine, given the context of dispossession and social upheaval.[30] Emma Kerr's first child, John Patterson, was born at Mount Hope Station circa

24 'Emma (Curr) Campbell (abt. 1853–1886),' WikiTree, accessed February 16, 2023, www.wikitree.com/wiki/Curr-21. Gary Murray, 'Biographies: Pastor Sir Douglas Ralph Nicholls and Gladys Naby Muriel Bux', Internet Archive, accessed February 16, 2023, web.archive.org/web/20160319023234/https://www.melbourne.vic.gov.au/SiteCollectionDocuments/nicholls-biographies.pdf.

25 Alfred Kelly acquired the run circa 1880. 'Giyakiki | Our story', Dja Dja Wurrung Clans Aboriginal Corporation, djadjawurrung.com.au/giyakiki-our-story/.

26 Paul Haw and Margaret Munro, *Footprints Across the Loddon Plains: A Shared History*, ed. Margaret Munro (Boort Development Inc., 2010).

27 From 1857 to 1883. R. V. Billis and A. S. Kenyon, *Pastoral Pioneers of Port Phillip* (Stockland Press, 1974), 61.

28 Molesworth Greene, Esq., 'Royal Commission on the Aborigines: Report of the Commissioners Appointed to Inquire Into the Present Condition of the Aborigines of This Colony, and to Advise as to the Best Means of Caring For, and Dealing With Them, in the Future; Together With Minutes of Evidence and Appendices,' Parliamentary Paper No. 76, Minutes of Evidence 1530, 25 May 1877 (John Ferres, Government Printer, 1877), 56.

29 For further discussion, see Uncle Roy Henry Patterson and Jennifer Jones, *On Taungurung Land: Sharing History and Culture* (ANU Press, 2020), doi.org/10.22459/OTL.2020.

30 Ann McGrath, 'The White Man's Looking Glass: Aboriginal-Colonial Gender Relations at Port Jackson,' *Australian Historical Studies* 24, no. 95 (1990): 195, doi.org/10.1080/10314619008595841; Amanda Nettelbeck, 'Intimate Violence in the Pastoral Economy: Aboriginal Women's Labour and Protective Governance,' in *Intimacies of Violence in the Settler Colony: Economies of Dispossession around the Pacific Rim*, ed. Penelope Edmonds and Amanda Nettelbeck (Palgrave Macmillan, 2018).

1869, and his surname probably refers to his biological father.[31] Emma was then engaged to Alick Campbell (1851 – circa1933) a young Barapa Barapa man from Gannawarra Station. The couple married at Coranderrk in 1873 after Emma's forced removal from Mount Hope.[32] In 1877, Alick Campbell testified to the Royal Commission on the Aborigines that he had spent most of his youth at Gannawarra, 'I was fourteen or fifteen years with him – brought up with him'.[33] Long-term residence of Aboriginal stock workers and accommodation of their families was common on Gannawarra. This co-occupancy occurred to a lesser extent on some neighbouring properties, a finding supported by data from the Tragowel Station journal. We now turn to this journal, which also records the happenings in the broader Loddon River district, including the rise of Christian settlement and infrastructure and interactions with Aboriginal people, from the diarist's point of view.

'Today my dear husband and father started with a mob of cattle to head for the diggings': Extractive landscapes in Bendigo's north

Tragowel Station was a key stop for travellers and locals on the busy Melbourne Road, perhaps because Abraham Booth, a trained butcher, regularly sold meat from the homestead butchery.[34] Booth moved to the district in 1840, first running the 112,000 acre Duck Swamp Station with Edward Argyle. In 1853, he acquired Tragowel Station with John Holloway and married Holloway's daughter, Hannah, in 1856.[35] Surviving volumes of Abraham and Hannah Booth's station journal began on 6 August 1856 with the 'commencement of [their] matrimonial Felicity' and ended in November

31 This research was originally commissioned by Uncle Roy Patterson, John Patterson's grandson. For discussion of surnames and station affiliation in Queensland, see Sally Babidge, Pamela J. Stewart, and Andrew Strathern, *Aboriginal Family and the State: The Conditions of History* (Ashgate Publishing, 2013), 92.

32 Diane Barwick, *Rebellion at Coranderrk* (ANU Press, 2024), 154. doi.org/10.22459/RC.2024.

33 Alexander Campbell, 'Royal Commission on the Aborigines: Report of the Commissioners Appointed to Inquire Into the Present Condition of the Aborigines of This Colony, and to Advise as to the Best Means of Caring For, and Dealing With Them, in the Future; Together With Minutes of Evidence and Appendices,' Parliamentary Paper No. 76, Minutes of Evidence 736, 22 May 1877 (John Ferres, Government Printer, 1877), 28.

34 'A Pioneer Dead,' *Argus*, 22 May 1902, 6, nla.gov.au/nla.news-article9072178.

35 'A Pioneer Pastoralist,' *Australasian*, 31 May 1902, 33, nla.gov.au/nla.news-article139759342.

1862.[36] John Holloway also makes occasional entries, and Hannah's brother George Holloway keeps the journal during a brief period of caretaking. These 76 months of entries document daily activities, major events and personal attitudes, including those towards the Djaara people working on Upper Loddon pastoral stations.[37]

Aboriginal employment in the Upper Loddon

The Tragowel diarists record mundane daily activities associated with their cattle business and interactions with neighbouring and more distant properties in the mid-Murray region. The journal records stock movement, commercial transactions, neighbourhood negotiations over infrastructure improvements and plans for community development, all managed by exchanging letters, couriered notes and personal visits. The small and limited window provided by the Tragowel journal includes a view of cross-racial employment practices in the district, as Aboriginal workers transacted with the Booth and Holloway families. The language used in the Tragowel journal reflect the values of the day, so Aboriginal workers are rarely named, and their national or clan affiliation is never mentioned. They are mostly referred to as 'blackfellows' or by their station affiliation, not by their individual identity.[38] Such language and concepts are unacceptable and offensive today, but nevertheless provide valuable indications of connection with pastoralists and to Country. Over the 76 months of journal entries, there are 63 interactions with Aboriginal people; 62 of these are with one or more Aboriginal men, and one engagement is with a group of Aboriginal women and children, who are unnamed and unenumerated. These interactions are seasonal: activity increased during spring, while summer was quieter. There is no recorded engagement with Aboriginal people in 29 of the 76 months, with the longest break between November 1858 and June 1859 (see Figure 2.1).

36 It is likely that more journals were kept by the couple, but they have not survived. According to Doust, the journal ends when the Booths left Tragowel to travel to England in 1862. Further journals by family members survive: the 'Oakover Log' 1884 to 1898, and the 'Dhulura Diary', mid-1893 to September 1897 recording farming on the Murrumbidgee. Janet Doust, 'Kinship and Accountability: The Diaries of a Pioneer Pastoralist Family, 1856 to 1898,' *History Australia* 2, no. 1 (2005): 4-1–4-14, doi.org/10.2104/ha040004.

37 Journal of Abraham and Hannah Booth 1856-1861 (MS 11834, Box F 2157–2), State Library of Victoria. This research also makes use of MS 9715, MSB 486, Journal of Mr and Mrs A Booth, typescript, State Library of Victoria.

38 For a nuanced discussion of derogatory racialised language usage on a Queensland pastoral station, see Cristina Lawrence and Jennifer Jones, 'Paying Aboriginal Rural Workers: Racism, the Labour Market and Worker Agency,' *Labour History* 125, no. 1 (2023): 55–84, doi.org/10.3828/labourhistory.2023.20.

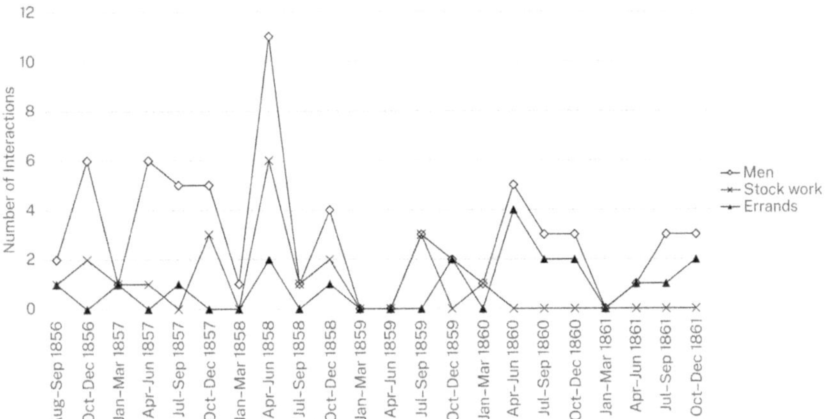

Figure 2.1: Interactions with Aboriginal men per quarter

Source: Compiled by Susan Poole and the authors.

Booth and Holloway did not employ Aboriginal people themselves, so their engagement is facilitated by business with other stations. On one occasion, Aboriginal workers are subcontracted when young George Holloway is in charge. All other new employees on the station are unracialised, presumably white.[39] The second form of engagement occurs when autonomous Aboriginal groups and individuals interact with the Tragowel Station family on their own terms. We elaborate on the nature of Aboriginal employment on other stations and engagement with Aboriginal people, including autonomous groups and individuals, to gain insight into the daily lives and priorities of Aboriginal people on Djaara land.

Results and discussion

Core station business drove engagement with Aboriginal people at Tragowel. Stock management, work-related travel and errands form 82 per cent of total encounters. Autonomous Aboriginal action accounted for the remaining 18 per cent, primarily in the form of self-sufficient travel and cultural activity.

As might be expected, stock work and droving accounted for 50 per cent of interactions with Aboriginal people. For example, on 18 November 1860, 'Mr Glasses French stockkeeper and blackboy came to the muster'.

39 The diarists repeatedly identify outsiders according to foreign race or national categories, including Jews, Germans and French men. It can be extrapolated that normative status is assigned to British whites.

Aboriginal workers often accompanied their employer on business, so work-related travel accounts for 17 per cent of interactions, such as on 13 October 1857, when the diarist records, 'Arch Campbell & blackfellow is here tonight with his horses going to the Bendigo market'. Running errands accounts for 15 per cent of interactions, as on 20 January 1857, when 'the blackfellow from Gardiners [came] with note regarding muster'. The remaining 18 per cent of entries refer to autonomous Aboriginal action, which are unrelated to settler objectives. These include travel and cultural activities. The key point here is that, on Djaara Country, within the settlers' purview, labour was subsumed into new Aboriginal-determined lifeways. We elaborate on this strategic engagement below.

Table 2.2: Named Aboriginal workers engaging with Tragowel, 1856–1861

Given name	Aboriginal name	Total interactions	Year	Employer	Station affiliation	Activity
Isacke	–	1	1856	Kirk	Pental Island	Droving
Harry	–	1	1856	Dr King	NA	Fetching horses
Mickey	Murtmeral	1	1856	Mr Morris	Unknown	Fetching horses
Paddy	–	3	1856	Dr King	Kerang Town	Work-related travel
Angus	–	1	1857	AM Campbell	Loddon Run	Work-related travel
Charley	Chalurmin	1	1857	NA	Autonomous	Gifting possum skin rug
Duke of Wellington	Morepin	1	1857	NA	Autonomous	Buying stores
Bobby	Younyourn	1	1858	Gardiner	Pericoota	Fetching horses
Jackey	Genbuckeroo	1	1858	Campbell	Lake Boga	Droving
Mooney	Carawook	3	1858	Cooper & Johnson	Avoca	Droving, fetching horses
Tommy	–	1	1858	Unknown	Unknown	Killed at the Kerang Pound

Given name	Aboriginal name	Total interactions	Year	Employer	Station affiliation	Activity
Robinson	Lanuremin	2	1856	Grey (Russell's Manager)	Serpentine	Droving
			1861	George Holloway	Autonomous	Bark cutting

Source: Tragowel journal and Henry Godfrey's 1863 census, compiled by the authors. See Paul Haw and Margaret Munro, *Footprints Across the Loddon Plains: A Shared History* (Boort Development Inc., 2010), 98–99.

Further analysis of the data shows that in 26 per cent of interactions with Aboriginal people in the journal, the Aboriginal worker is named (see Table 2.2). Half of these men are known Djaara identities who had built long-term associations with local settlers; hence, they escaped generic racialised descriptors as 'blackboy' or 'blackfellow'. Nevertheless, European names 'given' by settlers to Aboriginal men such as 'Duke of Wellington' indicate a style of affection, along with a degree of mockery or condescending superiority. Similarly, names such as 'Jackey', 'Mooney' and 'Tommy' reference the 'transformation of identity' in their 'bestowal from above', as the Djaara names of these men were known locally but were not used by the diarists.[40] Settler categorisation of particular Aboriginal men as trusted known entities who had 'come in' and were incorporated into station work regimes differentiates them from the unassimilated who stayed 'out bush', or from strangers.[41] Aboriginal people who were unfamiliar to settlers are also called 'warrigal blacks' in similar sources.[42] The language used by the Tragowel diarists reflects this division, as Aboriginal people who pursue their own cultural agenda are linguistically distanced via depersonalised and racist labels.[43] The diarist also ignores relationships between named Djaara stock workers and their unnamed kin. Given these people were living on and moving around Djaara Country and interacting with settlers 'as usual', it is likely that they held traditional affiliation with those lands.

40 Raymond Evans, Kay Saunders, and Kathryn Cronin, *Race Relations in Colonial Queensland: A History of Exclusion, Exploitation and Extermination* (University of Queensland Press, 1993), 113.

41 Veronica Strang, 'Moon Shadows: Aboriginal and European Heroes in an Australian Landscape,' in *Landscape, Memory and History: Anthropological Perspectives*, ed. Pamela J. Stewart and Andrew Strathern (London Pluto Press, 2002).

42 For example, by AM Campbell of Gannawarra, see Thomas Francis Bride, *Letters from Victorian Pioneers: Being a Series of Papers on the Early Occupation of the Colony, the Aborigines, … Addressed by Victorian Pioneers to His Excellency Charles Joseph La Trobe, Lieutenant Governor of the Colony of Victoria* (Robt. S. Brain, 1898), 143–144.

43 Liz Conor, *Skin Deep: Settler Impressions of Aboriginal Women* (UWA Publishing, 2016), 9.

Twenty-four stations are mentioned in the journal, mostly nearby. Fifteen of these employed Aboriginal workers and accommodated their kin (see Figure 2.2). Gannawarra Station accounted for 15 per cent of Tragowel's interactions with Aboriginal people (none of whom are named by the diarists, as shown in Table 2.2). In the Tragowel journal, Aboriginal workers are principally associated with Gannawarra while it was held by the Campbell family.[44] As noted above, Emma Kerr's partner, Alick Campbell, was from Gannawarra, reputedly AM Campbell's son.[45]

Other employers include medical practitioner Dr King, the Kerang public house known as 'Farmer's', the Kerang store owner and pastoralist Patchell, and Kerang merchant Mr Hill. These service providers are accompanied by Aboriginal people during 6 per cent of interactions recorded by Tragowel. White station worker Mick Galway also had significant associations with Aboriginal people.

Mick Galway worked for Pericoota, Gunbower and Tandarra stations in the period and maintained a long-term relationship with an Aboriginal woman, Alice Holmes, who lived at Mount Hope.[46] Galway is mentioned 29 times between December 1857 and October 1861. On five occasions, Aboriginal co-workers accompany Galway, as on 14 October 1861, when 'Micky Galway and the 2 blacks went out to single tree camp'. As discussed later, settler pressure that led to the removal of Aboriginal women from Mount Hope in 1869 personally impacted Galway.

Unaffiliated or independent movement accounts for seven per cent of engagements between Aboriginal people and Tragowel Station. Noteworthy is 7 December 1857, when the 'Blackfellow Duke Wellington bought 4/- worth of stores', presumably in preparation for cultural business in the Tragowel swamp, which is next to the Loddon River. This could also infer that bush tucker was insufficient to sustain a large group. The next day, 8 December, the diarist notes that 'a lot of Lubras & Pickaninies have been today begging as usual & have been noisy in the swamp. Have gone away toward Farmers' (*sic*). The phrase 'as usual' shows their routine presence and activity, which wasn't notable enough to gain habitual mention in the journal. In May the next year, the diarist condemned 'a lot of darkies [...] lounging about but are now gone'.

44 The Campbells appear in the journal until 1858; subsequent owners/managers Magarey, Hutchinson and Hughes appear less frequently.

45 Haw and Munro, *Footprints*.

46 Correspondence held by Pyramid Hill and District Historical Society, 6 McKay St, Pyramid Hill Victoria 3575.

In both instances, regular autonomous interactions and cultural activity is recorded using generic racialised language and an impatient, dismissive tone. By contrast, Booth and Holloway were comfortable with Charley, Duke of Wellington, and Robinson, who are recognised as local individuals and credited with autonomous action. Perhaps their routine station work, which contributed to settler aims, positioned them as Djaara people who had 'come in' from the bush and accepted incorporation into European regimes? Robinson worked for Serpentine Station in 1856 and collected bark for George Holloway in 1861, suggesting continuous residence, trusting relationships and participation in the settler economy.[47]

Aboriginal cultural purposes motivated another five per cent of exchanges, as suggested by the exchange on 22 July 1857, when 'Blackfellow Charley brought Mr H opossum rug'. Presented shortly after the birth of Hannah and Abraham Booth's first child, this cultural gift was likely designed to strengthen cross-racial relationships and reciprocity. The assumption that settlers are subject to both the benefits and demands of mutual obligation is also apparent in the behaviour of local Aboriginal women, noted above, as making regular requests for sustenance. Given that requests for sustenance are indicative of expectations for reciprocity and compensation for appropriated lands, it is understandable that these requests are persistent. Tragowel diarists characterised this as 'begging as usual'.[48]

These interpretations of interactions with Aboriginal people reflect colonial views that see land as property instead of kin, motivating the degree of surveillance and disquiet at sustained Aboriginal connections to the land.

The Tragowel diarists also record Aboriginal hunting activities; on one occasion (24 December 1857), they note 'some blackfellows was at the dam and stated they were going to the Banagar with Mr Hill fishing'. Given that Mr Hill was the owner 'of the Kerang store', this shared activity likely reflected an important alliance.[49] On another occasion, an unaccompanied 'native was here tonight', his business unstated.[50] These brief references to Aboriginal people indicate both continuity of traditional practices and adaptation to settler encroachment.

47 George Holloway 'engaged Robinson "Black Fellow" to get 100 sheets of bark for 1£', completing a new hut to accommodate travellers. 20 July 1861.

48 Jennifer Jones 'Acknowledging Sovereignty: Settlers, Right Behaviour and the Taungurung Clans of the Kulin Nation,' *Law&history* 8, no. 2 (2021): 117–143.

49 Journal of A and H Booth – typescript, Journal entry, Wednesday 28 October 1857 (MS9715, MSB 486), State Library of Victoria.

50 Journal of A and H Booth – Manuscript (MS11834, F Box 2157-2) State Library of Victoria; Journal of Mr and Mrs A Booth, typescript (MS9715, MSB 486), State Library of Victoria.

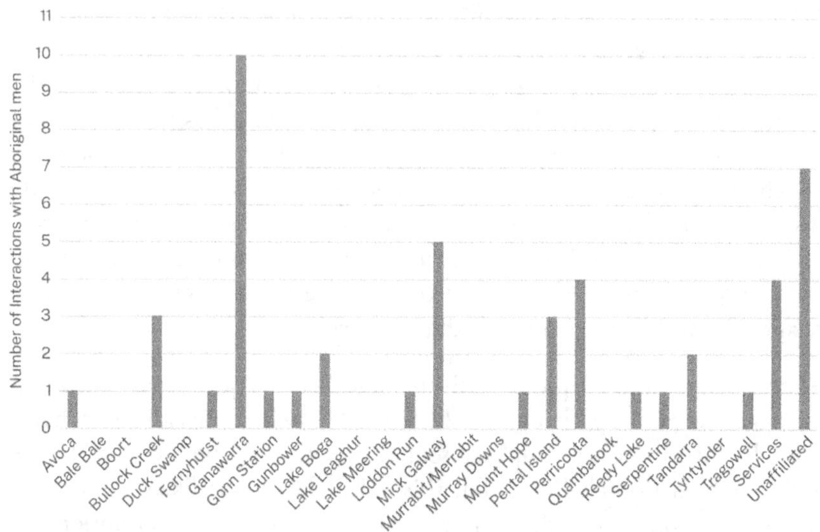

Figure 2.2: Documented interactions between Tragowel and Aboriginal people, by station affiliation

Source: Compiled by Susan Poole and the authors.

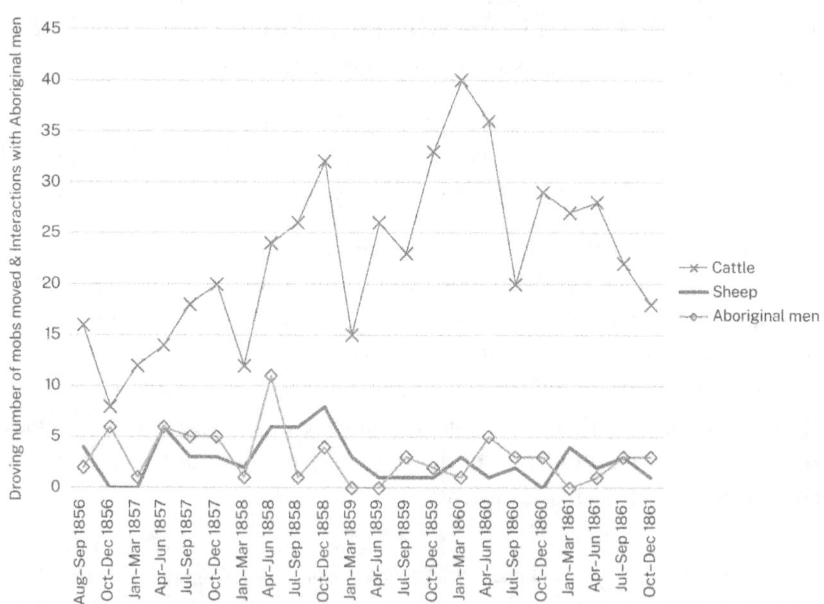

Figure 2.3: Stock movement in mobs per quarter, August 1856 – December 1861

Source: Compiled by Susan Poole and the authors.

The Tragowel journal reveals the continuous maintenance of Aboriginal relationships with their sacred land, juxtaposed with the growing impact of settlers who view the area as a resource for exploitation. Stock movement illustrates this increasing impact.

To contextualise the employment of Aboriginal stock workers in relationship to the volume of stockwork undertaken in the vicinity of Tragowel, stock movement was quantified over the 76 months of journal entries (see Figure 2.3). This reveals a gradual increase in cattle movement from an average of 10 to 15 mobs per quarter up to 25 mobs or more per quarter. The increase in cattle numbers did not correspond to a higher involvement of Aboriginal workers, despite the need for more hands. The trendline for Aboriginal involvement declines from four per quarter down to under two per quarter over the same period. Crucially, the increasing volume of cattle also holds implications for the environment. Over the passage of the diary, 499 mobs of cattle were driven within, through and from Tragowel station. Just 227 mobs (45%) were documented in number, leaving 55 per cent as unenumerated. Over the term of the journal, mobs averaged at 175 cows, but the size of the enumerated mobs varied from just one cow through to 1,200 cows, indicating huge variation in the size of the mobs. It is known that 8 to 10 mobs greater than 1,000 cattle were driven within, through and from Tragowel Station over the passage of the diary, an average of one very large mob per year. Sheep droving was more sporadic, but large mobs were more common, with 60 mobs – about 10 per year – averaging 3,072 in size. One extremely large mob of 17,000 sheep belonging to McReedy took two days to pass through Tragowel Station, 27–28 February 1860. Holloway and Booth were anxious to expedite their movement to protect their pasture, sending Edward Holloway and a station hand to 'look after' them on 27 February and noting they were 'still passing' the next day.

Squatters took action to curtail the impacts of droving stock and fenced their boundaries to manage incursions by neighbouring stock, even before Victorian Selection Acts forced squatters to 'protect their leases by investing in improvement'.[51] The first of these acts, the *Sale of Crown Lands Act 1860*, known as the *Nicholson Act*, was considered favourable to squatter interests, as was the second, which was known as the Duffy Land Act and passed in 1862. Scholars suggest that it was the third land act, of 1865, that encouraged pastoralists to reduce encroachment through freehold purchase

51 John Pickard, 'The Transition from Shepherding to Fencing in Colonial Australia,' *Rural History* 18, no. 2 (2007): 148, doi.org/10.1017/S0956793307002129.

and by fencing. This also fulfilled leasehold conditions.[52] Negotiations over boundary fences between Gannawarra, Gunbower, Mount Hope and Tragowel Stations began in the Upper Loddon much earlier, in 1858, before the *Nicholson Act* came into force. Fence construction commenced in earnest in 1861. Our findings suggest that awareness of environmental fragility and stock impacts spurred this early investment. With employment already declining, fencing represented an additional major impact upon Aboriginal people's land-based culture. This is because fencing can limit or block access to land and waters, which impacts spiritual practices and livelihoods.[53]

Pastoral infrastructure and Djaara adjustment

Boundaries are social constructs that are shaped by law and culture. Indigenous delineation of the 'limit of Country' was often maintained through spiritual practices: ephemeral ceremony like song and dance or metaphorically through paintings or carving.[54] The location of Aboriginal national boundaries may also be indicated by changes in vegetation or by watersheds, creeks and rivers. These delineations were slightly more familiar to settler understandings than the ephemeral modes. European squatters of Upper Loddon and mid-Murray marked, maintained and defended station boundaries by accessing cultural concepts and technologies. As early as 1858, this included fencing to prevent prolonged foraging by droving stock and unauthorised grazing by neighbours. Prior to fencing, boundaries between properties usually followed clear and well-defined natural features, including creeks and ridges. Boundaries were also marked by 'corner tree's' and furrow lines drawn by a plough. The agreed boundaries between Tragowel and neighbouring properties Mount Hope, Pental Island and Duck Swamp were re-drawn in July 1857, but stock frequently strayed over these boundaries with and without their owners' knowledge. Stock incursion had a detrimental impact on available

52 J. M Powell, *The Public Lands of Australia Felix: Settlement and Land Appraisal in Victoria 1834-91 with Special Reference to the Western Plains* (Oxford University Press, 1970); Pickard, 'The Transition,' 148.

53 Larissa Behrendt, 'White Picket Fences: Recognizing Aboriginal Property Rights in Australia's Psychological Terra Nullius,' *Constitutional Forum* 10, no. 2 (1999): 50–53; Christopher Mayes, 'Governmentality of Fencing in Australia: Tracing the White Wires from Paddocks to Aboriginal Protection, Pest Exclusion and Immigration Restriction,' *Journal of Intercultural Studies* 41, no. 1 (2020): 42–59, doi.org/10.1080/07256868.2020.1704228.

54 Andrew Turk, 'Representations of Tribal Boundaries of Australian Indigenous Peoples and the Implications for Geographic Information Systems,' in *Information Technology and Indigenous People*, ed. Laurel Evelyn Dyson, Max Hendriks, and Stephen Grant (IGI Global, 2007).

fodder and, hence, on neighbourly relations, as Booth and Halloway were aware. Of fourteen occasions recorded in the journal, Booth and Halloway were challenged about Tragowel stock straying over a neighbour's unfenced boundary twice (see Table 2.3).

Table 2.3: Unauthorised stock movement across station boundaries prior to fencing, 1857–1861

Date	Tragowel journal entry
27 February 1857	AM Campbells sheep [Ganawarra] was within ½ mile of our home (blow) feeding & the shepherd with them.
14 March 1857	Letter to Cameron [Lake Meering] about his sheep feeding on our run.
10 June 1857	Seen a many of Gardiners cattle [Perricoota] on our run.
13 August 1857	Saw Magarys sheep [Ganawarra] over the plough furrow again.
24 July 1858	Mr H has been running up the East Boundary to see if any of the Mt Hope Sheep has been over the boundary & finds they have been as far as the Clumps feeding.
13 August 1858	Saw Magarys sheep [Ganawarra] over the plough furrow again.
18 May 1859	Found Griffiths & Greens sheep [Mount Hope] feeding on our run.
19 May 1859	Found Mt Hope sheep again over the boundary.
6 July 1859	Magary sheep [Ganawarra] was nearly up to 2 mile Point this morning.
22 November 1859	Letter Chomley Mt Hope informing us that after next week he shall impound all our cattle found on MT Hope run & lay the largest damages on the act allows.
18 April 1860	Houston [Gunbower] was very cool about the cattle.
24 August 1860	Mount Hope sheep feeding about a mile over the line.
3 July 1861	Found some of Aitkens cattle [Tandarra] on the run & him there over the creek.
4 July 1861	Out at the Clumps & found Chomley sheep [Mt Hope] on our run & quite bare for some considerable distance. Shepherds excuse did not know the plough furrow.

Source: Compiled by the authors.

The remaining twelve record neighbouring stock feeding over the Tragowel boundary. Five of these occasions involve sheep from Mount Hope. The ill-feeling between neighbours is exacerbated by intentional trespass, as indicated on 27 February 1857, when the diarist expresses exasperation in brackets after finding Campbells sheep 'within ½ mile of our home (blow) feeding & the shepherd with them'. Worse still, the squatter, Aitken of Tandarra, is supervising the trespass himself on 3 July 1861. Relations with Mount

Hope similarly deteriorate when their shepherd allows his sheep to cross the Tragowel furrow in July 1858, May 1859, August 1860 and July 1861. Yet, when Tragowel cattle also stray over the Mount Hope boundary in November 1859, Chomley threatens Booth and Holloway with 'the largest damages on the act allows'. These exchanges reveal the motivation to protect and preserve available fodder, particularly when unauthorised sheep grazing makes the run 'quite bare for some considerable distance'. After reading these data on straying stock with reference to Table 2.4, which collates progress towards boundary fencing, it appears that straying stock may have informed decisions to fence station boundaries between Tragowel and Gunbower in 1860, and that the neighbouring squatter on Tandarra obstructs progress on fencing and benefits from stray feeding for as long as possible.

Table 2.4: Progress towards boundary fencing, 1857–1861

Year	Dates	Action
1857	24–29 July	Drawing boundary furrows between Tragowel, Mount Hope, Pental Island & Duck Swamp.
1858	23 June – 24 July	Negotiations over boundary fences between Tragowel, Gannawarra & Gunbower.
1860	18 April	Conflict over straying cattle, but no agreement on boundary fence between Tragowel & Gunbower.
1860	20 June	Drawing boundary line between Tragowel & Gunbower.
1860	19 September	Boundary fence erected between Mount Hope and Gunbower.
1860	28 September	Sourcing pines for boundary fence between Tragowel and Gunbower.
1860	27 October – 13 November	Seeking contract fencers.
1860	8 December	Contracted fencers working on boundary.
1860	29 December	Negotiating Tragowel & Tandarra boundary fence. Disagreement over fencing Rowen's Waterhole.
1861	3 January – 5 January	Agreement reached over Rowen's Waterhole.
1861	7 January	Contractors split and mortice fence posts.
1861	8 January	Drawing boundary to fence between Tragowel & Gannawarra.
1861	2 February	Drawing boundary to fence between Tragowel & Gunbower.
1861	9–16 March	Drawing boundary to fence between Tragowel & Tandarra. Renegotiating boundary.
1861	9–12 April	Drawing boundary to fence between Tragowel & Ganawarra; 8 miles and 52 chains.
1861	15–20 April	Negotiating boundary fence between Tragowel, Tandarra & Gannawarra.

Year	Dates	Action
1861	24 April	Fencing contractor's work inspected.
1861	3–16 May	Marking out fence with contractor.
1861	31 May	Negotiations over boundary fence Tragowel & Gannawarra.
1861	3 July	Conflict over straying cattle.
1861	4 July	Conflict over straying sheep.
1861	5 August	Ploughing boundary line.
1861	2 September	Assisting Garrett's stock (Bale Bale) through Ganley's fence (Serpentine).

Source: Compiled by the authors.

Squatters understood that Country was slow to recover if grasses were 'pulled up by the roots by the sheep' by the early 1840s.[55] Pickard notes that insufficient carrying capacity and overgrazing was solved in the early colonial period by 'simply moving further inland' or 'squatting on more land'.[56] Once land acquisition became difficult or expensive, squatters became more sensitive to stock impacts, including systematic straying by neighbours' stock, because unsustainable grazing led to land degradation and stock deterioration.

After boundary fences were erected, sustainable grazing in semi-arid ecosystems like the Upper Loddon could only be managed through adaptive stocking and control of native animals, first dingos, then kangaroos.[57] These more intensive European interventions resulted in a 'progressive loss of Aboriginal control over and access to resources', which increased proximity to and reliance upon settlers.[58] Prior to fencing, squatters entrusted one shepherd with 1,000 to 5,000 sheep on Gunbower and Lake Boga, for example, but after fencing, one boundary-rider cared for about 10,000 sheep.[59] Overall station staffing, including Aboriginal employment, reduced as a consequence of fencing.

55 Pickard quotes evidence given to the 1842 Select Committee on Immigration. John Pickard, 'Safe Carrying Capacity and Sustainable Grazing: How Much Have We Learnt in Semi-Arid Australia in the Last 170 Years?,' in *Land Degradation: Papers Selected from Contributions to the Sixth Meeting of the International Geographical Union's Commission on Land Degradation and Desertification, Perth, Western Australia, 20–28 September 1999*, ed. Arthur J. Conacher (Springer Netherlands, 2001), 278.

56 Ibid.

57 Judith Littleton, 'When Resilience Fails: Fences, Water Control, and Aboriginal History in the Western Riverina, Australia,' in *Hunter-Gatherer Adaptation and Resilience: A Bioarchaeological Perspective* ed. Christopher M. Stojanowski and Daniel H. Temple. (Cambridge University Press, 2018), 328–53, doi.org/10.1017/9781316941256.

58 Ibid., 338.

59 Ibid.

A related concern in the Tragowel journal is the drive to harness and preserve water resources in this semi-arid country. Rainfall on the Northern Plains is unpredictable, so the development of water infrastructure responded to both scarcity and abundance. Djaara and Barapa Barapa people drew upon ancestral knowledge that informed their sustainable land management strategies. This included engineered waterways, seasonal hunting and collecting, fire stick farming and patterns of social and territorial interaction that were responsive to climatic fluctuation. The changing landscape of pastoralism impacted all these socioecological strategies.

Table 2.5: Development of local weirs and dams, 1857–1860

Year	Dates	Watercourse	Action	Involvement
1857	25 May–20 June	Calivil Creek	Dam near 9 mile.	Booth and Holloway, Tragowel
1857	8–28 July	Pyramid Creek	Dam near 10 mile hut.	Booth and Holloway, Tragowel Mr Sheridan, Mount Hope
1857	16 November	Serpentine Creek	Negotiating cutting Serpentine Creek at Loddon junction.	Booth and Holloway, Tragowel Gardiner, Perricoota Grey, Serpentine
1858	20 May	Pyramid Creek	Negotiating construction of 1970-yard dam @ £165.	Booth and Holloway, Tragowel Gardiner, Perricoota Houston, Gunbower Greene, Mt Hope – refused
1858	15 July–28 August	Calivil Creek	Dam at Water Hole Camp.	Booth and Holloway, Tragowel
1858	2–25 September	Loddon River, Serpentine Creek	Negotiations to dam Loddon River, to flow Serpentine Creek. Collected £343-6-8 towards costs.	Association of neighbouring squatters. Later joined by McMillan, Lake Leaghur & Argyle, Gunbower
1858	2 November	Loddon River	Damming commenced.	Above 'Association of squatters'
1859	6 January	Loddon River	Lower dam washed away.	Booth and Holloway, Tragowel
1859	27 January	Calivil Creek	Raising dam wall.	Booth and Holloway, Tragowel
1859	27 June–12 July	Calivil Creek	Strengthening dam wall.	Booth and Holloway, Tragowel

Year	Dates	Watercourse	Action	Involvement
1859	13 August	Loddon River	Negotiations to survey drain from Loddon to Serpentine Creek.	Managed by Argyle, Gunbower
1859	26 September -2 November	Drain from Loddon to Serpentine Creek	Works commenced.	Association of squatters
1859	3 November	Drain from Loddon to Serpentine Creek	Dam breakage. Repairs 5–7 November.	Association of squatters
1859	14 November	Calivil Creek	Water running out of Calivil dam.	Booth and Holloway, Tragowel
1859	5 December	Calivil Creek	Repairs to dam commenced. Water stopped 13 December.	Booth and Holloway, Tragowel
1859	19 December – 6 January	Unclear, probably Calivil Creek	Working on dam.	Booth and Holloway, Tragowel
1860	12–14 April	Loddon River	Clearing cutting to Tragowel Creek.	Booth and Holloway, Tragowel
1860	16–28 April	Loddon River, Serpentine Creek	Reports on flood waters.	Booth and Holloway, Tragowel
1860	6–21 July	Loddon River	Concern over & works on upper and middle dams.	Association of squatters
1860	13–14 September	Loddon River	Works to keep creek water from flowing to the Loddon.	Booth and Holloway, Tragowel

Source: Compiled by the authors.

The Tragowel journal charts the negotiations, cooperative efforts and disagreements between squatters as they built dams on the Loddon River and attempted to redirect the flow to smaller creeks between 1857 and 1861 (see Table 2.5). Table 2.5 reveals repeated effort and investment to dam and redirect water flow, which impacted the ecologies of the Loddon River, Serpentine Creek and Tragowel Creek. The perceived benefits had a direct impact on contributions to water infrastructure works, as evident in the scaled financial support for a new dam on the Loddon, where primary beneficiaries invested £100 and others as little as £5 (see Table 2.6). These major stakeholders also invested in planning, lobbying and physical labour for the project. However, their lack of nuanced environmental knowledge meant they were soon disappointed by the effects of flooding rains. From August to November 1859, for example, the Tragowel pastoralists made concerted efforts to redirect water from the Loddon to the Serpentine Creek, but their technology proved insufficient (see Table 2.5). Brief extracts from the Tragowel journal in November 1859 reveal the trajectory from hope to disappointment:

> **1 Nov 1859** Have been to the dam & stopped the water for a time but occasionally made its escape, obliged to leave at noon because of rain & this afternoon carpenter has been & says water running through very fast.
>
> **2 Nov 1859** My Dear Husband did not return from the dam until midnight but was successful in stopping the water.
>
> **3 Nov 1859** Have had another breakage at the dam on account of the beam going across the water found a rent under so we took it out and now think it is secure.
>
> **5 Nov 1859** Been to the dam & to our horror found that it is broke away on this side of the frame & running a very strong stream & was quite useless to do anything to it.[60]

Table 2.6: Graded contribution to Loddon dam expenses, 1858

Promised contribution	Date	Amount
Ganley & Waite, Serpentine	18 September 1858	£100
Carmichael & Russell	18 September 1858	£100
Booth & Holloway, Tragowel	18 September 1858	£100
Rolf & Flinn	18 September 1858	£33-6-8
H. McNeil Campbell, Reedy Lake[?]	18 September 1858	£5
Garrett and Wheatley, Bale Bale	18 September 1858	£5
Henry Raines [on the Plain]	18 September 1858	'has promised something'
McMillan, Lake Leaghur	25 September 1858	'willing to do his portion'
Argyle, Gunbower	September 1858	'willing to do his portion'

Source: Compiled by the authors.

60 Journal of Abraham and Hannah Booth 1856-1861 (MS11834, Box F 2157-2), State Library of Victoria.

While private enterprise encountered many technical difficulties applying water management technologies in Victoria, this did not discourage sustained effort. Information available to prospective settlers encouraged local entrepreneurial water management schemes, holding that the Upper Loddon was 'well adapted for the storage of water, and extensive reservoirs might, from the precipitous and lofty nature of its banks, easily be formed'.[61] The need for central regulation and the coordination of rural water supplies arose due to the severe drought of 1877–1881. Land reform laws implemented at the end of the gold rush had increased the number of selectors occupying land around the Kerang and Pyramid Hill districts, with eighty selectors taking land on Tragowel Station by the end of the 1870s. These farmers were severely impacted by this drought.[62] As a result of their political agitations, a Water Conservancy Board was appointed to report on supplying water to the Northern Plains of Victoria for stock and domestic purposes. The passage of the *Water Conservation Act (1881)* and the *Irrigation Act (1886)* secured water redistribution rights for such farmers by allowing national works funded by government and implemented by local irrigation schemes.[63] The new Tragowel Plains Irrigation Trust, established in 1886, buoyed the perceived sustainability of local farmers by providing secure irrigation capacity.[64] The township of Tragowel, which developed during the 1880s, soon boasted a school, railway station, post office, cheese factory, telegraph office buildings and church. The Djaara people may have been the only group to fully understand the environmental consequence of water control, fencing and closer settlement – developments that had immediate and long-term effects on the delicately balanced Laanecoorie ecosystem.[65] By way of conclusion, we now turn to the short-term effects of closer settlement upon Djaara stewards, who had tenaciously maintained kinship ties with their Country.

61 Robert P. Whitworth, *Bailliere's Victorian Gazetteer and Road Guide: Containing the Most Recent and Accurate Information as to Every Place in the Colony* (F.F. Bailliere, 1865).

62 Edwyna Harris, 'State Administration versus Private Innovation: The Evolution of Property Rights to Water in Victoria, Australia,' *The Evolution of Markets for Water: Theory and Practice in Australia* (Edward Elgar Publishing Limited, 2005).

63 Public Record Office Victoria, 'Rural Water Supply,' accessed October 26, 2025. prov.vic.gov.au/archive/VF122.

64 David McKinna, *Gannawarra 2025: Taking up the Challenge* (Gannawarra Shire Council, 2010), 14.

65 Robyn Ballinger, 'Landscapes of Abundance and Scarcity on the Northern Plains of Victoria,' *Provenance* 7 (2008).

The rise of feminised Christian settler culture

Aboriginal employment on pastoral stations was influenced by the growing presence of settler women in the area and the expectations that male settlers adhere to cultural Christian moral standards and help to develop civic infrastructure. Until the late 1850s, male squatters took some pride in rough living and its associated freedoms. This included close association with Aboriginal communities and liaisons with Aboriginal women. In this early period, most Upper Loddon homesteads were established near important waterpoints and were reliant upon Indigenous resources, including labour from nearby camps. When Gerard Kreft, an officer in William Bladowski's scientific expedition, passed through the Upper Loddon collecting scientific specimens in 1856–1857, he noted 45 Aboriginal people living at Gardiner's Pericoota Station, with another 12 at an outstation. He observed 18 at Campbell's Gannawarra, 23 at Loddon Junction, 10 at Reedy Lake and 6 at Lake Boga.[66] These numbers diminished noticeably as settler society developed due to the combined impacts of dispossession, decreasing access to traditional lands and declining Aboriginal employment on the stations. Lake Boga provides an example of this process.

Prior to his marriage in 1859, Samuel Watson of Lake Boga had employed an Aboriginal man as a domestic worker. These arrangements changed a few days after his new wife took up residence. Mary Moore arrived in Melbourne as a first-class passenger on the Royal Charter, which docked on 22 July 1859. She wrote to fellow passenger Jane Brown of her new life in the 'comfortable homestead Lake Boga villa [which] looks over a beautiful lake about two miles each way', noting that:

> I have a splendid cook and imagine the first few days I was here I had a very smart black boy as my page and very well I liked him but Mr Watson has since engaged a married couple, they live a short way from us and the woman [comes] every morning to dust.[67]

66 Although, this number of Aboriginal people may have been inflated by the promise of trade. Kreft, as quoted in Littleton, 'When Resilience Fails'; Pickard, 'Safe Carrying Capacity.'

67 Mary Watson, Lake Boga, to 'My very dear Friend' [Jane], August 24, 1859, Papers of the Brown Family (as filmed by the AJCP), (M 858-863, File 310-312), National Library of Australia, nla.gov.au/nla.obj-743510385.

Men of rank traditionally apprenticed young male pages as their personal assistants. Mary Watson's description of their Aboriginal 'page', therefore, illuminates the operations of rank and race in the homestead. While domesticity was regarded as 'a force for civilizing and a sign of civilization', employing Indigenous domestic labour also posed risks to white women from 'the very subjects she must domesticate and civilize'.[68] Sam Watson likely relinquished this 'very smart black boy' in preference for a (white) married couple for this reason. But regular contact with female servants did not count as 'company'. As Mary revealed to Jane Brown:

> I have plenty to fill up my time. [As] Mr Watson is away all the day I require employments to keep me from feeling lonely. I have had no lady callers yet but gentlemen often visit.[69]

Mary Watson's lack of social contact indicates the absence of European social infrastructure, including churches, which would address this need. The Tragowel journal reveals the infrequency of religious gathering between 1857 and 1861 and associated work to develop community infrastructure (see Table 2.7). Booth and Holloway were Methodists whose reputation for 'excessive piety' suggests that their station journal would likely include any local opportunities for collective worship.[70] In 1858, the family recorded their financial support for a 'Wesleyan Bazarr' and the visit by Reverend Thomas Raston, a Wesleyan Minister from Castlemaine. Raston conducted a wedding service, a baptism and held Divine Service at two district stations during this visit (see Table 2.8). In November 1860, district squatters discussed appointing a minister and schoolmaster for the area, but no decision was made (see Table 2.8). The next religious service was conducted in May 1961 by Reverend Jacob Halley. A Congregational Minister assigned to the Lower Darling and Murrumbidgee region in 1860, Halley was already seeking a new situation by April 1861, but he did not gain sufficient local support to establish a circuit at Swan Hill and Kerang (see Table 2.8).[71] The district next welcomed Reverend Dickson to conduct religious services on 10 November 1861.[72] The population of Swan Hill and

68 Victoria Haskins, 'Domesticating Colonizers: Domesticity, Indigenous Domestic Labor, and the Modern Settler Colonial Nation,' *The American Historical Review* 124, no. 4 (2019): 1292. Amy Kaplan, 'Manifest Domesticity,' *American Literature* 70, no. 3: 591. doi.org/10.2307/2902710.

69 Mary Watson, Lake Boga, to 'My very dear Friend' [Jane].

70 Augustus Baker Pierce, *Knocking About: Being Some Adventures of Augustus Baker Peirce in Australia* (Yale University Press, 1924), 39.

71 *Memorials of Rev. J.J. Halley: Morning, Noon and Eventide* (Congregational Book Depot, 1910). Halley returned to Melbourne and later received an invitation from nearby Maryborough, in 1862.

72 Affiliation unknown, presumably dissenting.

the surrounding area was small, with 550 Europeans in the region by 1865, including 150 in the nascent town.[73] Improvements in transport, including the river steamboat trade that began in 1852, fostered competition between colonial governments, improving services and reducing isolation, like the provision of religious infrastructure.[74] Until the foundation of local churches, remote and sparsely populated districts were serviced by itinerant preachers who conducted services within a circuit. The Upper Loddon district did not enjoy regular ministry until 1875, when the Wesleyan Home Mission funded a local preacher for the North Loddon circuit, and a church was established at Durham Ox.[75]

Table 2.7: The rise of settler infrastructure in the Upper Loddon, 1857–1861

	1857	1858	1859	1860	1861
Communication	–	1	1	–	–
Education infrastructure	–	2	1	–	2
Health infrastructure	–	–	–	–	1
Land tenure	1	–	–	–	1
Religion	–	2	–	1	4
Responsible govt	–	–	–	1	–
Trade and transport	1	–	6	–	–
TOTAL	**2**	**5**	**8**	**2**	**8**

Source: Compiled by the authors.

Table 2.8: Efforts to create settler infrastructure, 1857–1861

Date	Topic	Citation
23 June 1857	Land tenure	A stranger passed to Mt Hope to survey their section.
20 July 1857	Trade and transport	Captain of the Melbourne Steamer on the Murray offering flour for sale at £27 at Swan Hill or Ganna.
17 June 1858	Religion	Mr Raston [Wesleyan Minister] from Castlemaine married Mr & Mrs Seward, John Booth christened. Fri 18th Mr H & Mr Raston have been down to Farmers & Dr Kings to arrange about holding Divine service either here or at Mr Farmers.

73 Littleton, 'When Resilience Fails.'

74 David Spurr, 'The River Murray as a Transport Conduit and Political Barrier: 'Following the Course of That Friendly River' in Trade, Transport and Diplomacy, 1836–1901' (PhD diss., La Trobe University, 2022).

75 'Wesleyan Home Missions', *Age* (Melbourne, 18 May 1875), 3, nla.gov.au/nla.news-article202135815; Brendan Monks, *A Land So Inviting: a History of the Shire of Gordon, 1885-1985* (Shire of Gordon, 1985), 26.

Date	Topic	Citation
22 July 1858	Education infrastructure	Mr Pascoe returned home this morning having been about a school being formed somewhere about Farmers.
23 July 1858	Communication	A young man from Farmers have been for our signature to a petition for a post office at the Loddon Inn.
3 September 1858	Education infrastructure	Attended a meeting at Farmers about a school formed somewhere at Kerang & a committee was formed to ascertain all particulars about it.
4 October 1858	Religion	Mrs Booth sent to Sewards a case containing a variety of things principally for the Wesleyan Bazarr.
9 March 1859	Trade and transport	Cobb & Co are going to run a coach 3 times a week from Sandhurst to Swan Hill.
16 April 1859	Trade and transport	Two men called to ask permission to erect a hut of the boundary of our run for the purpose of an eating house & also bought 16/6 worth of beef.
20 April 1859	Trade and transport	Cobbs coach passed before 9 oc full toward Bendigo.
27 April 1859	Education	A man called today that has been staying with Stevenson at the pound & wants to start a school at Kerang.
28 May 1859	Communication	Petition to Post Master General for a mail delivery 2 a week.
29 August 1859	Trade and transport	Have recd a letter from Seward asking our opinions about store at Durham Ox.
3 October 1859	Trade and transport	John has been to D Ox to see Mr Argyle about ground tor the store.
21 October 1859	Trade and transport	John & Seward been to Mt Hope to the man that is building Wool shed about taking the store to build at D Ox.
3 August 1860	Responsible government	Meeting having been called for the purpose nominating trustees for the County of Kerang.
22 November 1860	Religion	Called at Farmers to consult about a minister & schoolmaster for the neighbourhood but arranged nothing definite as yet.
13 April 1861	Religion	The Rvd Halley called today with a letter from Mr Pasco suggesting having him as a minister for Swan Hill District including Kerang-he has gone to Melbourne.
23 May 1861	Religion	Revd Mr Halley here this evening & has held service at our home.
10 July 1861	Health infrastructure	1 from Dct Gunmorrow Swan Hill about the hospital.

Date	Topic	Citation
26 August 1861	Land tenure	Mr Supholme came yesterday stayed all night left this morning for Ganawarra; sent by the Victorian Association for promoting the Interest of Squatters.
28 September 1861	Education infrastructure	A letter from Mr Pasco soliciting aid for a school building at Swan Hill.
20 October 1861	Education infrastructure	1 letter from Mr Pasco about a school at Swan Hill.
6 November 1861	Religion	A letter from Reverend Dickson that he will hold Divine Service on Monday night at Tragowel.
11 November 1861	Religion	Today Rvd Mr Dickson came from Lake Boga, having been to Swan Hill and preached this evening to 16 people.

Source: Compiled by the authors.

Survival: But not on your own land

Coexistence between Aboriginal people and settlers declined on local stations as rural society developed in the Upper Loddon. As expectations of conformity increased, cross-racial relationships like that between Mick Galway and Alice Holmes were subject to mounting social condemnation. In 1870, Molesworth Greene, owner of the Mount Hope Station, decided to act against 'two or three women at Mount Hope' (likely Alice Holmes and Emma Kerr) who he believed to be 'living as common prostitutes amongst his men'. Cross racial co-habitation was debasing in Greene's view, 'a bad thing for the station', so he asked the Chief Protector of Aborigines to have the women 'taken away'.[76] As a consequence, Reverend John Green visited Mount Hope Station in July 1870. He tried to convince the women and children to move off their Country to Coranderrk Aboriginal Station near Healesville. Reverend Green later testified that:

> they all seemed willing to come when I spoke to them about going the night I arrived, but next morning they were all gone (hid) … I found them during the day among the rocks … now they were not willing to go without one man (Sam), who was not there. I stayed all night again, hoping to induce them to go with me, but in the morning they were not to be found. I think some of the white men

76 Molesworth Greene, Esq., 'Royal Commission on the Aborigines,' Minutes of Evidence 1531, 25 May 1877, 56.

> who cohabit with them assisted them to get away. I left notice with Mr. Greene to write to the Central Board when they came back with Sam, and that I would return and take them.[77]

The group were eventually 'sent off to Coranderrk'. The pastoralist noted that the families left reluctantly, refusing to be separated. The squatter would 'have liked to have kept the men, but they would all go together'. He recalled:

> I had a great difficulty in getting them to go at all. I know that some of the half-caste women were living with some of the stockmen, and I had a great difficulty to get them away.[78]

Reverend Green admitted to the 1877 Inquiry that the Aboriginal women did not leave Mount Hope voluntarily. To the suggestion that, 'there was no coercion used in any case?', he replied, 'Two or three women at Mount Hope; a little was used there'.[79]

Connection to kin and Country is central to Aboriginal spirituality and wellbeing. At Mount Hope, Emma Kerr was close to Djaara land and her betrothal to a Barapa Barapa man likely availed kinship support. After Emma's forced removal, Alick Campbell 'came in' to Coranderrk 'of his own accord' because he wanted to marry Emma. Campbell testified in 1877 that he had wished to return to Gannawarra after his marriage, but Reverend Green 'would not let me go'.[80]

Why did Greene, who took control of Mount Hope in 1857, tolerate cross-racial households until 1870? Likely because extreme isolation on the early frontier undermined expectations of 'normal social and domestic environments' upheld in the metropole. Relationships between settler men and Indigenous women were, thus, tolerated until increased settlement exposed them to public notice. When these domestic arrangements were exhibited before incoming settlers, the squattocracy, who held themselves aloof from the standards applicable to the middle and working classes, felt it necessity to exert their control. The influx of Europeans drawn by closer settlement, as recounted above, reorganised landscapes through increased

77 John Green, Report, 16 July 1870, Seventh Report of the Board for the Protection of the Aborigines in the Colony of Victoria, Appendix 1, 5.

78 Molesworth Greene, Esq., 'Royal Commission on the Aborigines,' Minutes of Evidence.

79 Alexander Campbell, 'Royal Commission on the Aborigines,' Minutes of Evidence 728–36, 28.

80 Alexander Campbell, Minutes of Evidence 728, 28; See Barwick, 'The Board Takes Control', chapt. 6 in *Rebellion at Coranderrk*.

clearing, fencing and grazing, accelerated water control and the introduction of agricultural rather than pastoral enterprises. Alick Campbell, his new wife Emma Campbell and her children all remained at Coranderrk during those sixteen years (1870–1886) when Tragowel Station was reorganised and transformed by these forces of closer settlement.

The Campbell family eventually returned to Barapa Barapa Country, but on the New South Wales side of the border, which experienced closer settlement at a slower pace than Victoria to the south. Here, fencing was still limited, and native flora and fauna was still relatively abundant on pastoral stations. When Emma Campbell died in 1886, she was buried at Barham Station on Barapa Barapa Country. Her story illustrates Aboriginal efforts to stay connected to country despite settler incursion. These spiritual relationships were not extinguished by dispossession; they have been nurtured across the generations, and they are resurgent today.[81]

81 See for example 'Giyakiki | Our story', Dja Dja Wurrung Clans Aboriginal Corporation, djadjawurrung.com.au/giyakiki-our-story/.

3

Common law and religious difference in Bendigo courtrooms: 'The Chinese Oath'

In July 1894, those present in the Bendigo Supreme Court witnessed a protracted 'Chinese Oath' ceremony. After stepping into the witness box as a defendant on charges of perjury, a Bendigo resident, Ah Moy, was administered the oath. This meant that Ah Moy blew out a match after being told by the interpreter, Jack Ah Pong, that 'you come this Court and stand in this box there'. He then 'asked [Ah Moy] how his conscience is he said blow light out [*sic*]'.[1] Ah Moy's testimony, however, was found to conflict with that of other witnesses, and he was subsequently charged of perjury. Seven months after visiting the court as a witness, Ah Moy returned as a defendant. During this perjury trial, questions of religious equivalence were directly confronted. Another interpreter of Chinese descent who had been present at the first trial, James Ah Poo, also testified that:

> I do not know the Chinese word for God – The Chinese word Shunghi stands for God – Jack Ah Pong was interpreter in this case – He is in Gippsland now I think somebody brought him over here – I have heard witnesses sworn in Chinese Courts but not in China – Blowing the match out means to tell the truth.[2]

1 James Appoo, Depositions, *The Queen v Ah Moy*, Supreme Court, Bendigo, 25 February 1895, Perjury, Case 33, VPRS30/P0, Unit 1005, Public Record Office of Victoria (PROV).

2 Ibid.

As this story indicates, in oath ceremonies the courtroom became a public arena where religious difference was performed and where knowledge of the religions and faith traditions of people of Asian descent were produced and shared. Through a focus on oaths and perjury trials, this chapter explores how the drama of religious difference was performed in and via Bendigo courtrooms in the late nineteenth century, a time when the religious relativism characteristic of European imperial legal cultures was in tension with the growth of a self-consciously 'white' Christian nationalism. This chapter also shows how a space of religious plurality was far from one of religious equality. The Bendigo courtroom might be considered a space to encounter empire's 'multiculturalism', for it was a rare space that not only recognised the different religions of legal subjects but also attempted to authorise and formalise religious difference. And yet, religion was a form of legal alterity thoroughly modulated by the hierarchies of race.

Ah Moy's perjury trial, and the way it brought the question of Chinese testimony to public attention, was not an isolated instance. The Victorian Supreme Courts heard at least six perjury trials of Chinese men during the 1890s.[3] In each of these trials, the Chinese Oath was used to swear in the defendant, who gave their testimony 'in the Chinese language'.[4] These perjury trials highlight the importance of oath and testimony translation to the racial question of whether the testimony of people of Chinese and of South Asian descent could be rendered intelligible to English-speaking legal decision-makers, and therefore whether people of Chinese and South Asian descent could be equal legal subjects.[5] These questions, played out in the space of the Supreme Court, mapped onto the larger question of whether religiously diverse people designated 'Asiatic' had the right to enter and remain in the colony.

3 The archives of cases located at PROV include: *The Queen v Ah Boo*, Supreme Court, Melbourne, 17 August 1891, Perjury, Case 2, VPRS30/P0, Unit 853; *The Queen v Suey Lee*, Supreme Court, Melbourne, 17 April 1893, Perjury, Case 235, VPRS30/P0, Unit 928; *The Queen v Mow Tan*, Supreme Court, Melbourne, 17 April 1895 (5 May 1895), Perjury, Case 141, VPRS30/P0, Unit 1013; *The Queen v Lee Fook*, Supreme Court, Bendigo, 2 August 189, Perjury, Case 326, VPRS30/P0, Unit 1064; *The Queen v Ah Sing*, Supreme Court, Melbourne, 16 July 1894, Perjury, Case 342, VPRS30/P0, Unit 983. There were also at least two perjury trials of Indians: *The Queen v Isar Das and The King v Boota Singh*, Supreme Court, Melbourne, 15 February 1901, Perjury, Case 75, VPRS30/P0, Unit 1241. For a case preceding the 1890s, see Hock Fong, Depositions, *The Queen v Ming Toon*, Supreme Court, Melbourne, 15 May 1888, Perjury, Case 1, VPRS30/P0, Unit 720.

4 Charles Hodges, Depositions, *The Queen v Ah Sing*.

5 For instance, Chief Justice Higinbotham applauded Alfred Deakin's promotion of the federation of Victoria with the rest of the 'English-speaking race'. 'Banquet to the Hon. A Deakin,' *The South Australian Advertiser*, July 12, 1887, p. 5, nla.gov.au/nla.news-article37176499; For evidence of how identifying with the 'English-speaking race' entailed identifying with English law and with whiteness, see also 'The First Parliament of the English Speaking Race,' *The Bacchus Marsh Express*, January 28, 1893, p. 3, nla.gov.au/nla.news-article88192061.

Common law gained its authority by the legal fictions that it was universally liberating, that is, that every 'man' is equal before the law. This fiction was recurringly tested by a colonial setting that relied on structurally supported religious and racial inequality. In nineteenth century colonial Victoria, Christian religion – performed in the English language – had a privileged status in many spaces of daily public life. As such, this chapter continues to examine religious cohesion and its tensions as they placed out in particular Bendigo spaces, focusing on the spectacles performed in the 'theatres' of faith and religion that were courtrooms. How did the public negotiation of belief in courtrooms support and challenge the live and dynamic negotiations of religious difference? What kinds of understandings and legal powers of faith systems were made and challenged here?

Oaths, religious pluralism and liberalism

The liberal principle that all colonial subjects should be amenable to and equal before law saw people of diverse religious identities walk through the Bendigo courtroom doors, including those who practiced Taoism, Confucianism, ancestor worship, Islam, Sikhism and Hinduism. From the 1850s, significant numbers of South Asians lived in Bendigo and surrounding areas, and by the late nineteenth and early twentieth centuries, Muslims and Hindus had a particularly visible presence in Bendigo's public and legal life. In 1854, the Mount Alexander Mail reported that 'a native of Hindostan' was charged with stealing a child, and:

> in the absence of the waters of the Ganges, on which they were sworn in India, [the witness] repeated a solemn affirmation in India, declaring they would speak nothing but the truth, holding up their hand at the same time, in token of their sincerity.[6]

6 'Child Stealing,' *Mount Alexander Mail*, June 17, 1854, p. 2, nla.gov.au/nla.news-article202631387; This was evidently the practice for Hindu witnesses and defendants in courts across Victoria. For evidence of a witness sworn in 'on the water of the Ganges', see 'Purity of the Jury System: A Case Abruptly Closed', *The Argus*, November 26, 1898, p. 6, nla.gov.au/nla.news-article9862141; The racial category of 'Hindoo' was not defined in legislation, as 'Chinese' was. However, it operated in social and legal contexts as an adjective normally mapped to hawkers, and to indicate a subset of the 'coloured races' present in Victoria. While it might be mistaken as a religious category, it was used to refer to Hindu and Muslim Indians alike. For an instance where 'Hindoos' were compared to others of the 'coloured races', see 'Municipal Intelligence,' *The Argus*, March 1, 1893, p. 6, nla.gov.au/nla.news-article8521026. 'Hindoo' operated as a category in the license registers of the 1890s, which 'discriminated between Chinese, Hindoos (Afghans, Indian Muslims and Hindus) and Assyrians (Lebanese and Turkish), with a further unnamed category for British or local born', Andrew May, *Melbourne Street Life: The Itinerary of Our Days* (Australian Scholarly Publishing, 1998), 163.

Muslims were often sworn in to legal proceedings by the Koran in ways closely analogous to the Christian ceremony of taking a Bible-based oath.[7]

Judging whether a defendant sworn in on a non-Christian oath was culpable of perjury entailed deciding two related questions: had the oath been binding on the subject's conscience? And had their testimony been properly and accurately translated? These questions were crucial because if either a witness's oath was not binding or their testimony was inaccurately translated, they could be culpable for giving false testimony. The social meanings attached to the process whereby an interpreter rendered the oath binding on the conscience of a non-Christian witness or defendant can be traced in the history of the legal cultures of England, China and Victoria. It was also inherent to the liberal ideology of fairness that underscored colonial Victorian law. The principles by which British law should be applied to settler colonies were defined as early as the 1720s. These principles, so Jurist Blackstone outlined in the early nineteenth century, provisioned colonists to establish the rule of law in 'uninhabited' countries and explicitly allowed colonists to adapt British law to suit the needs of the particular colony:

> It hath been told that if an uninhabited country be discovered and planted by English subjects then all the English law then in being … should then be in force. Such colonists carry with them only so much as is applicable to their new situation.[8]

When Victoria gained its independence as a self-governing colony in 1851, it largely inherited its structures of law and legislature from New South Wales. These structures had been implanted from Britain and already adapted to colonial circumstances. Vitally, these included the legal fiction of terra nullius that claimed Australia to be empty of ownership, and also laws that specifically dealt with land legislation, lotteries and master–servant relationships, some of which targeted First Nations people.[9] Yet, just how Victorian settlers would deal with their new situation was by no means predetermined in 1851, nor was the question of how they would deal with the colony's racial and linguistic plurality.

Questions of cultural and linguistic difference had impinged upon the law's equal and universal application from the beginning of European colonisation. Barry Patton has argued that law, and the courts especially,

7 See *Bendigo Advertiser*, March 19, 1858, p. 3; *Bendigo Advertiser*, October 2, 1884, p. 2.

8 Alex Castles, 'The Reception and Status of English Law in Australia,' *Adelaide Law Review* 2, no. 1 (1963): 15.

9 Castles, 'The Reception and Status,' 19. See also Henry Reynolds, *The Law of the Land* (Penguin, 2003).

were essential mechanisms in the racialisation of Aboriginal and Torres Strait Islander people, that 'processes of Anglo-Australian colonial law skewed a supposedly impartial legal system'. Aboriginal legal subjects in colonial Victoria, Patton demonstrated, faced significant obstacles to having their evidence heard and admitted. Aboriginal subjects were denied substantive legal protection, especially in frontier periods.[10]

Throughout the 1890s, legal authorities remained significantly bound by liberal traditions, most strongly the idealisation of the rule of law as 'just' and 'equal', which obliged legal authorities to at least appear to give non-European defendants a fair trial and to recompense victims regardless of their gender, race or class. As historian Leigh Boucher has noted, in the context of nineteenth century Victoria, in the liberal tradition, 'there was little space for the admission that British subjecthood was hierarchically modulated by race'.[11] Such practices of linguistic relativism in British courts across the empire – underwritten, as they were with liberal principles – went together with practices of religious relativism. At base, to apply law to non-English-speaking people required the translation of their testimony so they could recollect the social events (including conversations) pertaining to the alleged crime. In practice, however, the translation of testimony required much more. Legal cultures of the nineteenth century, including that of the British and the Dominions, were steeped in racially codified practices that meant those who were not Christian or not Anglophone had a marked relation to common law.[12]

Oaths had been an important part of British culture at least since the English Reformation of the sixteenth century. They served as a mechanism to ensure the integrity and sincerity of a witness and thus the proper and so-called 'civilised' performance of law.[13] Like the Christian Oath, the invention of the Chinese Oath was entwined with British legal imperialism. There are reports of the ritual of beheading a chicken and drinking its blood to swear

10 Barry Patton, 'Unequal Justice: Colonial Law and the Shooting of Jim Crow,' *Provenance: The Journal of Public Record Office Victoria* 5, no. 4 (2006): 16–25.

11 Leigh Boucher, '"Whiteness", Geopolitics and the Settler Empire,' in *Re-Orienting Whiteness*, ed. Leigh Boucher, Jane Carey, and Katherine Ellinghaus (Palgrave Macmillan, 2009), 54.

12 In his study of language and law in Britain's plantation colonies in the Caribbean, Ogborn argued that 'the rules of oath-taking and evidence-giving – was part of the making of imperial and colonial identities and relationships dividing white and non-white, free and unfree'. Miles Ogborn, 'The Power of Speech: Orality, Oaths and Evidence in the British Atlantic World, 1650–1800,' *Transactions of the Institute of British Geographers* 34, no. 1 (2011): 109, doi.org/10.1111/j.1475-5661.2010.00412.x.

13 Jonathan Gray, *Oaths and the English Reformation* (Cambridge University Press, 2013); Richard S. Willen, 'Rationalization of Anglo-Legal Culture: The Testimonial Oath,' *The British Journal of Sociology* 34, no. 1 (1983): 109–28, doi.org/10.2307/590612.

in Chinese in Dutch Batavia as early as 1787.[14] This Batavian ritual, Paul Katz has suggested, was subsequently adopted in the British Straits Settlement in the early nineteenth century. It became the source of much discomfort and contest for European administrators. By the nineteenth century, British colonists in India, in conjunction with the metropole, had sanctioned the use of non-Christian oaths.[15] In the 1840s, judges in the Straits Settlement changed their approach to Chinese testimony following the *Indian Legislative Act V. 1840*.[16] The colonial Australian courts clearly borrowed judicial practices from the Straits Settlement and Hong Kong; however, from the 1850s, the forms of the Chinese Oath in Victoria, and seemingly also in the metropole and other Australia colonies, took a markedly different trajectory. By 1864, the Shanghai Mixed Court had 'fully adopted Western legal procedures' and did not allow the use of the Chinese Oath. Victorian courts, however, continued to use the Chinese Oath into the twentieth century.[17]

The court as a theatre of religious culture and relativity

The Bendigo Supreme Court was built in 1857–1858, early in the settler invasion, with settlers seizing Djaara land for pastoral use from 1851. In accordance with its function to consolidate the colonial state's power, the courts were originally located near police bases on Camp Hill (later site of Rosalind Park) in 1860.[18] In the year following Ah Moy's trial, the court would move into the imposing edifice of the new complex in the more central Pall Mall, backing onto Rosalind Park.[19] The colonial architecture of this and similar courts had multiple functions. Beyond providing a space that enclosed the bodies and voices of those participating in law, court buildings offered 'visible spectacles of European domination', both of the

14 Paul Katz, 'Ritual? What Ritual? Secularization in the Study of Chinese Legal History, from Colonial Encounters to Modern Scholarship,' *Social Compass* 56, no. 3 (2009): 332, doi.org/10.1177/0037768609338762.

15 Ibid., 334.

16 Ibid.

17 Paul R. Katz, *Divine Justice: Religion and the Development of Chinese Legal Culture* (Routledge, 2008), 129. For reference to the use of 'the Chinese Oath' in early twentieth century Britain, see Sascha Auerbach, *Race, Law, and 'The Chinese Puzzle' in Imperial Britain* (Palgrave Macmillan, 2008), 163.

18 Simone Bloomfield, *Crime and Punishment: A History of Bendigo's Law and Order* (Post Office Gallery, Bendigo, 2022), accessed October 29, 2023, www.bendigoregion.com.au/bendigo-art-gallery/publications/crime-and-punishment-a-history-of-bendigos-law-and-order.

19 For floor plans of the Pall Mall Bendigo Courts see Victorian Heritage Database Report, January 13, 2000, vhd.heritagecouncil.vic.gov.au/places/131/download-report.

landscape and of society.[20] The physical presence of the court building was to communicate the power of law and, as such, the power of the colonial state to judge and prescribe punishments for their subjects.

The internal spatial arrangement of the courtroom was further conducive to the display and enactment of legal power and social control. The Bendigo Supreme Court, as others across the British Empire, were rooms in which English-speaking male settlers, acting as magistrates and lawyers, controlled the order of sound and speech, managing who spoke when, where, and for how long.[21] Ah Poo's observation of Ah Moy's oath ceremony indicates how the Melbourne City and Supreme Courts functioned as theatres in which European and Chinese bodies and voices came into contact, and where the religious order of the colony was thereby acoustically performed.[22] The interior space of the court can usefully be examined as a theatre, as it involved a stage (the bench and witness stand), actors (magistrates, justices of the peace and license applicants) and a (polyglot, multi-racial) audience.[23]

Religious rituals and performances were regularly heard within the walls of the courts, where legal subjects participated in oath taking, evidence giving and the swearing in and use of interpreters.[24] The sound-absorbing walls of the Bendigo Supreme Court meant that only those inside the court could hear the words uttered there. But while these buildings could afford privacy, the courts' proceedings were, by principle, public affairs. 'Publicity to court proceedings is … warranted on the grounds that in the courts public justice is dispensed', noted a New South Wales newspaper editor when discussing divorce proceedings in 1898. Moreover, 'people should be free to note and to criticise the manner in which the proceedings are conducted'.[25] Reflecting this ideal of the courts as a space of transparency, the courtrooms in which

20 For discussion of the communicative function of British colonial buildings in this era, see Pramod Nayar, *Colonial Voices: Discourses of Empire* (John Wiley & Sons, 2012), 142–3. See also Peter Scriver and Vikramaditya Prakash, eds., 'Introduction,' in *Colonial Modernities: Building, Dwelling, and Architecture in British India and Ceylon* (Routledge, 2006).

21 For discussion of the linguistic culture of British colonial courts, see Ogborn, 'The Power of Speech,' 109–25. The first woman would be admitted to the magistracy in Victoria in 1985.

22 Ogborn, 'The Power of Speech,' 109–25.

23 Historians have looked at how race has been performed in the United States, for instance in *Staging Whiteness*, Mary Brewer looks at how racial identities have been performed in theatres and plays, and Stephen Hoelscher has analysed the public executions of black people under Jim Crow as performances of white supremacy. Mary Brewer, *Staging Whiteness* (Wesleyan University Press, 2005); Stephen Hoelscher, 'Making Place, Making Race: Performances of Whiteness in the Jim Crow South,' *Annals of the Association of American Geographers*, 93, no. 3 (2003): 657–86, doi.org/10.1111/1467-8306.9303008.

24 For discussion about how law is a linguistic process, see John Conley and William O'Barr, *Just Words: Law, Language and Power* (University of Chicago Press, 1998).

25 'Divorce Proceedings and Publicity,' *The Maitland Weekly Mercury*, January 8, 1898, p. 4, nla.gov.au/nla.news-article126320783.

people of various faiths and religious identities spoke were open to a public audience, including journalists, enabling the public access to the rituals performed inside the courts.

Religious diversity in Chinese Bendigo

By the 1890s, the regular spiritual meetings of Djaara in the city called 'Bendigo', with their ways of performing sovereign connection to Country by language, music and dance, often generically called 'corroberees', had been interrupted and displaced by the invading settlers.[26] The faith-scape of Bendigo was dynamic and changed in tandem with patterns of global and imperial migration. Europeans who practiced various Christian faiths lived side by side with people designated 'Asiatic', a category that included Chinese, Afghans, Syrians and people from current day India. The Chinese immigrants who began arriving in the 1850s practiced diverse faiths, including Confucianism, Taoism and ancestor worship. The Indians, Pakistanis, Bangladeshis, Afghans and Syrians (from an area that encompasses current day Lebanon) began arriving in the late 1870s and practiced variously Christianity, Hindusim, Sikhism and Islam. As for witnesses of Chinese descent, Hindu, Muslim and Christian witnesses were similarly sworn in according to an oath ceremony. Muslims were sworn on the Koran, Hindus by drinking a cup full of the symbolic water of the Ganges and Christians on the Bible.[27] Amid assimilationist attempts to convert Chinese people to Christianity, then, driven notably by European and by Christian missionaries, people of different faiths worked together, lived together and married in the daily intimacies of a diasporic context. Some of the faiths of Bendigo residents of Asian descent were more intelligible to Europeans than others. The ambiguity of whether there was a word for 'God' in Chinese languages was a particularly sore spot for the positivist culture of settler law, which venerated certainty.

26 Different nations had different names for 'corroborees'. For instance, the Kurnai who came to live on Ramahyuck called their form of corroberee 'Koonyero'; see Alistair Campbell, comp. and Ron Vanderwal, ed. *Victorian Aborigines: John Bulmer's Recollections: 1855–1908*, Occasional papers from the Museum of Victoria (1994), 46. See also Maryrose Casey, 'Theatre or Corrobboree, What's in a Name? Framing Indigenous Australian 19th Century Commercial Performance Practices,' in *Creating White Australia*, ed. Jane Carey and Claire McLisky (Sydney University Press, 2009), 125.

27 For instance, in a Victorian court, a Hindu oath ceremony was sensationalised; see 'Purity of the Jury System: A Case Abruptly Closed,' *The Argus*, November 26, 1898, p. 6, nla.gov.au/nla.news-article9862141; 'Victoria: Melbourne, Friday,' *The Sydney Morning Herald*, November 26, 1898, p. 9, nla.gov.au/nla.news-article14187013. For another Christian-dominated context where 'both Christian and Muslim legal texts recognized and established that Muslims swear by God', see Belen Vicens, 'Swearing by God: Muslim Oath-Taking in Late Medieval and Early Modern Christian Iberia,' *Medieval Encounters*, 20, no. 2 (2014): 117–51, doi.org/10.1163/15700674-12342162.

The colonial relations of religion

People of Chinese descent began arriving in Bendigo in the 1840s, within a decade of the start of British colonisation. The line between the 'settler' and the 'migrant' – so the works of Beenash Jafri, Samia Khatun, Andonis Piperoglou and others teach us – does not fit with colonial identity categories and liberal formulations.[28] In colonial Bendigo, 'settler' was, and is, a term 'creased by racialisation'.[29] Bendigonians of Chinese descent were treated ambivalently and were at once included in law and treated as perpetual foreigners, even as their religious precepts were translated into English, the language of the colony, and rendered intelligible to Anglophone listeners and legal authorities.

By the 1890s, there was little pretence that China-born people such as Ah Moy were equal subjects before colonial law. They had been disenfranchised and became the targets of legal discrimination under the *Shops and Factories Act 1890* and the *Chinese Act 1890*. Still, the imperatives to perform racially equal justice remained pertinent in Bendigo's courtrooms, if not in polling booths, workshops, bedrooms, factories and laundry rooms. The dramatic contrast between oath ceremonies as a symbol of the religious and racial fairness of law and the surrounding milieu of colonial racism was not lost on contemporary observers. Even during a time of heightened settler hostility towards Chinese people, hearing an interpreter translate law across religions and (often simultaneously) across languages was a spectacle.[30]

The 'Chinese Oath' was a spectacle consumed by Bendigo court audiences and by newspaper readership. Unsurprisingly, given the propensity for Europeans to hear Chinese speech as noise absent of meaning, this representation bore little resemblance to the actual words of the oath. In the fore-mentioned 1895 Bendigo Supreme Court perjury trial, the interpreter Ah Poo phonetically transcribed the oath as:

28 Andonis Piperoglou, 'Migrant-Cum-Settler: Greek Settler Colonialism in Australia,' *Journal of Modern Greek Studies*, 38, no. 2 (2020): 44, doi.org/10.1353/mgs.2020.0028; Samia Khatun, 'The Book Of Marriage: Histories Of Muslim Women In Twentieth-Century Australia,' *Gender and History*, 29, no. 1 (2017): 8–30, doi.org/10.1111/1468-0424.12258; Beenash Jafri, 'Desire, Settler Colonialism, and the Racialized Cowboy,' *American Indian Culture and Research Journal*, 37, no. 2 (2013): 76; For a discussion of Chinese belonging in Bendigo close to the case at hand, see Nadia Rhook, '"The Chinese Doctor James Lamsey": Performing Medical Sovereignty and Property in Settler Colonial Bendigo,' *Postcolonial Studies*, 23, no. 1 (2020): 58–78, doi.org/10.1080/13688790.2020.1727823.

29 See also Jodi Byrd's term 'arrivant' as opposed to 'settler' in her *The Transit of Empire: Indigenous Critiques of Colonialism* (University of Minnesota Press, 2011), 31.

30 'The Seamy Side. Before a Metropolitan Court.,' *Warragul Guardian*, September 22, 1893, p. 3, nla.gov.au/nla.news-article68601644.

Nee jew chung kong, in ho
You according to truth speak, don't
Kong tai wa, ku ku chun
Talk falsehood, everyword true
Nee ni jew chun kong
If you don't according to the truth speak
Sheng-ai jak nee
God punish you.[31]

For those in position of legal decision-making power, to hear the translation of Chinese speech and religion into English was to hear an interpreter render the Chinese witness susceptible to colonial law, and, hence, to colonial power.[32] Interpreters such as Ah Poo effectively worked as linguistic balms to ease the discomforting presence of Chinese people in the court. Mow Tan's oath ceremony was one instance among many where interpreters mediated affect and soothed the religious tensions of administering colonial law to people of Chinese descent.[33] Hence, when Ah Poo defended the oath's validity, he was speaking into a decades-long contest over the validity of the oath. When he testified in the Bendigo Supreme Court perjury trial, he used the present simple tense – a tense for statements and general truths – stating that: 'Blowing the match out means to tell the truth.'[34] His statement opens up the question of how often interpreters of Chinese descent were ready and willing to defend an oath founded in the approximation of so-called 'Chinese' religions? While it is difficult to gain a clear answer to this question from the historical record, what is clear is that, for Ah Poo and other people designated as Chinese in the courtroom, religious, social and legal belonging were inseparable.

From the founding of the Bendigo Law Courts, the use of disparate oaths had been contentious for observers of the judicial process, and, as in other British colonies, court oaths were subject to ongoing contestations. Though,

31 Exhibit B, *The Queen v Ah Moy*. Of course, this representation of the oath is not least an imperfect representation for the absence of tone markers.

32 For more on the linguistic and aural dimensions of settler governance in this era, see Nadia Rhook, '"The Chief Chinese Interpreter" Charles Hodges: Mapping The Aurality Of Race And Governance in Colonial Melbourne,' *Postcolonial Studies* 18, no. 1 (2015): 1–18, doi.org/10.1080/13688790.2015.1025353.

33 Hodges' role in various Chinese perjury trials was reported in the Victorian press and that of other colonies. For reference to his role in Lee Fook's trial, see 'Supreme Court Criminal Sittings,' *The Argus*, May 29, 1888, p. 7, nla.gov.au/nla.news-article6128338; 'The Law Courts,' *The Argus*, April 26, 1893, p. 10; 'Victoria. Melbourne,' *Newcastle Morning Herald and Miners' Advocate*, September 28, 1896, p. 6, nla.gov.au/nla.news-article135765638; 'Another Chinese Perjury Case,' *Bendigo Advertiser*, August 17, 1896, p. 3.

34 *The Queen v Ah Moy*.

the practice of blowing out a match was not the only oath ceremony that came under scrutiny during this era. Muslim and Hindu oath ceremonies were intermittently reported, but the Chinese Oath received the most public attention and was regularly ridiculed in public discourse.[35] From the mid to late nineteenth century, Europeans in Victoria intermittently ridiculed non-Christian oath ceremonies in ways that mapped onto broader questions about the validity of oaths. A critic wrote to the *Bendigo Advertiser* in 1858 that: 'The [oath] displays … of the present system are as ludicrous as the most grotesque customs of the most barbarous countries in the world'. They went on to lament that the way the courts applied oaths to so-called 'foreigners' was ineffective and ridiculous:

> In fact, as the law is based on the principle of swearing each man in the manner considered most binding on his religious conscience, the spectators in our Courts of Justice are entertained or disgusted, as the case may be, with the most ridiculous parodies of what are supposed to be the binding forms of swearing foreigners.[36]

By the time Ah Moy testified, Chinese oaths had evolved as a racial trope that implied Chinese people were prone to speaking untrustworthy words. As he sat in the Bendigo Supreme Court witness box, Ah Moy was participating in a ritual well established in Victorian courts, a ritual that the European settler public were conditioned to perceive as farcical.

This and similar perjury cases, thus, had significance beyond the legal proceedings. The representations of the trial fed into broader discourses that constructed people of Chinese descent and their languages as essentially unintelligible and therefore cast people of Chinese descent as incommensurable legal subjects.[37] Non-monotheistic faiths were particularly susceptible to being read as interrupting the settler legal order, which, as other chapters in this book demonstrate, was one in which Christianity was the privileged religion of public space and of the colony more widely. This distrust had legal implications. The Bendigo

35 For instances of racialisation through the Bendigo courts see 'Chinese Oaths,' *Mount Alexander Mail*, April 26, 1864, p. 3, nla.gov.au/nla.news-article197443398; 'Curious Oaths,' *Bendigo Advertiser*, October 13, 1900, p. 1, nla.gov.au/nla.news-article89431829.

36 'We occasionally hear of the cutting off of the head of some doomed rooster in the Court', 'The Swearing of Witnesses,' *Bendigo Advertiser*, June 10, 1858, p. 2, nla.gov.au/nla.news-article87981003.

37 In 1890, for example, two years before Ah Sing stepped into the witness box, the *Wagga Wagga Advertiser* reported court proceedings involving unnamed Chinese witnesses. 'Most of the witnesses in the case were sworn by the Chinese custom of blowing out a match', they told, 'and the evidence of some of them was very unintelligible "Slander,"' *Wagga Wagga Advertiser*, November 18, 1890, p. 2.

Advertiser reported the perjury trial in racist ways, casting Chinese people as generically untrustworthy: 'They did not … consider the blowing out of the match binding so they would please themselves whether they told the truth or not'.[38]

Performances of oaths in Bendigo courts highlight the necessity, under common law, of finding ways to breach the entwined religious and linguistic differences between Christian and non-Christian cultures and to, thus, accommodate social-religious diversity. It took concerted efforts of translation, miscommunication and communication to administer the oath to non-Christian subjects and to thereby subject them to settler legal structures. While the performance of common law in nineteenth century Bendigo courts was challenged by the multiple religious cultures of Chinese and other people of Asian descent, it could and sometimes did recognise, accommodate and trust them. However, legal authorities did so while working with invented approximations and appropriations of the multiple, deep and sacred religious traditions that lived across the private rooms, halls and public parks of Bendigo. As such, while it is tempting to describe the practices of religious relativity in nineteenth and early twentieth century Bendigo courts as an early form of multiculturalism, it is important to note the way these oath ceremonies were imperial creations and enforced by the state. To capitulate, rendering religious difference conspicuous enabled white settlers to regularly denigrate practitioners of non-Christian faiths by treating their (traditional and colonially invented) rituals as untrustworthy and laughable. It appears that those who followed polytheistic faiths were particularly susceptible to such denigration.

In the twentieth century, the rise of secularism saw these legal practices of religious relativity gradually, if haphazardly, pushed out of regular use, with either a Christian oath or a secular affirmation becoming the norm.[39] At times, non-Christians of Asian descent asserted their right to be sworn according to their religion. In 1926, Melbourne court officials were 'staggered' when a 'Hindoo witness desired to be sworn in on the water of the Ganges, but had to be content with drinking a glass of water instead'. From 1958, Victorian

38 'The Chinese Perjury Case: A Conspiracy Inferred,' *Bendigo Independent*, May 12, 1894, p. 4, nla.gov.au/nla.news-article178727929. See also 'A Chinaman Arrested for Perjury: Peculiar Case of Alleged Perjury,' *The Argus*, July 11, 1891, p. 10, nla.gov.au/nla.news-article8662041.

39 Further research is required to ascertain whether some Bendigonians began to prefer taking a Christian oath to avoid the courts doubting their testimony. For a case where a witness refused to participate in the match oath ceremony and requested to be sworn in on the Christian oath, see 'Me Do Dlink! Me Christian!' *Bendigo Independent*, May 15, 1912, p. 4, nla.gov.au/nla.news-article227955012.

law stipulated that witnesses should either swear a Christian oath on either the New or Old Testament, or a secular affirmation. There is evidence, however, that practices of non-Christian oaths persisted in Bendigo well into the twentieth century based on a culture outlined in the Clerk of Courts Manual.[40] In 1974, around four years before federal multicultural policies bound up with 'the long slow death' of the White Australia Policy would begin to roll out, a woman who identified as Hindu protested that 'while attending a Magistrates' court in Bendigo in connection with a car accident she was required, despite her initial objection, to take the oath on a glass of water'.[41] In May the same year, the Clerk of Courts Manual was amended to stipulate 'that a Hindu witness would in future make an affirmation instead of an oath.'[42] In 2002, the Victorian government performed an 'Inquiry into Oaths and Affirmations with Reference to the Multicultural Community' and recommended that the courts' swearing-in practices strike 'the right balance of freedom of expression … and a reliable system of oaths and affirmations', which would require cultural awareness training for legal officers that included learning about citizens' religions.[43] Today, the Bendigo Supreme Court accepts testimony sworn on a secular oath – as do courts across Australia – while its laws and ceremonies remain rooted in Anglo-Christian traditions.

40 *Evidence (Miscellaneous Provisions) Act 1958* (Victoria Current Acts, n.d.), austlii.edu.au//au/legis/vic/consol_act/epa1958361/.

41 The phrase 'long, slow death' is from the title of Gwenda Tavan's *The Long, Slow Death of White Australia* (Scribe, 2005). For discussion of the transition from the use of affirmation under the 1958 Oaths and Affirmations Act, see Mark Weinberg, 'The Law of Testimonial Oaths and Affirmations,' *Monash University Law Review*, 3 (1976): 25–27.

42 Weinberg, 'The Law.'

43 Federal multicultural policy began to roll out in 1978, and it has been overwhelmingly governed over by White Australians, where whiteness has operated as an (ethnically heterogeneous) position of structural privilege. See Ghassan Hage, *White Nation: Fantasies of White Supremacy in a Multicultural Society* (Pluto Press, 1998); *Government Response to the Victorian Parliament Law Reform Committee's Inquiry into Oaths and Affirmations with Reference to the Multicultural Community* (Victorian Government, 2002); for discussion of a calls for courts across Australia to use a secular oath, see 'National Call for Courts to Drop Religious Oaths,' *The Age*, August 1, 2002, www.theage.com.au/national/call-for-courts-to-drop-religious-oaths-20020801-gdug9r.html.

Popout One: Giving as cohesion: 'Hospital Sundays', religion, and medical philanthropy in fin-de-siècle Bendigo

It is Sunday, typically a day of rest in Christian goldfields time.[1] In the Bendigo Hospital, patients continue to be treated for illness, injury and disease. In the benevolent asylum, persons deemed 'insane' and 'unfit' face another day in basic, prison-like conditions.[2] Blocks away from these resource-pressured spaces, able-bodied people gather in the door-less church of Rosalind Park. The air is fresh. The atmosphere, festive. Today is not just any Sunday. It is Hospital Sunday, and the first to be held in Australia. The sky stretches above the elm trees planted decades earlier in Djaara Country. An estimated 10,000 people of various faiths and Christian denominations gather for the open-air universal church service to listen as Protestant priests and ministers take the stage. Multi-ethnic residents of Bendigo worship God and place money in collection bags. The carnival atmosphere and public display encourage their voluntary contributions. Organisers will in turn divide these funds between the hospital (given, this year, two thirds of the revenue) and the asylum (given one third) – much needed funds to supplement the settler state's thin budget for health and

1 For discussion of the 'diverse, but common, practice of rest on the Sabbath', see Timothy Jones and Clare Wright, 'The Goldfields' Sabbath: A Postsecular Analysis of Social Cohesion and Social Control on the Ballarat Goldfields, 1854,' *Journal of Religious History* 43, no. 4 (2019): 447–459, doi.org/10.1111/1467-9809.12626.

2 Valerie Lovejoy, 'The Things That Unite: Inquests into Chinese Deaths on the Bendigo Goldfields 1854–65,' *Provenance: The Journal of Public Record Office Victoria* 7 (2007): 17–29.

welfare.[3] Who donates, and how much, will be noted and published in local newspapers. This rewards donors with moral-religious capital and boosts communal views of benevolence and care in society.

'Hospital Sundays' began in England as once-a-year events where Christian churches and chapels collected funds at a charity service and donated them to hospitals.[4] The first was reportedly held in 1870 in Manchester, and variations were replicated in cities across England. The history of organised medical philanthropy in the Antipodean colony of Victoria, however, began earlier than this, with a distinct religious lineage. In November 1848, the Melbourne Jewish philanthropic society formed and held its inaugural meeting at the Rainbow Tavern, on Swanston Street.[5] This would be followed by a range of hospitals, orphanages, female rescue homes, aged care institutions, ladies' benevolent societies and services for people with disabilities, which together formed the basis for the colony's voluntarist approach to social provision. Historian Shurlee Swain tells how the colony of Victoria always relied on voluntary donations to deliver its medical services, with the government 'left to provide only for prisoners, psychiatric patients and some categories of neglected children'.[6]

Hospital Sundays emerged in a context where philanthropy was motivated by plural religious philosophies converging around the goodness of giving. These days became a thriving settler cultural institution, performed in Melbourne, Bendigo and other regional cities from the 1870s into the 1930s. Hospital Sundays were popular, growing bigger than their metropolitan counterparts. '[T]he large Australian cities', reported London-published *Hospital* journal in 1894, 'seem to show greater enthusiasm and collect larger sums than those yet realised in America or in any British cities.'[7] Bendigo led the way in this effort. In October 1873, the Bendigo Hospital Sunday committee declared that a great £1,004 has been raised at 'the first Australian Hospital Sunday'.[8] By the late nineteenth century, Hospital Sundays were considered

3 'The Bendigo Hospital Sunday,' *Bendigo Advertiser*, October 9, 1873, p. 2, nla.gov.au/nla.news-article88268868.

4 'The Early History of the Hospital Sunday at Saturday Funds,' *The Hospital* 16, no. 414 (1894), 451, www.ncbi.nlm.nih.gov/pmc/articles/PMC5263633/?page=1.

5 'Neither the government nor the philanthropic individuals on which it was dependent were prepared to admit that any citizen had a right to relief.' Shurlee Swain, 'Philanthropy,' *eMelbourne* (blog) July 2008, www.emelbourne.net.au/biogs/EM01139b.htm.

6 Swain, 'Philanthropy.'

7 'The Early History of the Hospital Sunday,' 451.

8 'The Bendigo Hospital Sunday,' *Bendigo Advertiser*, October 9, 1873, p. 2, nla.gov.au/nla.news-article88268868.

a tradition, and Bendigonians were particularly enthusiastic partakers. These 'Demonstrations' were celebrated as both 'noble' and entertaining, drawing crowds from hundreds into the tens of thousands.[9]

A festival of charity: Religious feelings beyond walls

Hospital Sundays were usually performed in Bendigo's central, grassy, tree- and flower-filled Rosalind Park. This open-air location enabled people of various faiths and Christian denominations to gather outside of the confines of church walls. The contributing churches included St Andrew's (Presbyterian), St Paul's (Church of England), All Saints' (Church of England), Forest-street (Wesleyan) and German Lutheran churches.[10] Members of St Kilian's (Roman Catholic) are present on the day. Although canon law prevented St Kilian's from participating in non-Catholic services, their support for Hospital Sunday indicates the 'social duty or honor' associated with the event.[11] Newspapers reported the sizeable Bendigo Hospital Sunday crowds. In 1881, for instance, on a day that 'threatened a heavy downpour', an estimated four to five thousand people attended in the adjoining Camp Reserve.[12] The following year, on a day when 'the weather was most beautiful indeed', an estimated ten to fifteen thousand people gathered.[13] It evidently felt good to give for the causes of health, and even better, to do so outside in sunlight with live music playing. The open-air location did make attendees vulnerable to the weather. In 1901, for instance 'the weather interfered with the collection', so that while there was 'a large attendance [once] a thunderstorm began the crowd had to disperse'.[14]

9 'The Bendigo Hospital Sunday,' *Bendigo Advertiser*, November 10, 1890, p. 2, nla.gov.au/nla.news-article88646668; At the time Hospital Sundays came to an end, England-born businessman, politician, and member of the Protestant Congregational Church, J. H. Abbott would be memorialised as initiating the movement: '[T]he late Mr. J. H. Abbott began this [Hospital Sunday] movement in Bendigo', see 'Hospital Sunday', *Shepparton Advertiser*, November 20, 1933, p. 4, nla.gov.au/nla.news-article168646437.

10 The total raised was 334 pounds. 'Bendigo Hospital Sunday,' *The Argus*, October 12, 1896, p. 6, nla.gov.au/nla.news-article9181878.

11 Can 1258, see Charles Augustine Bachofen, *A Commentary on the New Code of the Canon Law* (B. Herder Book Co., 1918), 92.

12 'Bendigo Hospital Sunday: The Open Air Service,' October 17, 1881, *Bendigo Advertiser*, Victoria, p. 2, nla.gov.au/nla.news-article88619342.

13 'Bendigo Hospital Sunday' October 16, 1882, *Bendigo Advertiser*, Victoria, p. 2, trove.nla.gov.au/newspaper/article/88577131/9077168

14 'Bendigo Hospital Sunday,' *The Argus*, October 21, 1901, p. 5, nla.gov.au/nla.news-article9613001.

Among rain and sunshine, church leaders leveraged biblical ideas of giving to the needy, encouraging those gathered to open their purses wide. During the Hospital Sunday of November 1890, one Reverend A. S. James preached from Deuteronomy; 'Thou shalt open his hand wide unto his brother, so thy poor, and so thy needy, in thy land.'[15] And during the Hospital Sunday of 1883, one Revered John Garlick delivered a lengthy sermon, reminding those gathered that 'God is always giving', linking God's generosity with the virtues of colonial institutions:

> now I trust that I need not ask your indulgence for inviting you to make a collection for the Bendigo Hospital and the Benevolent Asylum … The worth of these admirable institutions needs no comment of mine. There they stand before you, and you may look upon them with no small degree of pride. They are noble in their structure, noble in their object, and noble in their end.

Garlick concluded his multifaceted rationale to give by calling on a sense of loyalty to Bendigo, 'They are an honor to your city. Therefore I ask you to give largely to keep up its funds … Be Christ-like, He gave Himself for you.'[16]

Such self-sacrificial fusions of public health with Christian ceremony promoted civic goodness. Through the late nineteenth century, many states 'democratized ceremonial and celebratory events'.[17] Hospital Sundays emerged as what historian Ben Roberts calls a 'civic ritual': they entailed a physical expression of values that involves the 'embracement of recreation and public festivity'.[18] Here, the values centred around giving.[19] These days 'blurred the boundary between the sacred and the secular', between spaces of worship and religious learning and those of pleasure.[20]

15 'Bendigo Hospital Sunday,' *Bendigo Advertiser*, November 10, 1890, p. 2, nla.gov.au/nla.news-article 88646668.

16 'Bendigo Hospital Sunday,' *Bendigo Advertiser*, October 15, 1883, p. 3, nla.gov.au/nla.news-article 88521722.

17 Ben Roberts, 'Entertaining the Community: The Evolution of Civic Ritual and Public Celebration, 1860–1953,' *Urban History* 44, no. 3 (2017): 444–63, doi.org/10.1017/S0963926816000511.

18 Ibid.

19 Ibid.

20 Roger Ottewill, '"Alleviating the Sum of Human Suffering": The Origins, Attributes and Appeal of Hospital Sunday, 1859–1914,' *Studies in Church History*, 58 (2022): 352–371, doi.org/10.1017/stc.2022.17.

Faith-based philanthropy as a spectacle of belonging

Forms of social and religious capital were spectacularly bound together when it came to funding Bendigo's hospital and asylum. Givers watched how much others gave, and newspapers reported in detail the pounds donated at Hospital Sunday events, amplifying the idea of the Christian church's benevolence and care for society, for workers and for the poor.[21] The act of giving translated easily across faiths, notably, across Christian denominations and Confucianism. Medical philanthropy was intelligible as a God-like virtue, if not a godly one: a goodness at once religious and extra-religious. On these Sundays, giving was itself a form of faith, a trust that handing money to the hospital would benefit one's 'brother', implicitly, to the settlers' common benefit. The moral capital available through medical philanthropy and performances thereof was, however, racially variegated. For Europeans, it was a way to perform a social-religious belonging, but for people of Chinese descent, who donated variously as Confucians, Christians, church members, and citizens, it had distinct meanings.

Historians John Fitzgerald and Mei-fen Kuo have documented that for Chinese people living in diasporic contexts such as Bendigo, charity had dense functions, serving as 'an entrée into elite social and political circles and as a medium for cross-cultural negotiations'.[22] Chinese residents in Bendigo and across the colony were publicly shamed for, and expected to pay for the treatment of, their illness and diseases in a way that contemporary Europeans were not.[23] In a context where not all bodies and lives were treated as equal,

21 'Hospital Sunday,' *Bendigo Advertiser*, October 21, 1878, p. 2, nla.gov.au/nla.news-article88219733.

22 John Fitzgerald and Mei-fen Kuo, 'Diaspora Charity and Welfare Sovereignty in the Chinese Republic: Shanghai Charity Innovator William Yinson Lee (Li Yuanxin, 1884–1965),' *Twentieth-Century China*, 42, no. 1 (2017): 72–96, doi.org/10.1353/tcc.2017.0008; for more on the Confucian virtue of charity see Vivienne Shue, 'The Quality of Mercy: Confucian Charity and the Mixed Metaphors of Modernity in Tianjin,' *Modern China* 32, no. 4 (2006): 411–52, doi.org/10.1177/0097700406291788.

23 For a discussion of some of the structural and cultural barriers Chinese people faced in accessing European-run hospitals, see Lovejoy, 'The Things that Unite: Inquests into Chinese Deaths on the Bendigo Goldfields 1854-6.' For an instance of the racist medical neglect of a Chinese Bendigonian child, see '1881/1364 Edith Ah Quin: Inquest,' VPRS 24/P0000, 1881/1364, Public Record Office of Victoria, prov.vic.gov.au/archive/A134ABF1-F1BC-11E9-AE98-771848B5989B?image=1. With thanks to Natasha Joyce for sharing this source. The pressures for Chinese residents to prove they were not a burden on the medical system were enduring and compelled ongoing negotiations. In 1896, a decision was made by the Chinese community in Bendigo to circulate subscription books and thus to pay their own way to medical access and entitlement. 'Chinese Charity Subscription at Bendigo,' *The Age*, August 17, 1896, p. 6, nla.gov.au/nla.news-article190606051.

Chinese leaders and communities – as well as contemporary South Asian communities – leveraged diplomatic and political power through medical charity and its performances.[24]

Tensions about the park

The undeniably grave imperatives of health and welfare gave license for the Sabbath to verge into a day of enjoyment; however, these gatherings were not without tensions. The performance of non-Christian music, albeit usually military songs, added to the sensorial and social pleasures of Hospital Sundays. The crowd's palpable enjoyment was fuel for those concerned that these days were at odds with the Christian religious ideal that Sunday should be a time for sober learning and reverence. Christian Ministers intermittently threatened to discontinue their involvement in what the press described favourably as 'pleasant Sunday afternoon gatherings'.[25] The Argus reported in 1905:

> there seemed to be a tendency in Bendigo and elsewhere in connection with the Hospital Sunday movement to utterly destroy a great deal of work of the churches … The movement had been begun on a religious basis, but was now the means of disintegrating the work of ministers.[26]

In the 1930s, Hospital Sunday crowds across Victoria began to decline as new media such as radio became to compete with sermons as alternative forms of Sunday afternoon entertainment.[27] Bendigo crowds evidently remained convivial and generous in comparison to other centres. In 1933, the Shepparton Advertiser reported that the Bendigo gardens 'in the Lower Reserve were fragrant and gay in their spring dressing and perfumes and around the band rotunda there were shady promenades under elms and oaks'.[28] The Bendigo Base Hospital Board decided in 1934 to discontinue

24 For discussion of contemporary South Asian leaders leveraging the moral capital of medical philanthropy, see also Nadia Rhook, 'Affective Counter Networks: Healing, Trade, and Indian Strategies of In/dependence in Early "White Melbourne",' *Journal of Colonialism and Colonial History* 19, no. 2 (2018), doi.org/10.1353/cch.2018.0012.

25 'Hospital Sunday: Bendigo Clergy Object,' *The Argus*, July 4, 1905, p. 6, nla.gov.au/nla.news-article 9909469.

26 Ibid.

27 'Hospital Sunday,' *Shepparton Advertiser*, November 20, 1933, p. 4, nla.gov.au/nla.news-article 168646437.

28 Ibid.

Hospital Sundays. Growing critiques suggested that these days undercut traditional indoor church services, where numbers were already believed to be threatened by the popularity of home entertainments, including radio.[29] By the mid-twentieth century, the organisation of religious-based donation would shift toward an expectation of state-provided welfare and medical care, and the Bendigo Hospital began to seek secular funding.[30] In 1936, the hospital began an industrial fundraising tack. They appealed for farmers to donate wheat to help raise funds.[31] The life and death stakes of health and welfare, along with a blurring of demarcations between relaxed pleasure and strict reverence, had underwritten the success of Hospital Sundays as being celebrated as enduringly multi-faith, multi-denominational events.

29 'Bendigo,' *The Age*, April 18, 1934, p. 16, nla.gov.au/nla.news-article203836819.

30 'The Charities Board of Victoria, established in 1923 under the Hospitals and Charities Act 1922, was empowered to control the registration of all charitable institutions, including hospitals, and regulate their access to government support from the Hospitals and Charities Fund.' Brett Wright, 'Surgical Practice and Honorary Control at Bendigo Hospital 1892–98', *Health and History* 21, no. 2 (2019): 43, doi.org/10.5401/healthhist.21.2.0023.

31 See 'Bendigo and District: Novel Hospital Appeal,' *The Argus*, January 4, 1936, p. 14, nla.gov.au/nla.news-article11870524.

4

Jewish, British, middle-class: A history of Jewish adjustment on the Central Victorian Goldfields

Migrants of all creeds and nationalities travelled to Bendigo and Ballarat, on Victoria's booming central goldfields, as gold fever captivated communities across the globe in the mid-nineteenth century. Hopeful families and enterprising individuals sailed over vast oceans, then trekked through muddy tracks with packs and trunks following the lure of gold. Jewish migrants brought their Jewish faith, strengthening the small community already present in the colonies. The history of Jewish people in Australia began with the First Fleet, but the community did not thrive until the gold rushes of the 1850s.[1] The Jewish population increased tenfold during the 1850s, with three new synagogues established in Melbourne and dozens of other *shuls* created in outlying frontier and gold settlements.[2] These migrants mostly arrived from Jewish communities already undergoing social and cultural transformations, and their responses to conditions in the Victorian colony reflected these modernising trends.

1 Hilary L. Rubinstein, *The Jews in Australia: A Thematic History* (William Heinemann Australia, 1991), 76.

2 Anne O'Brien, 'Religion,' in *The Cambridge History of Australia*, ed. Alison Bashford and Stuart Macintyre (Cambridge University Press, 2013), 425–426.

Colonial Jewish communities were shaped by Anglo-Jewish ideals and Reform Judaism from Britain and Europe. The majority of Jewish people on the Central Victorian Goldfields were born in Britain (mostly in England) or in Central and Eastern Europe, in such places as Poland, Prussia and Germany.[3] Among these Central and Eastern European-born Jewish migrants were a minority who had spent some time in England before migrating to the colonies. In England, Jewish communal and institutional adherence became increasingly privatised and optional over the eighteenth and nineteenth centuries. This led to quick adaptation and the creation of unique Anglo-Jewish middle-class values that emphasised mobility, self-reliance and the nurture of the private family for increasing respectability.[4] By contrast, in Central and Eastern Europe, the prevailing political systems and antisemitism continued to disadvantage Jewish communities. Other Jewish groups in Europe experienced social and cultural transformation from the eighteenth century, a shift further facilitated through the Haskalah, an intellectual Jewish movement in Central and Eastern Europe that placed primacy on rationality and intellect.[5] Through the Haskalah, Reform Judaism became a new and major branch of Jewish practice that encouraged the modernisation of religion.

Drawing upon this longer history of change, Jewish people on the Central Victorian Goldfields altered their religious, social and cultural practices as they responded to the pervasive Protestant colonial frameworks, a lack of resources and their own shifting identity. Focusing on Jewish foodways, the Jewish Sabbath and synagogue worship, this chapter reveals how these cultural mediations were deeply entangled with the development of a colonial Jewish identity that was based upon strong ties both to Judaism

---

3 Elizabeth Offer, 'The Formation of Goldfields Anglo-Jewry: How Jewish Settlers Negotiated Judaism, Class, and Britishness on the Central Victorian Goldfields, 1851-1901' (PhD thesis, La Trobe University, 2021), 65. In both official and private records, Jewish people on the Central Victorian Goldfields relied upon such terms as Germany, Poland, and Prussia when describing certain areas in Eastern and Central Europe, yet their use of these terms could overlap or diverge individually. To account for this, this chapter incorporates all names, using, where possible, the location name given in the primary material to ensure a more accurate representation.

4 V. D. Lipman, *Three Centuries of Anglo-Jewish History: A Volume of Essays*, (Published for the Jewish Historical Society of England by W. Heffer, 1961), 82; Reinhard Rürup, 'Jewish Emancipation in Britain and Germany,' in *Two Nations: British and German Jews in Comparative Perspective*, ed. Michael Brenner, Rainer Liedtke, and David Rechter (Leo Baeck Institute, 1999), 50; Peter Bailey, 'White Collars, Gray Lives? The Lower Middle Class Revisited,' *Journal of British Studies* 38, no. 3 (1999): 273–90, doi.org/10.1086/386195.

5 Christhard Hoffman, 'Constructing Jewish Modernity: Mendelssohn Jubilee Celebrations within Germany Jewry 1829–1929,' in *Towards Normality? Acculturation and Modern German Jewry*, ed. Rainer Liedtke and David Rechter (Leo Baeck Institute, 2003), 30–31.

and to British colonial society. This chapter complicates current scholarly understandings of the relationship between Britishness, identity and religion in the nineteenth century, revealing the impact such negotiations had in shaping religious communities on Victoria's major goldfields.

Hebrew congregations and synagogues: Establishing Jewish institutions on the goldfields

The provisional living conditions of the early goldfields prompted many migrants to establish congregations and faith communities to create places of belonging where felt attachments and communal values could be expressed.[6] Hebrew congregations in Bendigo and Ballarat first gathered in hotel dining rooms or stores before building synagogues. The synagogue space and public worship emerged as a place and means to express and confirm divergent identities. As such, the synagogue and public worship could foster wider social and cultural inclusion for the Jewish community while also maintaining a sense of religious difference. Such mediations were evident as synagogues in Bendigo and Ballarat were established.

Local newspaper advertisements indicated that a Hebrew congregation with an acting committee had formed in Bendigo by 1855.[7] In his 1891 history of Bendigo, George Mackay placed the earliest organised gatherings for Jewish worship as 1854, though evidence suggests it may have formed even earlier.[8] Writing home to his family in England in 1853, Charles Hodges, a non-Jewish settler turned Chinese court interpreter who had recently left Bendigo for Melbourne, noted the presence of a synagogue among the various religious sects present on the Bendigo goldfields.[9] Hodges likely used the designation of 'synagogue' to refer to a gathered community rather than to a building, as no synagogue had then been built in Bendigo.[10] On 13 July

6 Alejandro Portes and Josh DeWind, 'A Cross-Atlantic Dialogue: The Progress of Research and Theory in the Study of International Migration,' in *Rethinking Migration: New Theoretical and Empirical Perspectives*, ed. Alejandro Portes and Josh DeWind (Berghahn Books, 2007), 19.

7 'Advertising,' *Bendigo Advertiser*, September 8, 1855, p. 1, nla.gov.au/nla.news-page8999609. The copies available of the local newspaper, the *Bendigo Advertiser*, only date as far back as September 1855, despite the newspaper being created in 1853.

8 George Mackay, *The History of Bendigo* (Fergusson & Mitchell, 1891), 171.

9 Charles Hodges, letter written home from Melbourne, Australia to his family, August 8, 1853, D7367/1, Gloucestershire Archives, catalogue.gloucestershire.gov.uk/records/D7367/1.

10 Ibid.

1856, the Bendigo Hebrew congregation celebrated the opening of their first synagogue, located in Dowling Street and built from wood, with a special ceremony taking place to mark this momentous occasion.

From its opening ceremony, the Bendigo synagogue emerged as a space that linked congregants to both Judaism and the wider imperial world.[11] After the opening, Israel Moses, one of the officers elected to serve at the synagogue, delivered a moving address to the gathered audience of Christians and Jews. He claimed that the synagogue was not only 'a temple of prayer, but … a schools [*sic*], to teach us our duties as a portion of the great family of mankind'.[12] The address referenced both international and imperial places, referring to the Jewish people as 'our nation' while also acknowledging a connection to 'our native England'.[13] Through this means, the Bendigo Hebrew congregation firmly acknowledged their place and attachment to the British Empire while also reaffirming ties to a separate non-British Jewish diaspora. In doing so, Jewish people in Bendigo worked seemingly disparate connections into a single identity, locating themselves within the British Empire but also beyond it. Though the synagogue was opened with much joy and celebration, one significant role had been left vacant: that of 'minister'.

The Bendigo Hebrew congregation did not employ their first Jewish minister until late in 1859, that being Isaac Friedman. Born in 1805 in Hungary, Isaac Friedman arrived in Australia in the early 1830s with his wife, Rebecca Netto, whom he married in London. Rebecca died in 1835 while the couple resided in Sydney. In the same year of Rebecca's death, Friedman married Maria Nathan, and by 1838, the new couple had made their way to Tasmania.[14] After another sojourn in New South Wales, as well as a brief return to Tasmania, Friedman was hired by the Bendigo Hebrew congregation. Friedman occupied a range of positions within the Bendigo Jewish community, as he acted to lead worship, to advise the community on *shehitah* (the religious laws surrounding the slaughter of animals for consumption) and to conduct marriages. The role of the Jewish minister

11 Tables of the Law refer to the stone tablets inscribed with the Ten Commandments and are usually displayed in synagogues.

12 'Opening of the Jewish Synagogue,' *Bendigo Advertiser*, July 14, 1856, p. 2, nla.gov.au/nla.news-article88051388.

13 Ibid., p. 2, col. 6.

14 'From the Hobart Town Gazette,' *Launceston Advertiser*, May 24, 1838, p. 4, nla.gov.au/nla.news-article84754267; 'List of Applications for Licenses Granted for the District of Hobarton,' *The Courier*, 3 September 1841, p. 4, nla.gov.au/nla.news-article2955674.

on the goldfields often extended beyond these roles to include teaching children Hebrew, delivering sermons, acting as *shochet* (ritual slaughterer) and performing rituals such as a *brit milah* (circumcision ceremony) and *bar mitzvah* (a coming-of-age ceremony for Jewish boys).

Friedman's extensive range of duties reflected recent shifts that had occurred as the synagogue *chazan* (or Reader), the person who leads group prayers through their melodic chanting in the synagogue, was transformed into a 'proper minister' who acted as pastor, preacher and public figurehead.[15] Heavily influenced by Protestant Christianity, this model for Jewish ministers was popular in the Australian colonies in the mid-nineteenth century, as it was across many English-speaking countries at the time. By the end of the century, the use of this ministerial model had decreased and would gradually disappear in the next century. Friedman served the Bendigo Hebrew congregation until 1868, when he moved to Melbourne with his family.[16] Another Jewish minister was not hired until the early 1870s, when Isaac Stone was employed, likely in response to the recent construction commissioned by the Hebrew congregation.[17] In the early 1870s, Bendigo had built an impressive new synagogue in the Byzantine and Moorish styles, a larger structure that would require a full-time minister to manage.[18] In the rapidly growing regional Victorian city of Ballarat, the local Jewish community was also busy establishing a Hebrew congregation.

A Hebrew congregation formed in Ballarat in the early 1850s and built a synagogue soon after. In an address presented in 1861, Charles Dyte dated the early beginnings of the Hebrew congregation to 1854, with gatherings for worship occurring in the Clarendon Hotel.[19] Dyte had arrived in Ballarat in 1853, although he initially moved between Melbourne and Ballarat to conduct business.[20] He quickly became an influential figure both within

15 Adam Mendelsohn, 'The Sacrifices of the Isaacs: The Diffusion of New Models of Religious Leadership in the English-Speaking Jewish World,' in *Transnational Traditions: New Perspectives on American Jewish History*, ed. Ava Fran Kahn (Wayne State University Press, 2014), 12.

16 'Advertising,' *Bendigo Advertiser*, June 23, 1868, p. 3, nla.gov.au/nla.news-article87896739; 'Family Notices,' *Bendigo Advertiser*, July 11, 1871, p. 2, nla.gov.au/nla.news-article87904934.

17 Much later in the 1880s, the Bendigo Hebrew Congregation hired Isidore Myers, then D. H. Harris, and then in 1890s, J. Goldstein.

18 'The Bendigo Advertiser,' *Bendigo Advertiser*, September 4, 1872, p. 2, col. 2, nla.gov.au/nla.news-article87975666.

19 'Hebrew Synagogue,' *The Star*, January 26, 1861, p. 4, nla.gov.au/nla.news-article66337060.

20 Parliament of Victoria, *Report from the Select Committee upon Ballaarat Riots – Bentley's Hotel* (John Ferres, Government Printer, 1857–1858), 24, nla.gov.au/nla.obj-70329844.

the congregation and in wider Ballarat society.[21] Within a year, the Ballarat Hebrew congregation opened their first, wooden synagogue in June 1855, located in Barkley Street.[22] While the land was officially reserved for Jewish religious purposes, the Ballarat Hebrew congregation soon faced a contest over possession of the land.

In 1856, the local municipal council sent the Ballarat Hebrew congregation a series of letters requesting their removal from the synagogue, as the land was required for a government building.[23] The congregation initially denied the request because the land had been consecrated. The council repeatedly asked the congregation to leave, which they agreed to, on the condition that another piece of land first be provided for the Jewish community. In 1859, a section of land was granted to the Hebrew congregation for another synagogue and a Hebrew school, located further down Barkley Street. The second reserve of land, however, was on Crown Land that was occupied by the Lloyd brothers, Frederick and Benjamin. The brothers refused to vacate, as they claimed that the land, for which they had been paying taxes, was theirs. Numerous court cases followed, mainly for trespassing, with the Lloyd brothers serving time in prison.[24] This dispute over the reserved land was not settled until late in 1860, and only after a physical altercation occurred between Charles Dyte and Frederick Lloyd.[25] After this confrontation, the two parties arrived at an agreement, and the Lloyd brothers left the reserve.[26] Construction work on the new brick synagogue quickly commenced upon their removal.

Like the Easter Parade and Hospital Sundays, discussed in our Introduction and Popout One, the new synagogue fostered social cohesion through shared celebration. The brick synagogue in Ballarat was officially opened

21 'News and Notes,' *Ballarat Star*, April 12, 1870, p. 2, nla.gov.au/nla.news-article219307719; 'News and Notes,' *Ballarat Star*, April 18, 1871, p. 2, nla.gov.au/nla.news-article197562019; 'Presentation to Mr Charles Dyte,' *Ballarat Star*, 28 May 28, 1872, 3, nla.gov.au/nla.news-article197629080.

22 'Ballarat,' *Geelong Advertiser and Intelligence*, June 11, 1855, p. 2, nla.gov.au/nla.news-article91870541.

23 Nathan Spielvogel, *Annals of the Ballarat Hebrew Congregation* (item box number AB175), B44 Australian Jewish Historical Society Institutional Archives, collections.ajhs.com.au/Detail/objects/7416.

24 'Eastern Police Court,' *The Star*, September 17, 1859, p. 2, nla.gov.au/nla.news-article66055341; 'News and Notes,' *The Star*, October 4, 1859, p. 2, nla.gov.au/nla.news-article66055662; 'News and Notes,' *The Star*, February 27, 1860, p. 2, nla.gov.au/nla.news-article72465277; 'News and Notes,' *The Star*, March 23, 1860, p. 2, nla.gov.au/nla.news-article72465781; 'News and Notes,' *The Star*, April 9, 1860, p. 2, nla.gov.au/nla.news-article72466078; 'Eastern Police Court,' *The Star*, May 29, 1860, p. 3, nla.gov.au/nla.news-article72467050; 'News and Notes,' *The Star*, August 13, 1860, p. 2, nla.gov.au/nla.news-article66057622; 'News and Notes,' *The Star*, October 30, 1860, p. 2, nla.gov.au/nla.news-article66059138.

25 'Eastern Police Court,' *The Star*, December 6, 1860, p. 4, nla.gov.au/nla.news-article66336148.

26 'News and Notes,' *The Star*, December 6, 1860, p. 2, nla.gov.au/nla.news-article66336157.

with a consecration service held on 17 March 1861, a Sunday afternoon. Built in the style of classical and Egyptian revival, the synagogue referenced the Eastern origin of Jewish people, as can be seen in Figure 4.1. The opening of the Ballarat synagogue was a significant community event, as local newspapers remarked on construction processes and later published articles on the first service. As one local newspaper commented on the opening ceremony, 'Jews from all parts of the world, and Christians of all denominations' were present.[27] This interreligious gathering in the synagogue became a common occurrence both in Ballarat and Bendigo. Christian ministers, visitors and persons of note were invited into the synagogue, often when a significant event was being celebrated, such as the Royal Jubilees held to commemorate Queen Victoria's reign. Through this means, the synagogue space was woven into the social and cultural fabric of goldfields society. Unlike Bendigo, the Ballarat Hebrew congregation had employed a Jewish minister before the first synagogue was completed.

Figure 4.1: Ballarat synagogue

Source: Photographed by Solomon & Bardwell, courtesy of State Library of Victoria.

27 'The Hebrew Synagogue,' *The Star*, March 18, 1861, p. 4, nla.gov.au/nla.news-article66337989.

In the early decades of the Ballarat Hebrew congregation, the synagogue employed three Jewish ministers. The first minister, David Isaacs, was hired in 1855 as the synagogue was nearing completion. Before arriving in the Victorian colony, Isaacs travelled to New Zealand and attempted to form strict Orthodox communities among settled Jewish people. In Ballarat, Isaacs remained with the congregation until the early 1860s. Samuel Herman became Ballarat's second Jewish minister, and when his short term expired in 1868, the congregational committee decided to select Israel Goldreich as the new minister.[28] Israel Goldreich was born in Poland in 1834, but it is unclear when he arrived in the Australian colonies. Before arriving in Ballarat, Goldreich had acted as the Jewish minister for the Hebrew congregation in Hobart Town, Tasmania. Like Bendigo's Jewish minister, Goldreich occupied multiple roles within the congregation and the Jewish community, acting as teacher, preacher, and officiant.

Goldfields Hebrew congregations formed during a pivotal period, as goldfields society was developing and Jewish migrants were experiencing other religious and social changes. These two factors influenced Jewish communities on early goldfields, affecting Hebrew congregations throughout the century as Jewish people navigated colonial frameworks, British identity, and the value of individual ambition to achieve middle-class status.[29] As follows, this negotiation and the related social, economic and religious integration of the Jewish community was particularly evident in issues of weekend labour and Jewish Sabbath adherence.

Desecrate the Sabbath or starve: Jewish Sabbath adherence and Sunday trading

Whether Jewish people decided to settle or sojourn on the goldfields, many became fully integrated into local economic life. Still, this process of integration raised serious (though by no means new) considerations regarding work, leisure and worship. In 1871, the Melbourne-based Jewish newspaper *Australian Israelite* complained of the rise in the desecration of the Jewish Sabbath across the Victorian colony, including the goldfields towns and cities. The writer highlighted the difficult position of Jewish people

28 The earliest evidence of Samuel Herman acting as Jewish minister in Ballarat is dated for 1865, 'Letter to the Editor,' *Ballarat Star*, January 15, 1868, p. 3, nla.gov.au/nla.news-article113600433.

29 Definitive work by Geoffrey Crossick discusses a slightly later period. Crossick, Geoffrey, *The Lower Middle Class in Britain, 1870-1914* (Croom Helm, 1977).

regarding their work habits, proclaiming that 'the Jewish workman is either compelled to desecrate the Sabbath or starve'.[30] To abide by both colonial law and *halachah* (Jewish religious law) meant ceasing from work for two days, Saturday and Sunday, which could have huge economic implications.

Sunday trading laws in colonial Victoria banned trade and most forms of paid labour on Sunday, making it illegal to conduct business on the Christian Sabbath. As a British outpost, the Australian colonies had inherited a body of statutes concerning the Christian Sabbath from England, such as the Westminster Confession of Faith, that encouraged Sunday Sabbath adherence by penalising non-observance.[31] Sunday trading was banned among these decrees. These statutes were extended in the Victorian colony over the nineteenth century, further limiting Sunday trading while banning shooting on the Sabbath and prohibiting theatre performances.[32] While colonial law prescribed Sunday Sabbath adherence, or at least a semblance of adherence, Judaism also outlined how the Jewish Sabbath should be observed.

In Judaism, the Sabbath occurs from dusk on Friday until dusk on Saturday.[33] *Halachah* surrounding the Jewish Sabbath is complex and multifaceted, specifying that activities such as writing, business transactions, shopping, lighting fires, cooking and laundry are not to be performed on the Jewish Sabbath.[34] Colonial and religious law complicated economic life for Jewish people on the goldfields, requiring ongoing negotiations. Such issues were further complicated by the type of occupations Jewish goldfields workers tended to engage in.

Jewish people on the Central Victorian Goldfields mostly worked in mercantile, commercial businesses or in skilled labour roles.[35] Pawnbrokers, storekeepers and publicans were the most popular occupations for Jewish migrants.[36] Hawking was also common, though more prevalent in the 1850s among those who were recently arrived, poor or experiencing illness.[37]

30 'The Sabbath and the Factory Act,' *Australian Israelite*, August 25, 1871, p. 4, nla.gov.au/nla.news-page29257580.

31 Timothy Willem Jones and Clare Wright, 'The Goldfields' Sabbath: A Postsecular Analysis of Social Cohesion and Social Control on the Ballarat Goldfields, 1854,' *Journal of Religious History* 43, no.4 (2019): 451, doi.org/10.1111/1467-9809.12626.

32 Jones and Wright, 'The Goldfields' Sabbath'; Geoffrey Serle, *The Rush to be Rich: A History of the Colony of Victoria 1883-1889* (Melbourne University Press, 1971), 158.

33 Michael J. Graetz, 'Sabbath.' In *Encyclopaedia Judaica*, edited by Michael Berenbaum and Fred Skolnik (Macmillan Reference, 2007).

34 *Encyclopaedia Judaica* s.v. 'Sabbath'.

35 Offer, *The Formation of Goldfields Anglo-Jewry*, 68.

36 Ibid.

37 Ibid.

Single and married Jewish women also participated in Victoria's booming goldrush economy, with storekeeping, tailoring and hotel-keeping proving viable occupations.[38] Jewish people on the Central Victorian Goldfields, concentrated in mercantile and commercial areas, likely faced disadvantages trading in a predominantly Protestant society. Such issues were further intensified on the goldfields, since Saturday was the most popular shopping day, and hence the most profitable day for business. Issues related to Sunday trading and Jewish practice were familiar to Jewish goldfields workers, as they had encountered similar challenges in England or seen their family members navigate English laws alongside Jewish practices.[39] The choices made by Jewish goldfields workers reflected these earlier practices in Britain and sometimes stood in direct opposition to colonial law.

The open transgression of Sunday trading laws, and the Christian Sabbath adherence they were meant to enshrine, often resulted in fines and social disapproval, testing the limits of goldfields social cohesion. In Ballarat, one Mr Bukh, a Jewish local business owner, frequently worked on Sundays, since he strictly observed the Jewish Sabbath.[40] Appalled by his actions, Bukh's neighbours reported him to the police, leading to his arrest and court appearance.[41] Represented by the previously mentioned Charles Dyte, Bukh objected to the charge; Dyte was overruled, and the bench imposed a fine of five shillings.[42] On the goldfields, few concessions were made for Jewish people in court. When such adjustments were made, they usually related to oath taking or rescheduling a missed court appearance if it coincided with a Jewish holiday.[43] Such allowances did not extend to Sunday trading.

38 'Jewish Emigration Society,' *Jewish Chronicle*, February 26, 1858, p. 84.

39 A significant number of studies have been conducted into the Saturday Sabbath and Sunday working practices of Jews both in Britain and North America. For some of this literature, see David Dee, 'Sport or Shul? Physical Recreation, Anglo-Jewry and the Jewish Sabbath, ca. 1890–1939' *Jewish Historical Studies* 44 (2012): 7–26; Sarah Mass, 'Sunday Rites or Sunday Rights? Anglo-Jewish Traders and the Negotiability of the Mid-Century Sabbath,' *History of Retailing and Consumption* 2, no.1 (2016): 68–83, doi.org/10.1080/2373518X.2016.1183879; Kerry M. Olitxky, 'The Sunday-Sabbath Movement in American Reform Judaism: Strategy or Evolution?' *American Jewish Archives* 34, no.1 (1982): 75–88; Annie Polland, 'Working for the Sabbath: Sabbath in the Jewish Immigrant Neighborhoods of New York,' *Labor: Studies in Working-Class History of the Americas* 6, no.1 (2009): 33–56, doi.org/10.1215/15476715-2008-044; Benjamin Kline Hunnicutt, 'The Jewish Sabbath Movement in the Early Twentieth Century,' *American Jewish History* 69, no. 2 (1979): 196–225; Heather A. McKay, *Sabbath and Synagogue: The Question of Sabbath Worship in Ancient Judaism* (Brill, 2001).

40 'The Argus,' *The Argus*, May 13, 1874, p. 4, nla.gov.au/nla.news-page237676.

41 Ibid.

42 Ibid.

43 'Mining Intelligence, Taking the Oath,' *Bendigo Advertiser*, March 7, 1866, p. 2, nla.gov.au/nla.news-article87959109; 'Country Court,' *The Star*, September 17, 1858, p. 2; 'Geelong Insolvent Court,' *Ballarat Star*, October 11, 1867, p. 4, nla.gov.au/nla.news-article112871073.

In Chapter Three, we saw that when it came to negotiating religious difference inside the courtroom, colonial law was compelled to practice religious relativity. Here, we see that outside of the courtroom, the application of colonial law could, on the contrary, be inflexible. For Bukh and other Jewish people, the law's normalisation of Protestant culture treated civil disobedience as religious dissent. Ignoring the Jewish meanings of Saturday meant that Jewish people were pressured to conform. When applied to all people within colonial society, Christian Sabbath observance and the laws surrounding Sunday trading acted as a form of Protestant social and religious control, with the law becoming a site for the navigation of religious difference.[44] In this way, social compliance was forced not by cultural assimilation but by threat of punitive action.

Some Jewish men continued to trade and work on Saturdays, to attend mining meetings or even engage in more leisurely pursuits. How Jewish women and children spent the Jewish Sabbath is unknown, as little evidence has survived regarding their weekend activity. A lack of primary sources makes it harder to uncover whether husbands laboured so that their wives and children could keep Sabbath, as other studies have suggested.[45] If they did, this adherence by women and children likely occurred away from Christian eyes, in the home or the synagogue, which, coupled with their abstention from work on Sundays, could be seen as symbolically heeding the Christian Sabbath. Jewish men or older children who worked on Saturdays in more visible communal and economic spaces may have demonstrated Christian work habits for their family. Although the reasons for these changes are not always clear, Jewish men on the goldfields modified their observances of the Jewish Sabbath. As an example, Henry Marks, an auctioneer and commission agent in Bendigo, auctioned goods on Saturday mornings from rooms in Pall Mall.[46] For men such as Marks, Saturday labour provided a way for Jewish people to meet their economic needs within the Protestant structures of the goldfields; it is unclear whether this was by choice or necessity. While colonial law could prove a powerful deterrent, this Saturday activity may have also been motivated by a desire to assimilate into the colony's cultural and social frameworks.

44 Jones and Wright, 'The Goldfields' Sabbath,' 451.

45 See Polland, 'Working for the Sabbath.'

46 'Advertising,' *Bendigo Advertiser*, November 22, 1855, p. 3, nla.gov.au/nla.news-page8999749; 'Advertising,' *Bendigo Advertiser*, December 15, 1855, p. 3, nla.gov.au/nla.news-page8999792; 'Advertising,' *Bendigo Advertiser*, April 26, 1856, p. 3, nla.gov.au/nla.news-article88049713. 'Advertising,' *Bendigo Advertiser*, June 7, 1856, p. 4, nla.gov.au/nla.news-page9000244.

Figure 4.2: Saturday night market in Ballarat, 1868
Source: W. H. Harrison, courtesy of State Library of Victoria.

Available evidence demonstrates that some Jewish people, such as Sydney Abraham and Isaac Davidson in Ballarat, shopped for clothes on Saturdays; an economic necessity, but much less pressing than work.[47] Shopping on a Saturday was not only possible but also socially and economically endorsed, as evidenced by crowds gathered at the night market in the above image.[48] As Jewish people increasingly entered the middle classes in colonial Victoria, they may have adapted their weekend habits, perhaps engaging in similar Saturday pastimes.[49] For some Jewish people, Saturday activity was a deliberate choice, one that incorporated not only economic decisions but also class, social and cultural aspects. At times, Jewish people engaged in similar negotiations regarding their food consumption.

47 'Eastern Police Court,' *The Star*, January 10, 1863, p. 4, nla.gov.au/nla.news-article72554054.

48 Weston Bate, *Lucky City: The First Generation at Ballarat 1851–1901* (Melbourne University Press, 2003), 172.

49 Linda Young, *Middle Class Culture in the Nineteenth Century America, Australia and Britain* (Palgrave Macmillan, 2002), 14.

Kashrut and *kosher*: Jewish food practices on the goldfields

Jewish people modified their observance of *kashrut* as they settled on the goldfields, a shift that reflects accessibility issues and acculturation. *Kashrut* refers to the set of dietary laws in Judaism that have their origin in the Torah.[50] According to the Torah, only mammals that chew the cud and have cloven hooves and fish that have both scales and fins are to be eaten. A certain set of birds, such as birds of prey, are forbidden, and meat and dairy are not to be consumed together. All animals must be slaughtered by a trained *shochet*, who must follow set rules and guidelines to ensure the meat is unblemished and to minimise pain caused to the animal.[51] The daily consumption of food makes *kashrut* an everyday practice, a mundane yet salient aspect of life.[52] Jewish women play an important role preparing food and keeping a kosher kitchen through a set of practices and observances.[53] How Jewish migrants negotiated such laws as they encountered Australian wildlife is unknown. They may have relinquished kosher observance or adapted their practices to accommodate local availability.

Newspaper evidence, though sparse, reveals how Jewish people navigated *kashrut* laws on the Central Victorian Goldfields. Institutionally supplied kosher foods were temporarily available on the goldfields during certain times of the year, mainly for religious holidays. Articles needed for Passover, mainly *matzah* (a type of unleavened flatbread), were available relatively early in Ballarat.[54] Local Ballarat or Bendigo papers made no mention of kosher food or meat through the rest of the year. This is not to assume, however, that Jewish people were not observing kosher at home. There may have been a kosher butcher present in the community who simply did

50 Panikos Panayi, 'The Anglicisation of East European Jewish Food in Britain,' *Immigrants & Minorities* 30, no. 2–3 (2012), 296, doi.org/10.1080/02619288.2010.502719.

51 Harry Rabinowicz and Rela Geffen, 'Dietary Laws.' *Encyclopaedia Judaica*, vol. 5, p. 650–59; For more in-depth information regarding *kashrut*, see Stanley Waterman, 'Eating, Drinking and Maintenance of Community: Jewish Dietary Laws and Their Effects on Separateness,' in *The Changing World Religion Map: Sacred Places, Identities, Practices, and Politics*, ed. Stanley D. Brunn (Springer, 2015); David C. Kraemer, *Jewish Eating And Identity Through The Ages* (Routledge, 2020); Ella Stiniguţă Laslo, 'Purity and Impurity in Judaism: Taboo Foods and the Kashrut Laws,' *Studia Judaica* 22, no. 1 (2017): 137–57.

52 Andrew Buckser, 'Keeping Kosher: Eating and Social Identity Among the Jews of Denmark,' *Ethnology* 38, no. 3 (1999): 203.

53 *Encyclopaedia Judaica* s.v. 'Dietary Laws.'

54 *Matzah* is unleavened flatbread and forms a significant part of the Passover celebration, especially the *seder*, the ritual feast.

not advertise, or individual Jewish people may have butchered their own animals. By the mid-1860s, kosher butchers and groceries became available in Melbourne, and goods could be transported by train to the outer regions.

The Jewish ministers employed by goldfields congregations often supplied kosher meat to the local community, although this provision may have been limited. Some Jewish people may have simply abandoned the practice, perhaps not viewing *kashrut* as a significant marker of their Jewish identity. A visiting rabbi in 1862, Rabbi Jacob Saphir, sheds further light on the observation of *kashrut* for goldfields Jewish communities. He stated that:

> I have noticed a sickness amongst Jews, who are god [*sic*] fearing, upright, who uphold Torah and go daily to synagogue, morning and evening, and yet regard the matter of shechita and dietary laws most lightly, because they have become accustomed to the practice of not eating kosher food, owning to the fact that when they first came to Australia there was no *shochet*.[55]

Saphir's remark provides insight into why such laws were no longer followed, citing the initial lack of Jewish institutions and religious knowledge. However, later evidence suggests that Jewish people continued to deviate from such laws later in the century when issues of access were largely resolved.

Some Jewish settlers appear to have deviated from or altered their kosher consumption as they increasingly identified with mainstream colonial society. An article published in the *Jewish Herald* in 1880 comments on this negotiation, noting:

> We are commanded to partake of none but Kosher food; we know the advantage derived from the observance of those laws ... How few of our most influential men have the moral courage to say, when sitting down at a public banquet to which they have been invited, 'I am quite sensible of the honour conferred upon me, but, professing Judaism, I cannot partake of viands that are not prepared in accordance with the laws of my religion.'[56]

Rising middle- or upper-class Jewish people likely felt some pressure to conform, particularly in such public scenarios where 'professing Judaism' would have marked them as different, whether or not they felt 'other'.

55 Joseph Aron and Judy Arndt, *The Enduring Remnant: The First 150 Years Of The Melbourne Hebrew Congregation, 1841-1991* (Melbourne University Press, 1992), 311.

56 'Is Judaism on the Wane?' *Jewish Herald*, November 19, 1880, p. 6, nla.gov.au/nla.news-article149435000.

The choices made regarding *kashrut* were at times also based upon the shifting ideas of the Jewish community, who increasingly identified as part of 'progressive' colonial society and ascribed to many of the reforming attitudes then apparent in much of the Western Jewish world. A newspaper article from 1884 further reveals this influence when it noted that 'the prohibition of eating meat with butter, and other Mosaic dietary laws, are looked upon as relics of an age of barbarism.'[57] Dietary laws in colonial Victoria could appear as out-of-date and non-reflective of their changing world and, as such, requiring reform.

This connection may have been influenced by the idea that British civilisation could both preserve ancient rites and reform its political institutions.[58] Jewish settlers in colonial Australia might have drawn upon similar ideas, believing that they could conserve Judaism through reform. Choices regarding kosher consumption were complex and layered, defined in part by access but also by changing views of Judaism, by acceptance into colonial society, and an idea that Judaism required reform. Similar choices also impacted worship in the local synagogue.

Singing hymns and playing organs: Decorum in the synagogue

On the Central Victorian Goldfields and other colonial synagogues, Hebrew congregations recast experiences of public worship by introducing new items and performance practices into the synagogue space. These shifts were entangled with wider social and cultural changes in contemporary colonial conceptions of class and behaviour, drawing upon middle-class notions of decorum and Jewish ideas of reform. In 1881, a letter to the editor of the *Jewish Herald*, a Melbourne-based Jewish newspaper, urged colonial Hebrew congregations to abandon traditional customs in favour of British practices in the synagogue. The author, who signed their name simply as 'N. B.', expressed concern regarding the 'babble and noise' of public worship and its effect on non-Jewish visitors.[59] Dismayed by the restless movement and sounds of synagogue worship, 'N. B.' hoped that

57 'Local and General Items,' *Jewish Herald*, October 3, 1884, p. 9, nla.gov.au/nla.news-article149549090.

58 Keith Robbins, *Great Britain: Identities, Institutions and the Idea of Britishness* (Longman, 1998), 236.

59 'To the Editor of the "Jewish Herald,"' *Jewish Herald*, October 7, 1881, p. 5, nla.gov.au/nla.news-article149433969.

colonial Hebrew congregations would create a more 'dignified form of worship', through the observance of British customs.[60] Such reform became increasingly important for Hebrew congregations, both in the colonies and overseas.[61]

The earliest move towards reform in British and European Jewish communities can be traced to the mid-eighteenth century, yet widespread changes were not enacted until the nineteenth century, as Hebrew congregations shortened liturgy and altered the chanting style of the *chazan*.[62] Reforming ideas were brought to the Australian colonies, where the distance from established Jewish institutions and limited resources allowed for changes in worship. Cultural shifts in colonial synagogues were further aided by the middle-class identifications of these communities and a desire to present such ideals to wider circles.

As Jewish people settled on the goldfields and became an integrated part of local society, many maintained a middle-class position and identity. This social location sometimes raised concerns within the Jewish community about settler views on Judaism. While synagogue services varied according to religious holidays, the day of the week and even by the season, public prayer in Judaism was individualistic and loudly participatory, as adherents were encouraged to seek their own rhythmic pattern of movement and prayer.[63] Religious services in Judaism also included a *chazan* or cantor (one of the many roles occupied by Jewish ministers in colonial Victoria). Reading of the Torah, the pivotal event of public worship, demanded extensive congregational involvement.[64] Some Christians perceived the simultaneous prayer chants during synagogue services as chaotic and noisy.[65] Jewish colonialists were evidently aware of such perceptions.

60 Ibid.

61 The lower case 'reform' refers to changes made according to ideas of improvement, and not the uppercase Reform, which concerns a branch of Judaism formed at the mid-nineteenth century in Germany. Sue Silberberg also discussed the changes that occurred in ritual and worship in Melbourne's synagogues in the nineteenth century, Silberberg, *A Networked Community: Jewish Melbourne in the Nineteenth Century* (Melbourne University Publishing, 2020), 47.

62 Todd Endelman, *The Jews of Britain, 1656 to 2000* (University of California Press, 2002), 111. A *chazzan*, also known as a Reader, leads the synagogue congregation in prayer through melodic chanting.

63 Karla Goldman, *Beyond the Synagogue: Finding a Place for Women in American Judaism* (Harvard University Press, 2009), 4–5.

64 Ibid., 4–5.

65 Todd Endelman, *Broadening Jewish History: Towards a Social History of Ordinary Jews* (The Littman Library of Jewish Civilization, 2011), 74.

Across Victoria, Jewish adherents expressed anxiety about the viewpoint of 'stranger[s] of our own faith' or 'ministers of another religion' who witnessed synagogue worship and argued for change in service practices.[66] Such views indicate the desire to convey an image of conformity via solemn, reverent and genteel worship to others rather than improve worship for the benefit of the congregation. This does not imply that changes in synagogue practice were only about appearances. Shifts in synagogue worship in the Victorian colony were also deeply entangled with ideas of reforming Judaism to reflect the modern subjecthood of Jewish colonists and ensure its survival in a colonial setting, where the boundaries defining Jewish identity were increasingly blurred.[67] Changes to synagogue services were influenced by a range of factors, including desires to propagate and maintain social cohesion across middle-class colonial society. Middle-class Jewish colonists shaped synagogue services by drawing upon values such as decorum that were shared across religious divides.

Decorum in this context relates to personal conduct during public worship, though usage and connotations varied slightly within the Jewish community and outside in wider settler society. Decorum, as a British ideal, was particularly important to Protestants and signified body governance, cleanliness, modesty and moral discipline.[68] Decorum reflected middle-class views, disapproving of aristocratic excesses and the unsophisticated habits of the working class.[69] Among the colonial Jewish community in Victoria, Jewish people connected decorum with synagogue worship and used the term to incorporate ideas of good behaviour that required certain degrees of orderliness, propriety and reverence.[70] This conception included being quiet or at least limiting noise that might disturb the prayer of others.[71] Local correspondents often characterised goldfields synagogue services with terms like decorum, indecorum and solemnity. These descriptors were not

66 'Synagogue and Decorum,' *Jewish Herald*, November 12, 1897, p. 12, nla.gov.au/nla.news-article 147278127; 'Synagogue Decorum,' *Jewish Herald*, July 30, 1880, p. 3, nla.gov.au/nla.news-article14943 5152.

67 Offer, *The Formation of Goldfields Anglo-Jewry*, 131.

68 Leonore Davidoff and Catherine Hall, *Family Fortunes: Men and Women of the English Middle Class, 1780–1850* (The University of Chicago Press, 1987), 90, 91, 421.

69 Davidoff and Hall, *Family Fortunes*, 21, 91.

70 'Synagogue and Decorum,' p. 12, 'Synagogue Decorum,' p. 3, and 'Decorum in our Synagogues,' p.5, *Jewish Herald*, October 7, 1881; 'Divine Service,' *Jewish Herald*, 8 August 1884, p. 8–9, nla.gov.au/ nla.news-article149434680.

71 'Decorum in our Synagogues,' p. 5.

only used by the congregations themselves but also served to contextualise and define synagogue conduct.[72] Achieving this ideal of decorous worship, however, also required the introduction of new objects and practices.

The most notable change in synagogue worship was the introduction of choirs and organs across the second half of the nineteenth century. This change that was likely influenced by recent shifts in England and Europe both within and outside the Jewish community. In England, the Methodist revival contributed to the popularity of choral music, significantly influencing the tradition of singing in both urban and rural areas of Britain.[73] This tradition, which varied according to denomination, was carried to the colonies.[74] Organ music and choirs first entered synagogue worship in the early nineteenth century in Europe and Britain, though this is not to suggest that this was the beginning of communal singing in the synagogue.[75] Group chanting, in which the entire (male) congregation participates, has always been central to synagogue services, though individual prayer was highly regarded. Choirs and organs, however, emerged as a more distinct phenomenon in Hebrew congregations in the mid-nineteenth century, just as Reform Judaism advocated for such shifts. Colonial Jewish people across Victoria supported the introduction of choirs and organs to services. When the Hebrew congregations in Ballarat and Bendigo opened a new synagogue, choirs and organ music were often included as a highlight of the event.[76]

Choirs and organs were increasingly regarded as central to synagogue worship and promoted the decorum and good behaviour desired by many adherents. In a letter to the editor of the *Australian Israelite* in 1871, the writer argued that a choir was 'absolutely necessary', explaining that

72 See 'Jewish Wedding,' *Bendigo Advertiser*, December 2, 1899, p. 4, nla.gov.au/nla.news-article 89471816; 'The Bendigo Advertiser,' *Bendigo Advertiser*, October 4, 1881, p. 2, nla.gov.au/nla.news-page9127919; 'The Bendigo Advertiser,' *Bendigo Advertiser*, October 2, 1894, p. 2, nla.gov.au/nla.news-article89005120; 'Ballarat Courier,' *Ballarat Courier*, November 29, 1870, p. 2, nla.gov.au/nla.news-page 21557042; 'Ballarat,' *Jewish Herald*, September 22, 1882, p. 4, nla.gov.au/nla.news-article149435315; 'The Synagogues,' *Jewish Herald*, September 24, 1880, p. 2, nla.gov.au/nla.news-article149434296.

73 Derek B. Scott, 'Music and Social Class in Victorian London,' *Urban History* 29, no.1 (2002): 68, doi.org/10.1017/S0963926802001062; Helen J. English, *Music and World-Building in the Colonial City: Newcastle, NSW, and its Townships, 1860–1880* (Routledge, 2021).

74 Andre de Quadros, *Focus: Choral Music in Global Perspective* (Routledge, 2019), 15; David Martin, 'Music and the Aesthetic in Worship and Collective Singing: England since 1840,' *Society* 53, no. 6 (2016): 652, doi.org/10.1007/s12115-016-0078-5.

75 Joseph A. Levine, 'Judaism and Music,' in *Sacred Sound: Experiencing Music in World Religions*, ed. Guy L. Beck (Wilfrid Laurier University Press, 2006), 45.

76 See 'Consecration of the Ballarat Synagogue,' *Jewish Herald*, September 23, 1881, p. 6, nla.gov.au/nla.news-article149434529. 'Sandhurst—Consecration of the New Synagogue,' *Australian Israelite*, October 4, 1872, p. 3, nla.gov.au/nla.news-article261974927.

'the intent of a choir [was] to add *solemnity* to the service' (their emphasis).[77] Choir and organ music discouraged individual chanting, hence ordering worship and creating a unified service. Such accompaniments also added a special feeling to synagogue services, potentially elevating the atmosphere of reverent solemnity. When the Bendigo Hebrew congregation celebrated the consecration of their new synagogue in 1872, the ceremony did not include a choir, as noted by the *Australian Israelite*. The writer, a local Jewish observer, believed that the proceedings 'therefore, lacked the spirit which would have been engendered had there been the sweet singing which generally accompanies such ceremonies'.[78] While this term 'the spirit' could hold various meanings, including communal togetherness, it does suggest that choirs were important to religious ceremonies. Incorporating musical instruments and choirs into synagogue services shifted understandings of worship and with it, the sounds, sights and emotions of public services. The goldfields Jewish community used choirs and organs to connect with broader social values, subtly fostering social cohesion. The next century, however, brought significant challenges to the goldfields Jewish communities.

Decline and loss beyond 1900

From 1900, the Jewish population on the goldfields rapidly reduced, as out-migration that had begun in the 1870s continued. Public services were held regularly at the Bendigo synagogue until about the 1920s, when a *minyan*, the ten men above the age of thirteen required for public services, could no longer be gathered. In 1925, representatives of the Bendigo Hebrew congregation applied to the Governor of Victoria to dispose of the land and the long unused and decaying synagogue.[79] Once approved, the land and synagogue were sold and the funds held in trust for destitute Jewish people until 1950, when it was donated to the Montefiore homes, a residential aged care service in Melbourne. Over in Ballarat, the Jewish congregation maintained some strength in numbers during the early twentieth century but suffered from communal infighting, leading to a temporary split in

77 'The Choir,' *Australian Israelite*, October 6, 1871, p. 3, nla.gov.au/nla.news-article261974162.

78 'Sandhurst—Consecration of the New Synagogue,' p. 3.

79 Act 201 First Schedule, Bendigo Regional Archives Centre, Bendigo, 1925.

1908. The Ballarat Hebrew congregation reunited by 1914, maintaining regular public worship but diminished numbers.[80] The coming decades would, however, sorely test the Ballarat Hebrew congregation.

In the 1930s and 1940s, economic collapse, war and increased migration significantly affected Australian Jewry. During these decades, Jewish migration to Australia increased as Jewish people sought to escape the Holocaust or leave Europe in its devastating aftermath.[81] Many perceived the incoming Jewish people as racially distinct and unable to assimilate or acculturate.[82] Anglo-Jews who had already assimilated were considered as white, yet Eastern European Jewish migrants were deemed to be non-white. Immigration forms included questions designed to identify and prevent the migration of converted Jews.[83] While the impact on the daily life of Anglo-Jews in Australia may have been negligible, these racialised discourses were troubling for many. The pre- and post-war migrants who arrived from Europe diversified the Australian Jewish community and stimulated Jewish consciousness and religious practice, as Orthodox forms of Judaism began to predominate.[84]

The Ballarat Jewish community gradually decreased over the mid-twentieth century, as Jewish people relocated or enlisted in the Second World War, though the American soldiers posted in Ballarat briefly boosted synagogue attendance.[85] In 1946, the Ballarat Hebrew congregation numbered only thirty paying members, with an average of ten meeting on Friday nights.[86] No Hebrew school was maintained, nor any services conducted.[87] Most incoming Jewish migrants settled in metropolitan centres or its outer suburbs rather than smaller regional cities. Attendance at weekly synagogue services decreased further in the 1950s.[88] The Ballarat synagogue survived thanks

80 See 'Ballarat,' *Jewish Herald*, April 24, 1914, p. 4, nla.gov.au/nla.news-article150067963; 'Central Hebrew Synagogue,' *Ballarat Star*, October 4, 1909, p. 6, nla.gov.au/nla.news-article218793514.

81 Andrew Markus, 'Jewish Migration to Australia 1938–49,' *Journal of Australian Studies* 7, no.13 (1983): 18–19, doi.org/10.1080/14443058309386871.

82 Jon Stratton, 'The Colour of Jews: Jews, Race and the White Australia Policy,' *Journal of Australian Studies* 20, no. 50–51 (1996): 55, doi.org/10.1080/14443059609387278.

83 Ibid., 56, 78.

84 Suzanne D. Rutland, 'Debates and Conflicts: Australian Jewry, the Claims Conference and Restitution, 1945–1965,' *Dapim: Studies on the Holocaust* 28, no. 3 (2014): 156, doi.org/10.1080/23256249.2014.944023.

85 *Ballarat Hebrew Congregation Committee Report 1942*, (Ballarat Hebrew Congregation Committee, 74Vv6d8JX2xZ, 1942), State Library of New South Wales.

86 Questionnaire Ballarat Hebrew Congregation, AB175, Australian Jewish Historical Society Archive, Sydney.

87 Ibid.

88 Ibid.

to the untiring efforts of a small committee of dedicated members, such as Nathan Spielvogel and Marcus Stone, who oversaw the synagogue grounds and conducted worship. Through their efforts, the Ballarat synagogue endured, becoming the oldest synagogue on the Australian mainland.

Today, the Jewish communities on the Central Victorian Goldfields celebrate their enduring connection to the early goldfields, their place and their history.[89] The early struggles and strengths of Bendigo and Ballarat's Jewish communities are worthy of celebration. The social, religious and cultural negotiations that Jewish settlers undertook were complex, influenced by a longer history of change overseas and an emerging identity based upon strong ties to both Judaism and Greater Britain. On those fields of gold, Jewish people found a way to be Jewish, British and middle-class, adjusting their values and faith practices to become significant and integrated members of society.

89 At the time of writing this chapter, another Hebrew congregation has formed in Bendigo, *kehillat s'dot zahav* (The Congregation of the Fields of Gold), which is a progressive community that welcomes interfaith connections. The Hebrew congregation and synagogue in Ballarat continues to hold services with members from Melbourne or nearby and gather monthly for worship and High Holidays.

Popout Two: Spatial organisation and hierarchies of prejudice in Central Victorian goldrush cemeteries

The White Hills Cemetery is situated on a gentle slope that descends to a strip of flat ground where the Bendigo and Long Gully Creeks meet. Once known as the Junction Cemetery, the first burials took place at the top of the rise in 1853. This site, non-consecrated ground that was not aligned with religious organisations, illustrates how an early goldrush burial ground evolved into a municipal cemetery with strict denominational boundaries. Heritage historian Celeste Sagazio characterises cemeteries as valuable sources of evidence that reveal societal shifts in cultural attitudes and religious influence.[1] Migrants from various faith traditions in the mid-nineteenth century Victorian goldfields practiced burial customs as part of their ritual observances. During the 1850s, most newcomers arriving in Port Phillip were Christians from the British Isles who likely encountered unfamiliar cultures, ethnicities and faiths at the goldfields for the first time.[2] European and British Jews were also attracted by goldrush potential, as were some Chinese Buddhists, 'Afghan' Muslims and Sikhs.[3] This population boom created an equal need to accommodate the living and the dead. In this context, frontier

1 Celestina Sagazio, 'Cemeteries: Their significance and conservation,' *Historic Environment* 12, no. 2a (1996), 14.

2 Charles Fahey, 'Peopling the Victorian Goldfields: From Boom to Bust, 1851–1901,' *Australian Economic History Review* 50, no. 2 (2010), 149, doi.org/10.1111/j.1467-8446.2010.00298.x; Weston Bate, *Victorian Gold Rushes: Themes in Economic and Social History* (McPhee Gribble, 1988), 27.

3 Hilary Carey, 'An Historical Outline of Religion in Australia,' in *The Encyclopedia of Religion in Australia*, ed. James Jupp (Cambridge University Press, 2009), 315.

pragmatism overshadowed the burial reforms then occurring elsewhere in the colony and in Britain and Europe.[4] As the frontier society stabilised, however, early unsegregated burial grounds evolved into formally divided cemeteries that mirrored the theological divisions and social hierarchies of the community they served. The spatial configuration of the cemetery landscape functioned as a mechanism for socially excluding marginalised communities whose burial customs differed from the prevailing cultural practices. The location, development and diverse burial traditions of White Hills Cemetery serve as a microcosm of Bendigo's broader civic development and gradual entrenchment of prevailing prejudices, as illustrated below.

Figure P.1: View from the upper section of White Hills Cemetery looking south east, downslope toward the Chinese and Jewish sections on the creek flat

Source: Photographed by Natasha Joyce

4 Patricia Jalland, *Australian Ways of Death: A Social and Cultural History 1840–1918* (Oxford University Press, 2002), 304.

From chaos to order

Life on the early goldfields unfolded at a frantic pace, and necessity influenced burial management above preference or prejudice. Camps were densely populated, and newspapers reported the practice of 'burial among the tents' before official cemetery land was designated.[5] Bendigo's first recorded interment occurred in 1853 at the Old Sandhurst Burial Ground atop Camp Hill, where government officials established a presence to manage the new settlement. The original burial ground operated for less than a year before new legislation mandated that cemeteries be removed from the population.[6] The high demand for prime real estate in the rapidly expanding town led to the old site being filled in and developed, then largely forgotten. The nearby White Hills Cemetery, however, established in similarly hasty circumstances, underwent expansion despite significant natural challenges.

In 1852, government officials tasked with managing the Central Victorian Goldfields established their primary camp at White Hills, choosing a piece of flat ground where the Bendigo Creek, already fed by four minor waterways, converged with two additional tributaries. The site came to be known as Junction Camp, and the subsequent ad hoc burial ground, the Junction Cemetery. In heavy downpours, the gullies and creeks feeding the central Bendigo Creek quickly fill, and their junction is prone to flash flooding.[7] This tendency to flood was a well-recognised challenge for those living on the goldfields, and mishaps drew regular attention from across the colonies. In October 1852, Tasmanian newspaper the *Cornwall Chronicle* reported 'a very heavy flood of rain covering all the flats around Bendigo Creek'.[8] Official efforts to address the issue were also noted, with the *Adelaide Observer* highlighting government construction of 'a substantial timber bridge, sufficiently arched to render it safe from trees and other bodies carried down by occasional floods'.[9] In February 1856, 'the whole of the

5 'The Diggings,' *Mount Alexander Mail*, August 3, 1855, p. 2, nla.gov.au/nla.news-article202635869.

6 Rita Hull and John Kelly, *Bendigo's Bridge Street Burial Ground* (John Kelly, 2010), 6.

7 The Bendigo Creek rises near Crusoe Reservoir at Kangaroo Flat and is fed by fourteen tributaries. The Tipperary Gully, Golden Gully, Spring Gully and Back Creeks flow into the central Bendigo Creek before it reaches White Hills, where it meets with the Long Gully and Ironbark Gully creeks. Chris Beardshaw, Julian Skipworth and Ky Tran, *Bendigo Urban Flood Study* (North Central Catchment Management Authority and City of Greater Bendigo, 2013).

8 'A Few Words from the Diggings at Bendigo Creek.' *Cornwall Chronicle*, October 16, 1852, p. 672–3, nla.gov.au/nla.news-article65580388.

9 'Latest News from the Victoria Diggings,' *Adelaide Observer*, September 4, 1852, p. 5, nla.gov.au/nla.news-article160110548.

flat in the vicinity of the Junction Camp was under water', and again in May 1858, flooding 'very nearly destroyed' the bridge going to the cemetery and washing away the Sexton's home.[10] These accounts underscore the widespread awareness of the Creek's flood risks. At Marong, near Bendigo, accounts mention a junior government surveyor who did not follow his senior's advice: to avoid the flood-prone Bullock Creek when selecting the cemetery site.[11] The account is corroborated by modifications on an 1855 survey map for Marong, which indicates that the original site next to the creek has been crossed out and relocated 200 metres above sea level, one kilometre away.[12] Thus, authorities were not only aware of the creek's susceptibility to flooding, they were also inclined to avoid flood-prone areas when they could.

Burial reforms

At the turn of the eighteenth century, the population shifts associated with the Industrial Revolution caused an overcrowding crisis in British and European burial grounds, mostly located in churchyards.[13] Public health concerns about the proximity of bodies to waterways were among the factors that influenced burial reforms. These improvements included the creation of intentionally arranged cemeteries removed from population centres.[14] Philosophies of the Enlightenment and Romantic movements influenced functionally aesthetic layouts that aimed to balance appreciation of nature with faith and offer spiritually enriching sanctuaries for Christian contemplation.[15] The British reforms significantly shaped burial arrangements in Australia, as the rapid expansion of Melbourne and Sydney created similar congestion issues.[16] By the 1840s, burials were

10 'The Storm and the Flood,' *Bendigo Advertiser*, February 9, 1856, p. 2, nla.gov.au/nla.news-article 88048812; 'The Late Flood,' *Bendigo Advertiser*, April 30, 1858, p. 2, nla.gov.au/nla.news-article8798 0120; Fiona Stanton, *White Hills Cemetery Bendigo: A Reflection* (Bendigo Historical Society Inc, 2018), 4.

11 Ken James, 'The Surveying Career of William Swan Urquhart, 1845-1864,' *Provenance*, no. 8 (2009).

12 Richard Larritt, surveyor, *CEM203: Marong Cemetery Res; Marong*, Historic Plan Collection (VPRS8168/P0002), Public Record of Victoria. The map is signed by the surveyor for the area, Richard Larritt, and the junior surveyor mentioned may have been Henry Grimes.

13 Sandra F. Hayward, 'Colonial Expressions of Identity in Funerals, Cemeteries, and Funerary Monuments of Nineteenth-Century Perth, Western Australia,' *Genealogy* 2, no. 3 (2018): 2, 23, doi.org/10.3390/genealogy2030023.

14 Lisa Murray, '"Modern Innovations?" Ideal vs. Reality in Colonial Cemeteries of Nineteenth-Century New South Wales,' *Mortality* 8, no. 2 (2003), 136, doi.org/10.1080/1357627031000087389.

15 Celestina Sagazio, *Cemeteries: Our Heritage* (National Trust of Australia [Victoria], 1992), 9–13.

16 Jalland, Australian Ways of Death, 306.

moved out of churchyards into separately allocated denominational plots positioned side by side within cemetery precincts, which evolved into single cemeteries containing religious demarcations.[17] The boundaries were not, however, solely determined by differences within Christianity.

Cemetery divisions extended beyond Christian denominations and included race, ethnicity, class, age and cause of death. Garden historian Susan K. Martin notes that 'their divisions mirrored the living social distribution, and even arrangement, of denominations and classes'.[18] Christian graves were separated from Jewish ones. Aboriginal and Chinese burials were racially combined without regard for faith or ethnicity.[19] Hindu and Muslim individuals were often interred in Chinese sections, erasing their faiths.[20] Paupers, 'lunatics' and infant deaths shared space with criminals, disregarding individual belief systems.[21] Funerary historian Julie Rugg contends that while denominational divisions within cemeteries may reflect societal division, the presence of exclusive sections designated for minority groups indicates 'that cemeteries, for the most part, accommodate all'.[22] However, while cemeteries accommodate (almost) all the dead, they do not do so equally.

The original cemetery at White Hills was located on a slight elevation above the creek flats, where burials occurred without consideration for religious or racial differences. The natural rise can still be observed today. The slope of the land can be seen in Figure P.1, where the photograph has been taken from the highest point of the cemetery, looking down toward the Chinese and Jewish sections on the creek flat. Local authorities in rural northern England sometimes installed new cemeteries adjacent to pre-existing burial.[23] Likewise, the original Junction burial ground was extended

17 Murray, '"Modern Innovations,"' 130.

18 Susan K. Martin, 'Monuments in the Garden: The Garden Cemetery in Australia,' *Postcolonial Studies* 7, no. 3 (2004): 336, doi.org/10.1080/1368879042000311115.

19 Don Chambers, *The Melbourne General Cemetery* (Hyland House, 2003), 18.

20 Chambers, *The Melbourne General Cemetery*, 18.

21 Infantile death refers to pregnancy losses, stillbirths and babies who die soon after birth. Chiara Garattini, 'Creating Memories: Material Culture and Infantile Death in contemporary Ireland,' *Mortality* 12, no. 2 (2007), 193–206, doi.org/10.1080/13576270701255172. For further discussion of Australian burial sites and practices, see Kenneth Stanley Inglis and Jan Brazier, *Sacred Places: War Memorials In The Australian Landscape* (The Miegunyah Press, 2008); Robert Nicol, *At The End Of The Road: Government, Society, And The Disposal Of Human Remains In The Nineteenth And Twentieth Centuries* (Allen & Unwin, 1994).

22 Julie Rugg, 'Defining the Place of Burial: What Makes a Cemetery a Cemetery?' *Mortality* 5, no. 3 (2000): 263, doi.org/10.1080/713686011.

23 Julie Rugg, Fiona Stirling, and Andy Clayden, 'Churchyard and Cemetery in an English Industrial City: Sheffield, 1740–1900,' *Urban History* 41, no. 4 (2014), doi.org/10.1017/S0963926814000285.

to become the official municipal cemetery; land was allocated for future expansion, and formal denominational divisions were mapped out. The higher ground of the rise was designated for Church of England and Roman Catholic burials. The Chinese section of the cemetery was adjacent to the creek.[24] The biographer of the cemetery's first Sexton, Fiona Stanton, noted that Chinese sections were often positioned to the rear of a cemetery or in the least desirable locations.[25] At White Hills, the natural topography of the cemetery landscape supported the imposition of social hierarchies based on race, ethnicity and class.

Several colonial cemeteries in Victoria have extensive Chinese sections, some marked with gravestones, while others remain unmarked.[26] The first known Chinese burial at the White Hills site was recorded in 1854; however, the nearby Ironbark and Emu Point settlements of Chinese nationals suggest there were likely many earlier burials that went unrecorded.[27] Traditional practices typically required that the remains of Chinese nationals be returned to their home village in fulfilment of their ancestral faith systems.[28] For numerous Chinese goldfields sojourners, such obligations were challenged by the vast distances involved.[29] Posthumous repatriation of exhumed remains was sometimes possible, but immigrants were more likely to be laid to rest in the places where they died.[30] Interment at the base of the rise at White Hills presented additional challenges. Graves were subject to flooding, which elevated the risk of damage, dislodgment and the destruction of remains. As at Marong, officials were aware of the risks associated with the proximity of graves to watercourses and the regularity of flooding of the Bendigo Creek at the Junction site.

24 *CEM365: White Hills Cem; Sandhurst*, Historic Plan Collection (VPRS8168/P0002), Public Record of Victoria, proposed further extension.

25 Stanton, *White Hills Cemetery*, 4.

26 Susan Lawrence and Peter Davies, *An Archaeology of Australia Since 1788*, (Springer, 2011), 344–6.

27 Bendigo Chinese Association Museum Inc., *Chinese Memorials & Memories: The White Hills Cemetery - Bendigo* (Golden Dragon Museum, 2001). Further reading: Valerie Lovejoy, 'Reading Remains: Recovering Chinese Lives in Nineteenth Century Bendigo,' *Historic Environment* 23, no. 3 (2011).

28 Valerie Lovejoy, 'The Things that Unite: Inquests into Chinese Deaths in The Bendigo Goldfields 1854-65,' *Provenance*, no. 6 (2007).

29 Although the term sojourner is applied in this instance, as highlighted by Keir Reeves and Benjamin Montford, the Chinese were not the only 'temporary' immigrants to Victoria, and those who remained formed significant communities. Keir Reeves and Benjamin Mountford, 'Sojourning and Settling: Locating Chinese Australian History,' *Australian Historical Studies* 42, no. 1 (2011): 111–25, doi.org/10.1080/1031461X.2010.539620; Lawrence and Davies, *An Archaeology*.

30 'White Hills Burial Register 1858–1880 records 31 exhumations in 335 burials between 1858 and 1880', in Lovejoy, 'The Things that Unite', note 98.

Conclusion

Colonial authorities tasked with reforming early gold rush cemeteries adapted British burial practices to local contexts. In the process, they incorporated the landscape's natural topography to establish spatial hierarchies that were influenced by prejudice. As a result, goldfield burial grounds evolved from unregulated and intermingled settings into controlled spaces shaped by both practical and ideological considerations. This transformation had significant implications for the burial of Chinese nationals. Initially, they were interred as part of a burgeoning community in unsegregated burial grounds. However, the topography allowed the placement of dominant Christian sections at an elevated distance from socially marginalised groups. Chinese graves were literally and physically marginalised, and were vulnerable to physical damage and destruction. As well as serving the entire community, Rugg lists a further fundamental purpose of cemeteries: the memorialisation of the individual identity of the deceased.[31] Repeated flooding at White Hills Cemetery denied this commemoration to the many Chinese nationals buried in this section.

31 Rugg, 'Defining the Place of Burial,' 261.

5

Divine intention and family misfortune on the Central Victorian Goldfields: How 'Providence orders all things well'

> 'Providence orders all things well and to Him I decide to commit the sacred care of us all'.[1]
>
> Jane Brown Hamilton

On Christmas Day in 1864, Jane Brown Hamilton wrote from the Bendigo goldfields to her family in Scotland, voicing anxiety for her five-month-old baby, Jessie. She had been wheezing and coughing for ten days and was 'such a sweet little thing', Jane wrote, that 'I would like ill to lose her'. Jane's concern about Jessie's condition increased after the sudden death of an infant next door, and she was therefore 'prompt to do all for her that I can'. In the context of the family correspondence, doing 'all for her' implied that (contrary to family expectations) Jane continued to breastfeed on demand.[2] This was an adaptive action that Jane defended six months later, when

1 Jane Hamilton to Mother, Sister and Brother, 24 August 1862, Letter 390, Papers of the Brown Family, Acc12100, National Library of Scotland (hereafter NLS). This substantial collection of original letters was accessioned in 2014. The collection was first made available on microfilm under the Joint Copying Project (JCP) at the National Library of Australia (hereafter NLA) in 1978. The JCP copies are now available online. Both the original letters from the NLS and the JCP microfilm and online copies have been consulted for this chapter. All transcription is by the author.

2 Jane Hamilton to Mother, 25 December 1864, Letter 467, Papers of the Brown Family, Acc12100, NLS.

environmental conditions on the goldfields had worsened and 'darling Jessie' was still 'very fragile'.[3] Local newspapers then heralded the onset of drought; 'sickness prevailed to a large extent' due to 'an impure and short allowance of water', and some gold crushing operations were suspended.[4] Frontier conditions affected both business and personal life in ways little understood by distant families, effectively depriving Jane of needed comfort and support.

Jane Hamilton's Scottish family continued to offer breastfeeding advice that reflected their temporal and geographical distance. Sister-in-law Kate Brown, who was (involuntarily) childless but settled comfortably in urban Scotland, suggested in January 1866 that it was irresponsible of Jane 'to continue nursing your little girl so long'. Prolonged breastfeeding, according to Kate, was 'hurtful to both you and her', and she was 'absolutely sure that if you weaned her you would find the child would grow stronger'.[5] Although maternal breastfeeding was then widely practised by the British middle classes and sentimentalised as a womanly domestic duty, public discourses warned that 'excessive suckling' weakened the mother and risked her health.[6] In late February 1866, at the height of Bendigo's summer, Jane contextualised her choice to persist with breastfeeding. Writing to her mother, she noted that although the weather 'keeps as trying as ever', she felt much stronger, despite still having 'the pull upon me of nursing Jessie':

> You will blame me for this but I could not do otherwise. Humanly speaking I believe she couldn't have got through this fearfully trying season without her cup of comfort – many a day she would look for nothing else. However I shall wean her as soon as winter sets in if she is no worse.[7]

Jane explained that breastmilk alternatives were scarce due to lack of fodder, 'country dairy people are giving up milking' and 'there's much distress about here and great death of infants'. A baby in their family circle then

3 Jane Hamilton, Bendigo to Mother, Brother and Kate, 24 June 1865, Letter 443, Papers of the Brown Family, Acc12100, NLS.

4 'The Drought.' *Bendigo Advertiser*, December 6, 1865, p. 2, nla.gov.au/nla.news-article87928600.

5 Kate Brown to Jane Hamilton, 25 January 1866, Letter 68, MS 862-3, Brown Family Papers, Australian Joint Copying Project, NLA.

6 Tamara S. Wagner, '"Nature's Founts": Breastmilk in Victorian Popular Culture,' *Victorian Review* 45, no. 1 (2019), 18–22, doi.org/10.1353/vcr.2019.0026; Jessica Cox, 'The "Most Sacred of Duties": Maternal Ideals and Discourses of Authority in Victorian Breastfeeding Advice,' *Journal of Victorian Culture* 25, no. 2 (2020): 230, doi.org/10.1093/jvcult/vcz065.

7 Jane Hamilton to Mother, 23 February 1866, Letter 478, Papers of the Brown Family, Acc12100, NLS.

died of whooping cough, and the *Bendigo Advertiser* reported that although 121 children were born in the town of Sandhurst (as Bendigo was then known) in December 1865, 59 children under the age of five had also died in the same month. While this 'recently excessive rate of mortality' was attributed to the long drought, the editor declared that not even the desiccating power of the goldfields atmosphere could 'nullify the impurities', which were:

> ever seething in our undrained and untended town … Let anyone walk through the town … and he will go to his bed thankful to that Providence which has so long preserved this place from widely devastating disease.[8]

In the absence of civic improvements, Divine Providence or God's preordained plan seemed the only protection available to Bendigo residents. Reference to Providential regulation of the world, including health and illness, was then common in public and private discourse. Although gold mining depended on luck, which conflicted with Calvinist opposition to gambling, dissenting congregations thrived on the goldfields. Pews were filled with miners determined to gain their independence by discovering valuable deposits near the surface.

Jane Hamilton had expressed belief in God's preordained plan during trying times in 1864, when she declared that 'Providence orders all things well and to Him I decide to commit the sacred care of us all.'[9] But to what extent did such belief shape the way Australian colonists and their families planned their lives and negotiated daily events? Examining how a family maintained religious solidarity while negotiating their individual experience (as well as differing needs and perspectives) answers scholarly calls for more nuanced historical interpretation of the intersections between religion and agency in daily life.[10] Because members of the Brown family were resident in both industrialised Glasgow and the upturned mining-scape of Bendigo, their embodied processes of family making give insight into the workings of both local and international networks. The Brown family letters also reveal how

8 Bendigo's Big Hill reservoir ran dry in 1865, and water was carted 42 kilometres from Elmore (then known as Runnymede) on the Campaspe. Frank Cusack, *Bendigo: A History* (Heinemann, 1973), 135; 'Sanitary Reform,' *Bendigo Advertiser*, January 18, 1866, p. 2, nla.gov.au/nla.news-article87957800.

9 Jane Hamilton to Mother, Sister and Brother, 24 August 1862, Letter 390, Acc12100, NLS.

10 Andrew Blaikie, 'Rituals, Transitions and Life Courses in an Era of Social Transformation,' in *A History of Everyday Life in Scotland, 1800 to 1900*, ed. Graeme Morton and Trevor Griffiths (Edinburgh University Press, 2010), 92.

material living conditions and opportunities for children were impacted by the perceived operations of Providence, reflecting tensions and negotiations between spiritual and material domains.

The Brown family correspondence is a substantial collection held in the National Library of Scotland, including letters sent and received by multiple members of the extended family who migrated to the Victorian goldfields from 1852 to 1869.[11] These correspondents are articulate and informed thanks to a religious culture that prioritised literacy and self-improvement. Although dissenting United Presbyterians, the correspondents were educated in the Cumnock Parish school controlled by the established church in Scotland, which had delivered a form of national schooling since 1696 and made Scotland a world leader in population-wide education.[12] The Brown family correspondence exemplifies this influence. Patriarch Robert Brown (1795–1847) was raised on an Ayrshire tenant farm, 'Winpark', owned by the Duke of Portland. He was ordained as a Secession Church minister in 1824.[13] His son James Brown (1835–1890) followed in this vocation and was ordained a United Presbyterian minister in 1859. He gained a doctorate in Divinity in 1878.[14] James Brown's sisters, Jane (1827–1895) and Maggie (1830–1859), both exhibited active interest in their faith and in elevating family prospects through relocation. Maggie's husband James Hoey (1832–1865) began the migration chain to Australia in 1852, two years prior to their marriage. He was accompanied by his brother Tom Hoey and Andrew Hamilton (1816–1870), the widower of their older sister. Andrew Hamilton later married Jane Brown, who left her role as a governess in Germany to nurse her ailing sister Maggie, arriving in Australia just prior to Maggie's death in 1859.

This chapter focuses on one family's interpretation of their colonial circumstance and how their adaptive actions were influenced by a shared Providential world view. As United Presbyterians, a denomination that,

11 A microfilm copy is held by the NLA, made available by the Australian Joint Copying Project in 1978. This research accessed both collections, as indicated.

12 The Act for Settling of Schools established schools in every parish funded by the Church of Scotland and local landowners. Callum Brown, *The Social History of Religion in Scotland since 1730* (Methuen, 1987), 98; Ryan Mallon, 'Scottish Presbyterianism and the National Education Debates, 1850–62,' *Studies in Church History* 55 (2019): 363–380, doi.org/10.1017/stc.2018.5.

13 The Secession Church later amalgamated with other dissenting denominations to become the United Presbyterian church; James Brown, *Sermons: With a Biographical Sketch by His Son* (James Maclehose and Sons, 1892). Winpark was still farmed by a relative in 1855. See *Ayrshire Ordnance Survey Name Books, 1855-1857*, Ayrshire volume 33, OS1/3/33/70, Scotland's People.

14 Brown, *Sermons*, 14.

in broad terms, embraced the Calvinist theology of the Westminster Confession, the Brown family drew upon current social understandings of Providential design while also believing that individual action was directed by free will.[15] This focus deepens understanding of life on the goldfields, taking readers into the little-known female worlds of domestic distress to counter triumphal accounts of goldfields history. The lens of religion offers a nuanced understanding of lived experience on the goldfields and provides powerful insights into the human cost of economic development.

In 1866, Bendigo was a chaotic, filthy and dangerous mining town that still awaited sanitary reform. As noted in Popout Two, necessity shaped infrastructure development more than design or management best practices. By this time, the ubiquitous canvas tent of the initial rushes had been replaced by slab and bark huts, and as Katrina Dernelley suggests, domestic comfort had improved.[16] But when inveterate traveller Anthony Trollope visited Bendigo in 1872, there was still ample evidence of frontier improvisation in terms of civic amenity. While Trollope predicted 'a handsome city, with fine streets, imposing banks, public gardens and well-built public edifices', during his stay, the town appeared 'repulsive. Everything was crowded, unfinished and uncomfortable.'[17] It was as if the town had been 'scratched up violently out of the body of the earth by some infernal deity, who had left everything behind him dirty, uncouth, barren and disorderly!'[18]

Exposure to Bendigo's literal and metaphorical 'underworld' was evident in the 'excessive mortality' (as it was understood at the time) suffered by Jane Hamilton's family. These losses included little Jessie, who continued to decline despite extended breastfeeding, and died in August 1866. In the early 1860s, under-five mortality comprised half of all deaths in Australia and were 'always higher … in the summer months, when food- and water-borne infectious diseases took their greatest toll'.[19] Table 5.1 below, 'Antipodean deaths in the Hamilton-Hoey families 1859–1869', collates these family bereavements. It reveals that the extended family suffered the loss of five infants, two young mothers and all three male breadwinners

15 Chad van Dixhoorn, 'The Westminster Standards,' *The Oxford Handbook of Reformed Theology*, ed. Michael Allen and Scott R. Swain (Oxford University Press, 2020).

16 Dernelley refers here to the nearby goldfield town of Castlemaine. Katrina Dernelley, 'Our Land of Adoption: Seeking Home in a Gold Rush Landscape,' *History Australia* 18, no. 3 (2021): 505–506, doi.org/10.1080/14490854.2021.1956340.

17 Anthony Trollope, *Australia and New Zealand*, vol. 1 (Chapman Hall, 1873), 428.

18 Trollope, *Australia and New Zealand*, 418.

19 Michael Willem de Looper, 'Death Registration and Mortality Trends in Australia 1856–1906' (PhD thesis, The Australian National University, 2014), 260, hdl.handle.net/1885/16791.

before the surviving widows and children left Bendigo in 1869. Rudimentary conditions on the Central Victorian Goldfields in this period, including insanitary housing and irregular incomes, were among the factors that increased the risk of maternal and infant mortality:

> there was a dearth of grandmothers to pass on mothering skills; sanitation was primitive; hot summers, flies, and scant and polluted water supplies nourished gastrointestinal diseases; and financial insecurity and unstable personal relationships undermined domestic security.[20]

The prevalence of epidemics and high mortality associated with water-related communicable diseases in Australia was reduced by public health measures, including the provision of clean water and sewerage infrastructure, in the late nineteenth century.[21] Before then, babies born to mothers who were single, deserted or married to men who could not provide were particularly exposed to illness and death. This suggests that infant mortality was a social as well as a medical problem.

The vulnerability of women and children on the goldfields was exacerbated by the debilitation of male breadwinners exposed to mining-related disease, such as miner's phthisis, now known as silicosis. This occupational disease became increasingly common as Bendigo's mines were industrialised from the 1860s, and poor dust control and ineffective ventilation led to increased adult male mortality.[22] Collins and Kippen note that until the early twentieth century, the disease was widely attributed to the predilection of individual miners or to their negligent behaviour.[23] In 1865, Jane Hamilton considered it 'strange how rife this chest disease is in my circle' and noted how her 'cousin' Tom Hoey 'has also been attacked and I fear in a very serious form … although he

20 Janet McCalman et al., 'Colonial Health Transitions: Aboriginal and "Poor White" Infant Mortality Compared, Victoria 1850–1910,' *The History of the Family* 16, no. 1 (2011): 68, doi.org/10.1016/j.hisfam.2010.09.005.

21 Michael Willem de Looper et al., 'Sanitary Improvement and Mortality Decline in Sydney, New South Wales, 1857–1906: Drinking Water and Dunnies as Determinants,' *The History of the Family* 24, no. 2 (2019), 227–248, doi.org/10.1080/1081602X.2018.1550725; Hanbo Wu, 'Mortality Transition in Nineteenth Century Australia: A Further Investigation' (MA thesis, The Australian National University, 2017).

22 Sandra Kippen, 'The Social and Political Meaning of the Silent Epidemic of Miners' Phthisis, Bendigo 1860–1960,' *Social Science & Medicine* 41, no. 4 (1995): 491–9, doi.org/10.1016/0277-9536(94)00374-3; Wu, 'Mortality Transition in Nineteenth Century Australia,' 99.

23 Kippen, 'The Social and Political Meaning of the Silent Epidemic of Miners' Phthisis, Bendigo 1860–1960'; Yolande Collins and Sandra Kippen, '"A Social Disease with Medical Aspects": Miners' Phthisis and the Politics of Occupational Health in Bendigo, 1880s–1910,' *Journal of Australasian Mining History* 6, no. September (2008): 70–89.

is better and thinks lightly of it'.[24] Given that Tom Hoey's mining ventures had failed, and his family had 'less than nothing of the needful', Jane hoped that Providence would 'direct the course and send prosperity'.[25]

Table 5.1: Antipodean deaths in the Hamilton-Hoey families, 1859–1869

Name	Relationship	Year of death	Age	Cause of death	Place of burial
Henry Hoey	Son of Maggie and James Hoey	August 1859	11 months	Unspecified	White Hills Cemetery Bendigo
Maggie Brown Hoey	Sister of Jane Brown Hamilton, wife of James Hoey	November 1859	29 years	Heart disease	Brighton General Cemetery
Catherine (Kate) Hoey	Twin infant of Nena and Tom Hoey	April 1862	5 months	Unspecified	White Hills Cemetery Bendigo
Mary Mortley Hoey	Second wife of James Hoey	March 1864	21 years	Childbirth	New Zealand
James Harvey Hoey	Brother-in-law of Jane Hamilton, brother of Tom Hoey	November 1865	36 years	Lung disease	White Hills Cemetery Bendigo
Catherine Hoey	Third child of Nena and Tom Hoey	February 1866	About 1 year	Whooping cough	White Hills Cemetery Bendigo
Jessie Brown Hamilton	Second child of Jane and Andrew Hamilton	September 1864 – August 1866	23 months	Unspecified	White Hills Cemetery Bendigo
Thomas Hoey	Brother of James Hoey, husband of Nena Hoey	April 1867	31 years	Lung disease	White Hills Cemetery Bendigo
Little Tom Hoey	Fourth child of Nena and Tom Hoey	September 1868	About 1 year	Tuberculosis	White Hills Cemetery Bendigo
Andrew Hamilton	Husband of Jane Hamilton	16 December 1869	53 years	Lung disease	White Hills Cemetery Bendigo

24 James Hoey described Jane Brown Hamilton as his 'cousin', but their biological relationship is unclear. James was married to Jane's sister Maggie, and James and Tom Hoey's sister Janet was Andrew Hamilton's first wife (deceased). See James H Hoey to Mrs Brown, 25 November 1860, Letter 114, MS 862-3, Brown Family Papers, Australian Joint Copying Project, NLA.

25 Jane Hamilton to Mother, Brother and Kate, 24 June 1865, Letter 443, Acc12100, NLS.

This hope in Divine Providence helped to abate a fear of the future and motivated individual and corporate action to support family members. As noted above, Jane Hamilton's family were active United Presbyterians, a denomination then characterised as 'liberal evangelical Calvinist' in tenor.[26] Family letters reflect a shared belief in the Calvinist doctrine of predestination, which posits that all life events (including eternal salvation or damnation) are willed by God.[27] As Fergusson argues, the doctrine of predestination could provide comfort to believers because their destiny was considered 'safe in the hands of God'.[28] But because election to salvation was also a 'high mystery' and known only to God, believers were never sure of their status. Scottish Presbyterians who adhered to harsher versions of Westminster Calvinism commonly viewed an individual as either 'elect' and predestined for heaven, or 'reprobate' and foreordained to hell. This severe doctrine was under review during the long nineteenth century, as ascendant evangelicalism broadly understood God's love and the message of salvation as 'directed towards all people and not merely some', as predestination implied.[29] The United Presbyterian church was at the forefront of this liberalisation. The United Presbyterian Synod passed the Declaratory Act in 1879 that qualified the Westminster Confession to leave more room for free-will conversion and hence evangelical mission.[30] The doctrine of predestination was nevertheless influential across the nineteenth century, fostering humility and diligence among United Presbyterian congregants. Adherents searched for signs of election in their lives, which included the capacity to find consolation or 'Christian contentment' in suffering.[31] A rebellious response to the arrangements of Providence was actively discouraged because complaint or 'murmuring' could indicate reprobation. Indulging in murmuring was believed to anger and potentially provoke God to harsher measures, that 'may incur not only greater suffering in this world but damnation in the next'.[32]

26 Eric G. McKimmom, 'The Secession and United Presbyterian Churches,' in *The History of Scottish Theology, Volume II: From the Early Enlightenment to the Late Victorian Era*, ed. David Fergusson and Mark Elliott (Oxford University Press, 2019), 336.

27 See Jennifer Jones 'Faith and Failure on the Australian Goldfields: Gendered Interpretations of Piety and the 'Good Death',' *Journal of Religious History* 43, no. 4 (2019): 460–77, doi.org/10.1111/1467-9809.12627.

28 David A. S. Fergusson, 'Predestination: A Scottish Perspective,' *Scottish Journal of Theology* 46, no. 4 (1993): 461, doi.org/10.1017/S0036930600045245.

29 Ibid., 470.

30 Ibid.

31 Ibid., 465.

32 Tobias Gregory, 'Murmur and Reply: Rereading Milton's Sonnet 19,' *Milton Studies* 51 (2010): 22, doi.org/10.2307/26396001.

Correspondence between members of the Brown family reveals that they actively supported each other to submit to God's will and monitored their thoughts and behaviour to resist murmuring. This reading accepts that the goldfields writers used acceptable religious language to articulate their embodied experiences for an international readership unacquainted with its place-based nuances. Their choice of religious language also draws attention to other 'prohibited' knowledges, including religious doubt and grumbling against God, that are subject to veiled reference or epistolary silence.[33] This held implications for the management of unexpected events, including the contingency plans developed by the family in response to the debilitation and death of male breadwinners. The need to protect vulnerable mothers and children resulted in an exchange of letters that gave voice to goldfields women and children as they responded to lost hopes, pragmatically adapted to present realities and negotiated future-focused religious belief.

Murmuring

Members of the extended Hamilton-Brown family had multiple occasions to reveal and obscure their response to affliction and the temptation to murmur. Murmuring (in a religious sense) expresses impatience with the workings of Providence through complaint or grumbling against God's ultimate authority. Biblical references to murmuring are numerous and include the Israelites muttering about Moses' leadership as they wandered through the wilderness. Grumbling against authority indicates unequal power and dependency. Tradition holds that Israel's lack of faith and impatience angered God and provoked their punishment. As Van Der Walt notes, the Israelites had failed to trust that Yahweh (who 'even hears "silence"') would acknowledge their circumstances and 'meet the need and sustain those with unheard voices'.[34] A more righteous response to suffering was exemplified by the patriarch Job, who refused to murmur or 'charge God foolishly' for unfavourable Providential design.[35]

33 Julie A. Bokser, 'Sor Juana's Rhetoric of Silence,' *Rhetoric Review* 25, no. 1 (2006): 5–21, doi.org/10.1207/s15327981rr2501_1; William Merrill Decker, *Epistolary Practices Letter Writing in America Before Telecommunications* (University of North Carolina Press, 1998).

34 J. S. van der Walt, 'Unheard/Heard Voices in Exodus 1-17 and Some Thoughts on Poverty in South Africa,' *Acta Theologica* 27, no. 1 (2019): 16, supp. 27.

35 Job refused to murmur despite numerous calamities visited upon him by God to test his faith, including the death of all his children and the loss of his wealth and status. Russell M. Hillier, 'The Patience to Prevent That Murmur: The Theodicy of John Milton's Nineteenth Sonnet,' *Renascence: Essays on Values in Literature* 59, no. 4 (2007): 257, doi.org/10.5840/renascence200759418.

This serious issue prompted believers to offer each other support to resist murmuring, or to reference their murmuring obliquely as they encountered difficult circumstances.[36] For example, when Andrew Hamilton's Melbourne business failed in 1861, his brother-in-law William Stewart wrote from Scotland to offer the family solace. Financial and reputational losses were less painful, he assured Andrew and Jane Hamilton, 'when we are conscious of having honestly done our best for ourselves and others, we have a satisfaction even in adversity that many who are prosperous cannot have'.[37] Stewart expressed confidence that both good *and* bad outcomes were sent by God:

> And that conclusive question of the patriarchs quells all inclination to murmur 'shall we receive good from the hand of the Lord and not receive evil also' the fact of it coming 'from the hand of the Lord' is, or ought to be, sufficient for us.[38]

Stewart quotes Job 2:10 to amplify his reasoning and to encourage the core Christian virtue of patience. This reflects the belief that God provided believers with sufficient strength to endure suffering. Jane Hamilton voiced concord with these sentiments. After her baby Jessie died in 1866, she referred to God's generous provision of 'sustaining grace':

> I have not begun yet to fret after my little lamb, to sustaining grace be the glory, but I sometimes fear, if heaven appears by and by more distant, I might be tempted to murmur yet I trust not.[39]

Jane confesses that despite this God-given composure, she feared that she 'might be tempted to murmur'. This reference to murmuring allows readers to gauge the extent of her distress over the loss of Jessie, as a lapse into grumbling held potentially eternal consequences. Yet Jane reassures her readers that right-thinking and hard work help to steady her resolve:

> Beside trying to let my mind rest on the thoughts and comforts best for me, I have also done what I could otherwise to cheer and occupy myself. In fact I felt after first my arms were left empty I must work and work hard too.[40]

36 Published sermons, popular hymns and Christian literature discouraged murmuring and advocated patient submission.

37 William Stewart, Paisley, to Jane Hamilton, 25 October 1861, Letter 355, Papers of the Brown Family, Acc12100, National Library of Scotland, Edinburgh; Hillier, 'The Patience to Prevent That Murmur,' 252.

38 Ibid.

39 Jane Hamilton to Mother, 26 September 1866, Letter 486, Acc12100, NLS.

40 Ibid.

Jane Hamilton resorts to culturally sanctioned patterns of behaviour, which included diligent application to her earthly calling as a wife and mother. Encapsulated by the Weberian 'Protestant Work Ethic', Jane Hamilton gained a degree of contentment through hard work and hence 'comforting self-conviction' that her behaviour manifested godly virtue (which indicated salvation).[41] Jane's work, however, soon extended beyond the realm of domestic duties. The continued decline of her husband, Andrew Hamilton, compelled her to earn an income, so she opened a private school in Eaglehawk.[42] Jane drew upon the concept of Providential provision to reconcile difficult elements of this forced adaptation, which climaxed after the birth of her third child in 1868. Yet Providential direction was sometimes opaque. This is evident in the actions of both Andrew and Jane Hamilton (in Bendigo) and James and Kate Brown (in Paisley, Scotland). Both couples believed that God's plan for their nuclear family included gaining or retaining custody of orphaned nephew Robert Brown Hoey. The lengthy negotiations that ensued provide insight into their subjective interpretation of Providence, which (temporarily) resolved James and Kate Brown's unwanted childlessness and provided Andrew and Jane Hamilton with options when their circumstances worsened. Acceptance of unwelcome female financial headship was also central to this Providential path.

Interpreting Providence and ensuring family survival

While James Hoey lay on his deathbed in 1865, he made plans for the care of his children, Robert and Maggie. Although his sister-in-law Jane Hamilton had cared for Robert and Maggie Hoey since their mother's death in 1859 and loved them as her own children, James Hoey wanted the family patriarch, James Brown, to raise his son in Scotland. Young Maggie Hoey was to remain in Bendigo with Andrew and Jane Hamilton. Jane considered this transfer of responsibility to be 'a solemn duty which I owe both to the dead and the living', but her husband Andrew Hamilton disagreed. He argued that it was 'wrong to separate R from his sister and break up ties

41 Sam McKinstry and Ying Yong Ding, 'Alex Cowan & Sons Ltd, Papermakers, Penicuik: A Scottish Case of Weber's Protestant Work Ethic,' *Business History* 55, no. 5 (2013): 724, doi.org/10.1080/00076791.2012.745069.

42 See Jennifer Jones, 'A Tale of Two Widows: Marriage, Widowhood, and Faith on Bendigo Goldfield, 1859–1869,' *Journal of Religious History* 43, no. 2 (2019): 234–50, doi.org/10.1111/1467-9809.12583.

which have long existed'.[43] Jane Hamilton wrote of her duty to relinquish Robert Hoey but deferred any action for three years after James Hoey's death. This vacillation was contextualised by James Brown's happy news of March 1866. He and his wife Kate had finally become parents. James Brown nevertheless reassured Jane that his desire to adopt Robert had not waned. Referring to the working of Providence, he argued that the birth was God's reward for submission:

> We had as you may guess quite made up our minds that we were to go childless and had accepted what had seemed to be God's will without murmuring, but there were away down in our hearts a longing desire which we did not express to others and not very often to one another, but it is God's will that we might have got a little child to love- when the proposal came that we should take little Robert we both thought that it was sending him to us that God was answering our desire. No sooner however had we made up our minds most thankfully to take him than this other prospect began to dawn upon us.[44]

Here, James Brown admits to the pain of unwilling childlessness in a culture that positioned infertility as a shameful inadequacy. But keeping silence about childlessness, from his perspective, reflected submission to God's will and a deliberate choice not to murmur.[45] This decision was rewarded, as God answered their unspoken 'longing desire' for a 'little child to love', first through the promised custody of Robert Hoey and then, unexpectedly, through conception. James Brown broke the socially expected silence over reproductive difficulties to assure his sister that his welcome for Robert was not dampened by the surprise pregnancy, 'but rather confirmed my resolution and increased the heartiness with which I affirmed it', as their home would now ring with childish laughter. Following the birth of Mary Agnes, their Scottish family would therefore be akin to Robert's family life in Australia.[46] All misgivings on the custody matter were resolved from James Brown's point of view, and the couple expected Robert Hoey to be duly dispatched. Their anticipation only heightened when news of the

43 Maggie Hoey was Jane's sister. Jane Hamilton to Mother, Brother and Sister, 26 April 1867, Letter 203, Acc12100, NLS.

44 James Brown to Jane Hamilton, 25 March 1866, Letter 53, MS 862-3, NLA.

45 Christina Benninghaus, 'Silences: Coping with Infertility in Nineteenth-Century Germany,' in *The Palgrave Handbook of Infertility in History: Approaches, Contexts and Perspectives*, ed. Gayle Davis and Tracey Loughran (Palgrave Macmillan, 2017).

46 James Brown to Jane Hamilton, 25 March 1866, Letter 53, MS 862-3, NLA.

Hamilton's financial crisis arrived, yet Robert Hoey did not. Kate Brown, who was characteristically direct in her correspondence, wrote to Jane in June 1867, declaring:

> We feel however that Robert should be with us now. You have had him a long time- could you not by enquiry hear of any one with whom you could entrust him home to us?[47]

Kinship structures frequently provided orphaned children and widowed mothers with 'forms of cushioning' in this period, when premature death was still prevalent.[48] Phillip Batman has shown that, with the inducement and support of close relatives, working-class Irish families used migration to England as an effective survival strategy for vulnerable or under-resourced kin.[49] The Brown family had discussed the possibility of the Hamiltons' return migration, urging Andrew and Jane to consider Scotland if his health allowed. They also suggested sending Robert Hoey in advance. Historians concur that the social and economic survival of middle-class family units then required the pragmatic negotiation of family values and preferred customs. This included contravening the 'domestic ideal' to support female economic independence and female-headed households when necessary. Gordon and Nair chart a rising number of female-headed households in Glasgow in the second half of the nineteenth century and argue that women's financial independence had become increasingly respectable among the middle classes.[50] Negotiations within the Brown family support this argument. Although Kate Brown expressed sorrow for Jane, that 'dull times necessitate exertion beyond your household duties', she surmised that 'such occupation was far more congenial to you and even less toilsome than those said household duties as you describe them'.[51] Kate Brown also expected Jane to earn a family income, even if she returned to Scotland:

> I only wish that Mrs Hamilton's Seminary was in dear old Scotland and you were reaping the fruits of your labours beside us for I can tell you that such institutions here are highly remunerative.[52]

47 Kate Brown to Jane Hamilton, 25 June 1867, Letter 501, Acc12100, NLS.

48 Blaikie, 'Rituals, Transitions and Life Courses in an Era of Social Transformation,' 102.

49 Philip A. Batman, 'A Comparison of Kinship Family Survival in York and Swaledale in the Nineteenth Century' (PhD thesis, University of Leicester, 2020).

50 Eleanor Gordon and Gweneth Nair, 'The Myth of the Victorian Patriarchal Family,' *The History of the Family* 7, no. 1 (2002): 125–38, doi.org/10.1016/S1081-602X(01)00100-2.

51 Kate Brown to Jane Hamilton, 25 June 1867, Letter 501, Acc12100, NLS.

52 Ibid.

Kate Brown's enthusiasm suggests awareness that her husband's modest United Presbyterian stipend would not stretch to support Jane Hamilton and all her dependants upon their return to Scotland.[53]

James Brown's proposed adoption of Robert Hoey may have also reflected his desire for a male heir. The respectability of middle-class Victorian men included demonstrating their capacity to comfortably support a wife and then to produce an heir, both in a timely manner.[54] Christian ministers were also expected to exhibit ideal standards of Christian domesticity in their family arrangements. But Andrew and Jane Hamilton's inaction stalled these plans. They disagreed over the relative advancement opportunities available for boys in Scotland and Australia. Andrew held the view that 'a boy gets on slowly at home', but Jane Hamilton felt sure 'R is better suited at home than here'.[55] Andrew Hamilton perhaps made veiled references to James Brown's limited remuneration and hence his capacity to assist in successful 'male self-making'.[56] James Brown held an influential and respected position as a minister of religion, and although a modest United Presbyterian stipend was often supplemented by 'in-kind' benefits including clothes, books and housing, this removed a degree of control over finances. Ministers were not only vulnerable to congregational power but also expected to exercise appropriate Christian self-denial in the financial realm.[57] The impasse over Robert Hoey's future thus continued until the Providential path seemed more obvious.[58]

The issue was finally pushed towards a resolution by a serious decline in Andrew Hamilton's health, ten days after the birth of Jane Elizabeth. Andrew woke his wife in the night, haemorrhaging from the lung, and, 'there was no time to lose- the blood was gurgling up so fast':

53 Sawkins notes that although highly educated, ministers in non-established Presbyterian denominations that relied upon voluntary giving received a wage equivalent to that of a middle ranking clerk. John W Sawkins, 'Ministerial Stipends in the Free Church of Scotland: Edinburgh 1843–1900,' *Scottish Church History* 41, no. 1 (2012): 71–112, doi.org/10.3366/sch.2012.41.1.5.

54 John Tosh, 'What Should Historians Do with Masculinity? Reflections on Nineteenth-Century Britain,' *History Workshop Journal* 38, no. 1 (1994): 179–202, doi.org/10.1093/hwj/38.1.179.

55 Jane Hamilton to James and Kate, 2 February 1868, Letter 205, Acc12100, NLS.

56 Catherine Jamieson, '"It Is Not Good for the Man to Be Alone?" Irish Protestant Missionary Bachelorhood and Changes in Missionary Marriage Trends in the Late Nineteenth Century,' *Gender & History* 29, no. 2 (2017): 389, doi.org/10.1111/1468-0424.12295.

57 James Brown's congregation was generous, paying for several months recuperation in the south of France when required for his health in 1861; see Kate Brown to Jane Hamilton, 22 September 1861, Letter 261, Acc12100, NLS; Andrew Landale Drummond and James Bulloch, *The Church in Victorian Scotland, 1843–1874* (Saint Andrew Press, 1975), 50.

58 Jane Hamilton to James and Kate, 2 February 1868, Letter 205, Acc12100, NLS.

> It was a strange sad night, the joy over the birth and my safety so suddenly checked by the dark shadow of we knew not what. What thoughts crowded into my mind as I sat by the fire- not overstrong myself and my dearest husband thus struck down ... But ... the Lord never forsook me in any trying hour yet and that night I felt unusually upheld- my bodily frame needed that and 'as thy day is, thy strength shall be' was once more found true. God seemed to calm and support my dear Andrew wonderfully too.[59]

By referring to Deuteronomy 33:25 and the provision of strength to meet daily challenges, Jane Hamilton demonstrates her 'Christian contentment' even in these trying circumstances. She also, however, identifies the gap between cultural ideals of protected new motherhood and the stark realities of goldfields life. In this period, cultural perceptions of pregnancy included association with disablement and death, which encouraged women to hide their condition from loved ones.[60] The Brown family correspondents shielded others from worry by announcing a birth some weeks or months after the safety of mother and child seemed secure. Such was the case when Jane Hamilton announced the arrival of baby Jane Elizabeth, then three weeks old. Jane was quick to 'banish all anxiety from your mind at once by telling' her mother:

> how very well we both are ... The weather being very hot I have not quite come to my strength, but then I tell you I have driven twice to Eagle Hawke (yesterday I had baby with me), you will judge that I am not very weak.[61]

Yet five days after writing this buoyant letter, Jane disclosed the extent of her vulnerability to her cousin Jane Frew. Describing the family crisis ten days after the birth, Jane noted that she was 'not overstrong' and needed to be 'unusually upheld' by God.[62] Driving herself and baby Jane twice to Eaglehawk perhaps reflected business necessity rather than personal vigour. Other post-partum adjustments included finally agreeing to relinquish Robert Hoey. Jane disclosed her vacillation to James Brown, noting:

59 Jane Hamilton to Jane Frew, 2 February 1868, Letter 529, Acc12100, NLS.

60 It was held that only the woman could confirm true gestation, from knowledge associated with 'quickening' or movement of the foetus at around five months; Cynthia A. Huff, 'Chronicles of Confinement: Reactions to Childbirth in British Women's Diaries,' *Women's Studies International Forum* 10, no. 1 (1987): 67, doi.org/10.1016/0277-5395(87)90095-1; Barbara Duden, 'Quick with Child: An Experience That Has Lost Its Status,' *Technology in Society* 14, no. 3 (1992): 335–44, doi.org/10.1016/0160-791X(92)90011-X.

61 Jane Hamilton to MA Brown, 24 January 1868, Letter 204, Acc12100, NLS.

62 Jane Hamilton to Jane Frew, 2 February 1868, Letter 529, Acc12100, NLS.

> Although it is almost heart-breaking to let him go, still to me it seems a solemn duty which I owe both to the dead and the living … I cannot therefore decide day to day that dear Robert will be sent … I feel it is strongly impressed on my own mind that he ought to be and it seems as if Providence had laid the means in my hand by all of your kindness lately.[63]

Remittance from family members, notably her brother (and her cousin Jane Frew), enabled Jane Hamilton to pay for Robert Hoey's passage. Remittances, which usually flow from the migrant back to the home country, are recognised as a form of 'welfare solidarity' that reflect a degree of altruism, self-interest and an investment in family contractual relationships.[64] Jane Hamilton identified remittances flowing from Scotland to Australia as Providential provision because the money resolved her indecision over Robert. Jane admitted in an earlier letter that, 'I don't see that he could be brought up so here- this land is anything but prosperous'.[65] Jane and her family had suffered during the 'bust' phase of Bendigo's gold mining industry. After the depletion of shallow alluvial gold in the 1850s, underground quartz reefing developed in the 1860s. Mining companies, including Andrew Hamilton's 'St Mungo', encountered difficulty and expense as quartz reefing advanced. Costly pumps were needed to prevent flooding after the water table was struck, and as Charles Fahey notes, the quartz industry then struggled to attract capital sufficient for further exploration.[66] Andrew Hamilton's health declined just before rich lodes in Bendigo's quartz reefs were discovered. This encouraged investment and fostered a mining boom in 1870 to 1871. These developments came too late for Andrew Hamilton, who died on 16 December 1869. By 1870, the family had relinquished their mining interests, and newly widowed Jane returned to Scotland with her dependent children.[67] Identifying signs of a Providential path proved difficult and stressful for Jane. She finally sent Robert Hoey to Scotland in February 1868, but soon openly doubted her actions. Reflecting upon her decision-making processes, Jane wrote to her mother:

63 Jane Hamilton to James and Kate, 2 February 1868, Letter 205, Acc12100, NLS.

64 João Estêvão, 'Remittances, Welfare Solidarity, and Monetarization: The Interaction Between Personal and Economic Relations in Cape Verde During the Colonial Period,' *Portuguese Literary and Cultural Studies* 23/24, (2013): 55–73, doi.org/10.62791/2xsxrz51.

65 Jane Hamilton to MA Brown, 24 January 1868, Letter 204, Acc12100, NLS.

66 Charles Fahey, 'Peopling the Victorian Goldfields: From Boom to Bust, 1851–1901,' *Australian Economic History Review* 50, no. 2 (2010): 155, doi.org/10.1111/j.1467-8446.2010.00298.x.

67 'Deaths,' *The Age*, December 18, 1869, p. 2, nla.gov.au/nla.news-article188570998.

> I have done what I thought Providence indicated [but] there are points in our lives in which we would fair consult the Oracle as they did of old … I feel anxious and impatient to know what changes may be making amongst you; then dear James also being unwell is a source of care and sad reflection to me [that] makes me ask was I wise to send [Robert] away?[68]

Jane's brother, like his father before him, enjoyed indifferent health. But news of recent illness unsettled Jane as it undermined the security of his family. That Jane questioned Providential intent in writing is a measure of her disquiet. While female financial headship was supported by this family, not all women were judged as suited to 'such a sphere of usefulness'. When Jane Hamilton returned to her teaching vocation, her sister-in-law Kate Brown admitted that 'I fear were I left alone or dear James unfitted for duty I would make but a poor find!'[69] Yet Robert Hoey had been incorporated into this household, which now appeared more vulnerable. This correspondence is remarkable for the candid and unusual insight it provides into inter-family politics and personal agency. Jane's refusal to send Robert Hoey had functioned as a form of agency at a time when she had so little. Jane reflects upon the fragility of life and the wisdom of her Providence-led decisions, preferring to maintain honest family intimacy over the righteous image at other times presented to the outside world.

James Brown experienced no such doubts. Writing to Jane in June 1869 to announce the birth of a son, who was also named Robert (after their father), James attributes the shift in family fortune to his submission to divine intention by adopting Robert Hoey:

> we are very glad to have him [their new baby son] and very thankful to the giver of all good that we who before were childless have now a household of three. It was coincidentally after I had determined that Robert come to us that Mary made her appearance and it was on that occasion twelvemonth that Robert came to us that this small person arrived. I cannot but see the hand of Providence in this-Robert has been to us the bringer of goodluck.[70]

68 Jane Hamilton to MA Brown, 23 April 1868, Letter 537, Acc12100, NLS.

69 Kate Brown to Jane Hamilton, 25 June 1867, Letter 501, Acc12100, NLS.

70 James Brown to Jane Hamilton, 17 June 1869, Letter 557, Acc12100, NLS.

The arrival of a biological son (who even bore the same name) did not seem to perturb thirteen-year-old Robert Hoey. He wrote to Aunt Jane about his summer holiday plans:

> Mary Agnes and Aunt are pretty well. Aunt has got a little boy now. He is about three weeks old. I am going to sell my rabbits very soon as I am going away very soon. We have a pair of pigeons but they are Mary's.[71]

Small animals including rabbits and birds were common childhood pets among the British working and middle classes. They occupied little space, offered valuable lessons in responsibility and, in straitened times, could become financial or food resources.[72] Robert Hoey's transactional discussion of his pet rabbits suggests awareness of financial need and perhaps adult expectations of his behaviour. Although Robert uses the term 'we' to describe corporate possession of pigeons, he immediately notes that the birds belonged to cousin Mary. There is no indication that Mary Agnes, the couple's first biological child, would relinquish her pets when the family removed to their seaside holiday.

The priority afforded a biological male child is also evident twelve months later, when James writes to condole with Jane upon her widowhood and return migration. Writing from abroad while undertaking a holy-land tour, James reflected upon the family reunion:

> I wish I had seen you when [my children] were first presented to you. Isn't Mary an old fashioned little lassie and the son too – he is a fine specimen to be the heir of the headship of our family.[73]

Robert Hoey returned to Scotland as the eldest male child in the family, but the assumptions of primogeniture ensured that the 'appropriate socialisation' of headship went to baby Robert Brown.[74] Although Robert Hoey gained an education and resources for adulthood, he arguably lacked the 'culturally mediated opportunities' that may have flowed if baby Robert had not arrived.[75] A family descendant, Mary Agnes Alison Walker Weir, understood Robert Hoey in this light, noting that he 'took accountancy

71 Robert B Hoey to Jane Hamilton, 18 June 1869, Letter 325, MS 862-3, NLA.

72 Julie-Marie Strange, 'When John Met Benny: Class, Pets and Family Life in Late Victorian and Edwardian Britain,' *The History of the Family* 26, no. 2 (2021): 214–235, doi.org/10.1080/1081602X.2021.1897028.

73 James Brown, Constantinople to Jane Hamilton, 3 May 1870, Letter 235, Acc12100, NLS.

74 Sarah Blaffer Hrdy and Debra S Judge, 'Darwin and the Puzzle of Primogeniture,' *Human Nature* 4, no. 1 (1993): 1, doi.org/10.1007/BF02734088.

75 Hrdy and Judge, 'Darwin and the Puzzle of Primogeniture,' 22.

exams in Glasgow but never flourished'.[76] Robert Hoey's views on his forced migration are unknown, but he continued to describe Bendigo as 'home' twelve months after his relocation.[77]

Members of the Brown family ventured to the Victorian goldfields hoping that God would send them health and prosperity, or at least protect them from misfortune. When they encountered suffering instead of bounty, family members found consolation through welfare solidarity and kinship-care. Although preferring the security of patriarchal structures, they also accommodated women's financial headship. These adaptive actions were acknowledged as the work of Providence. As Calvinists, the Brown family saw prosperity and a flourishing family as reward for submission and evidence of predestination. But they also acknowledged tragedy, including failed patriarchal arrangements, as God-sent. James Brown indicated such when he wrote to console Jane Hamilton in 1870:

> That you were a widow and your children fatherless affected me much. You have certainly had your cross to bear in life. I trust and hope that according to the days in which God has afflicted you and the years in which you have seen evil so will He make you glad.[78]

Understanding Jane's affliction as divinely intended imposes a form of 'compulsory optimism' upon believers. The family, therefore, rallied to preserve their Godliness while managing the harsh goldfields environment and multiple family tragedies. Significantly, this Providential optimism fostered personal agency that contravened family expectation. Jane Hamilton adopted improvised and non-preferred behaviours like child-led breastfeeding in her alien circumstances. This aligned her embodied knowledge with God's will. Members of the extended family also followed non-traditional Providential urgings, providing monetary and emotional resources to support female economic independence and to solve the misfortune of infertility. Such arrangements ultimately reminded the family that God might afflict or bless his faithful servant. Jane affirms this knowledge in her last letter from Bendigo, written ten days before Andrew Hamilton's death, noting to her family 'All our steps are ordered by the Lord. … When he sent me to this distant land … I know he has not said "Go" without adding "and I am with you"'.[79]

76 Mary Agnes Alison Walker Weir, *A Family History for the Brown-Hamilton Letters, with CD*, Folder 61, Acc12100, NLS.

77 Robert B Hoey to Jane Hamilton, 18 June 1869, Letter 325, MS 862-3, NLA.

78 James Brown, Constantinople to Jane Hamilton, 3 May 1870, Letter 235, Acc12100, NLS.

79 Jane Hamilton to Dearest Friends, 6 December 1869, Letter 229, Acc12100, NLS.

6

Building an Irish-Roman Catholic Church on the goldfields and Northern Victoria, 1852–1914

In March 1852, a German priest, Father Henry Backhaus, celebrated mass for gold seekers at Bendigo using a rough bush altar. For the next two decades, Backhaus was the goldfield's most important Catholic cleric. An astute investor and speculator in urban and rural land, when Backhaus died in 1882, his probated estate placed him in the top one per cent of property holders. Also unusual for a Catholic priest, Backhaus took a leading part in public life, often inciting local controversy and sectarian tensions.

These atypical roles of cleric, local community activist and wealthy speculator have intrigued local historians. Father John Hussey, a priest in the Sandhurst Diocese, thought Backhaus 'saved money, but he also saved the faith.'[1] The journalist William Dobson was less complimentary to Backhaus: 'whilst being conscious about his priestly duties', he was also 'censorious, irascible and avaricious, a clerical enigma'.[2] Mal Nolan, the most recent biographer of Backhaus, was intrigued by the terms of his will, which unsuccessfully attempted to exclude the controlling influence of Martin Crane, the first Bishop of Sandhurst, and his successors.[3]

1 John Hussey, *Henry Backhaus, Doctor of Divinity, Pioneer Priest of Bendigo* (St Kilian's Press, 1982), 65.

2 W. T. Dobson, 'Cloth of Gold,' (n.d.), Foreword. Manuscript held in the Sandhurst Diocesan Archives. I am grateful to Dr Donna Bailey, the Diocesan Archivist, for providing me with a copy of this manuscript.

3 M. J. Nolan, *The Enterprising Life of Dr Henry Backhaus, Bendigo Pioneer* (M.J. Nolan, 2008).

This chapter will argue that, although Backhaus played a prominent part in establishing the Catholic Church on the Bendigo goldfield, the character of Bendigo's Catholicism developed deeper and more enduring roots in the forms of devotion that were brought to goldfields with the arrival of Bishop Crane and his associate Stephen Reville. While Backhaus set up the first Catholic Church in Bendigo, Crane and Reville brought to Bendigo a system of devotional practice that had its roots in their native Ireland. They followed the forms that have been labelled by historians as the 'Devotional Revolution'. Moreover, while Backhaus was a successful investor in land, very little of his capital was used to build the infrastructure that a strong Catholic community needed. Coming to Bendigo, Crane and Reville had oversight of an area larger than this goldfield. They were charged with administering a new diocese that extended from the Northern Plains as far west as the Loddon River, up into the high country of the north-east. They arrived at a particularly important time, when the agricultural potential of this region was being tested by the arrival of land selectors. A large proportion of these settlers were Irish Catholic migrants, and Crane and Reville found a fertile region to implant their Rome-centric vision of Catholicism. This contrasted the relaxed and independent character of Backhaus' ministry.

Dr Backhaus comes to Bendigo

Henry Backhaus was born on 12 February 1812, the son of Anton Backhaus, a boot merchant of 'modest but secure means'. Anton married twice: the first marriage produced two children and the second, to Maria Margarita, five children. Henry Backhaus was the oldest son of this second marriage. Educated first at a local school, Backhaus finished his schooling at Paderborn Gymnasium and enrolled at the University of Würzburg in 1831. After a year of study, he decided to train for the priesthood, and, with the help of a local priest, he entered Rome's College of the Propagation of the Faith. Here, Backhaus studied under Father Karl-August von Reisach. Elevated to the Bishopric of Bavaria in 1836, Reisach returned to Rome to ordain Backhaus on 24 August 1836. A year later, at the age of 25, Backhaus was awarded his doctorate in theology.[4]

For the next sixteen years, Backhaus worked as a priest in Calcutta, Sydney and Adelaide. Ministering to British troops in the Hazaribagh district, he came for the first time in contact with poor Irishmen, and he also recruited

4 Dobson, 'Cloth of Gold,' 3–4.

nuns from Ireland in late 1840. During his Indian sojourn, Backhaus also mixed with the local mercantile community, which may have given him a taste for business life and fostered his love of property speculation. In his Indian years, he also clashed with the local clerical hierarchy, establishing a trend that he maintained in Australia. Citing poor health, Backhaus departed from India and arrived in Sydney in November 1846 via Singapore and Indonesia. His stay in Sydney was brief, and in October 1847, he made his way to Adelaide via Melbourne.[5]

Backhaus was invited to Adelaide by an old friend, Dr Francis Murphy, who had been appointed the inaugural Bishop of Adelaide in 1843. Established on Wakefieldian principles of systematic settlement, Adelaide lacked a large Irish Catholic population, and Murphy struggled to establish an enduring diocese. When gold was discovered in Victoria in late 1851, the Adelaide diocese was in dire financial straits. Murphy was forced to terminate the services of most of his priests, including Backhaus. During his four-and-a-half-year stay in Adelaide, Backhaus commenced his Australian career of land acquisition. William Dobson suggests that Backhaus may have acquired his initial capital through a friend from India, Count John Lackenstein. In Adelaide, Backhaus mixed with the colonial elite. He attended government house levees, and in March 1851, he was invited to stand for the local legislature. Although Backhaus politely refused this offer, it did presage his future involvement in public affairs.[6]

Like thousands of his fellow South Australian settlers, Backhaus abandoned the struggling South Australian colony, and in March 1852, he sailed for Melbourne. Arriving in Melbourne, Backhaus offered his services to Dr Patrick Bonaventure Geoghegen, the Vicar General of the Melbourne Catholic Diocese, who led the local church while its Bishop Goold was overseas. Geoghegen toured the goldfields for three weeks in March 1852, and on his return, he requested that Backhaus take charge of the goldfields, which he did so by early April. A brief journal, kept on route, plots Backhaus' journey. Catholics had been deprived of ministers in the former pastoral districts of Victoria, so as he travelled to Bendigo, Backhaus ministered to the Catholic community by baptising babies and young children. Backhaus visited Kyneton and Mt Alexander before celebrating his first mass at Bendigo on 15 April 1852. Backhaus initially divided his services between

5 Ibid., 5–10.
6 Ibid., 11–13.

the Mt Alexander and Bendigo goldfields and spent alternate weeks in each centre. By April, it was probably clear to most diggers that Bendigo had greater prospects, and Backhaus settled into life on this field.[7]

Arriving in Bendigo, Backhaus found a Catholic community that was largely Irish, with a leavening of European Catholics chiefly from Italy and Germany. In the early 1850s, his flock was largely composed of pre-goldrush migrants, either assisted migrants brought to Victoria to provide labour for the pastoral industry or convicts from New South Wales or Tasmania who had served their time. A distinctive group was young women who had been orphaned by the potato famine of 1847 and were settled in the colonies by a scheme devised by the Colonial Secretary Earl Grey. In a society with a large imbalance of men, the orphans group rapidly found marriage partners and provided the first flood of Catholics seeking Backhaus' ministry. The majority of Backhaus' congregation were products of post-famine migration.[8]

Irish migration to Australia and the 'Devotional Revolution'

Australian historians have argued that the impact of the famine on migration to Australia was more complex than a simple flight from mass poverty and death. In his study of the Irish and Catholics in Sydney and Melbourne, Chris McConville argues that Irish migration to Australia was largely a phenomenon of the post-famine economic and population adjustments of Ireland.[9] Despite a jump in departures from Ireland between 1853 and 1855, migration, McConville argues, was more important after 1860. The Irish population grew impressively after a famine in 1740–1741 and reached a peak in 1841 of 8.5 million. Population growth was sustained by the remarkable capacity of the potato to feed a growing population. With access to small plots of land, labourers could grow potatoes for food to supplement low wages. The Great Famine of 1847 to 1851 resulted in the death of one million, and massive emigration further reduced the population.

7 Ibid., 15–21.

8 For the Irish Orphans, see Trevor McClaughlin, *Barefoot and Pregnant? Irish Famine Orphans in Australia* (Genealogical Society of Victoria, 1991). The Bendigo experience is based on genealogical investigations undertaken by Dr Donna Bailey, Sandhurst Diocese Archivist.

9 Chris McConville, 'Emigrant Irish and Suburban Catholics: Faith and Nation in Melbourne and Sydney, 1851–1933,' (PhD thesis, University of Melbourne, 1984); for his argument on later migration, see Chapter 2 '"Tip'rary so far away" – Ireland and the Emigrants,' 30–79.

In the wake of the famine, agriculture turned from labour-intensive cereal cropping to pastoralism. Small holdings were consolidated, and the number of agricultural labourers dropped dramatically. Remaining tenant farmers were reluctant to subdivide their farms and had fewer children through delayed marriage and celibacy to achieve these aims. By 1861, the Irish population had fallen to 5.8 million.[10] Migration offered escape from these demographic and economic constraints.

In this period of agricultural modernisation, the practice of Catholicism was also reformed. Ireland experienced what the historian Emmet Larkin labelled a 'devotional revolution' that made 'practicing Catholics of the Irish people' in the decades after 1850. Mass attendance was low before the famine, he argued, also noting considerable local variations of religious practice. These ranged from 'idiosyncratic to the heterodox' and included belief in fairies and the efficacy of magic. Popular religion included 'patterns', local festivals held at holy wells or significant locations, and 'wakes', festivities held around the dead body prior to burial. Another uniquely Irish practice was that of 'stations', in which the sacraments were administered in private houses on a rotating basis. During the second half of the nineteenth century, the Irish Catholic Church largely eradicated these practices. Historians have debated the timing and the part played by Cardinal Paul Cullen in the imposition of these changes in Ireland in line with 'a current of opinion in the Catholic Church which favoured papal over national or diocesan authority'.[11] The significant point is that after 1850, Irish Catholicism was distinctly ultramontane, closely following the dictates of Rome. This 'ultramontanism' was translated to the Australian colonies by Irish bishops.

Under Cullen's direction, the Irish church completed the abolition of stations and continued and intensified a program of church building. Mass attendance rose significantly, and the clergy placed emphasis on taking communion and making confessions more frequently. Devotion to the

10 For population and demographic change in Ireland, see Timothy W. Guinnane, *The Vanishing Irish: Households, Migration, and the Rural Economy in Ireland, 1850-1914* (Princeton University Press, 1997). For an overview of population, see 3–33, and for rural Ireland after the famine, see 34–58. The disappearance of the agricultural labourers is analysed in David Fitzpatrick, 'The Disappearance of the Irish Agricultural Labourer, 1841–1912,' *Irish Economic and Social History* 7, no, 1 (1980): 66–92, doi.org/10.1177/033248938000700105.

11 Emmet Larkin, 'The Devotional Revolution in Ireland, 1850–75,' *American Historical Review* 77, no. 3 (1972): 625–652, doi.org/10.1086/ahr/77.3.625. See also D.W. Miller, 'Irish Catholicism and the Great Famine,' *Journal of Social History* 9, no. 1 (1975): 81–98, doi.org/10.1353/jsh/9.1.81. For an argument on pre-famine religion, see S.J. Connelly, *Priests and the People in Pre-famine Ireland 1780-1845* (Gill Macmillan, 1982).

Sacred Heart was encouraged, and Marian practices – the praying of the rosary and the devotion to the immaculate conception – were encouraged by the clergy, who took a dominant part in the lives of Catholics. Lay persons were encouraged to join sodalities and confraternities to promote religious observance under ecclesiastical direction. Mixing with Protestants was discouraged, and mixed marriages were vigorously opposed. In Ireland, the clergy had firm control over education, and the Catholic youth were schooled apart from the Protestant young.[12] Critically, as Colin Barr has shown, Cullen was influential in Rome and remarkably successful in placing Irish bishops in charge of Australian dioceses.[13] But in the case of Bendigo, this influence was delayed for almost 25 years.

Henry Backhaus and the Bendigo Catholic Church

Father Backhaus was not uncritical of gold seeking. He warned gold seekers that gold might appear a blessing but could be a curse. George Dunderdale, a digger in 1852, recalled in the 1880s that Backhaus initially preached from the top of a packing case in front of a tent:[14]

> You go what you call on the spree; you find the sly grog; you get drunk and are robbed of your gold: sometimes you are murdered: or you fall into a hole and are killed, and you go to hell dead drunk.

In a letter to Bishop Goold in April 1853, Backhaus complained that 'the Catholics merely hear mass. The Sacraments seem to be entirely lost sight of in their covetous pursuit of gold'.[15] While the number who took communion and went to confession cannot be determined, Backhaus' meticulous record keeping demonstrates that he very soon conducted marriages, baptisms and funerals. In his second year in Bendigo, Backhaus, the lone Catholic cleric, conducted 17 marriages, 152 baptisms and 61 burials. This pace grew during the next ten years (Figure 6.1).[16]

12 For an overview of the debates on religion in nineteenth century Ireland, see Sean Kelly, *Religion and Society in Nineteenth Century Ireland* (Duandalgan Press [W. Tempest], 1985).

13 Colin Barr, '"Imperium in Imperio": Irish Episcopal Imperialism in the Nineteenth Century,' *The English Historical Review* CXXIII, no. 502 (2008): 611–650, doi.org/10.1093/ehr/cen161.

14 Quoted in Dobson, 'Cloth of Gold,' 20.

15 Ibid., 45.

16 Baptismal, Marriage and Burial Registers, Parish of St Kilian's, Sandhurst Diocesan Archives. Thanks to Dr Donna Bailey, who extracted figures for this chapter and provided an Excel spreadsheet for the author's use.

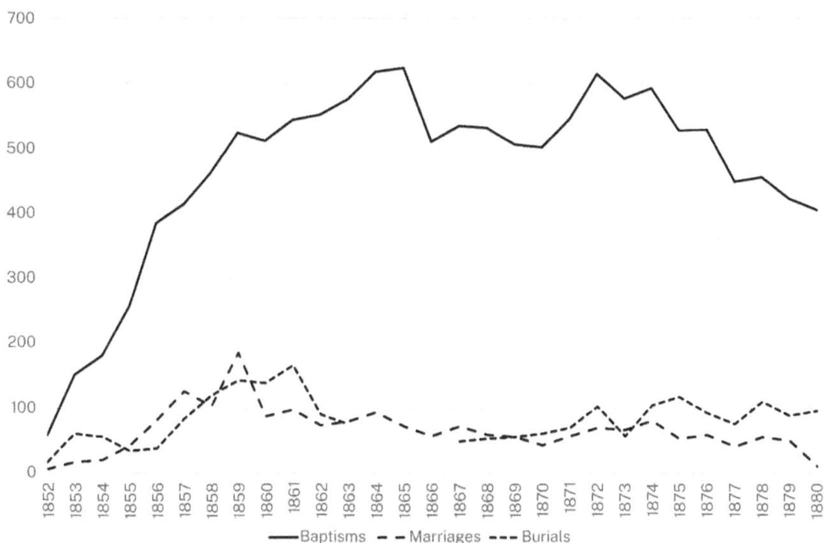

Figure 6.1: Marriages, baptisms and burials conducted at St Kilian's parish, 1852–1880

Source: Compiled by Donna Bailey and the authors.

The covetous pursuit of wealth was not confined to the laity. When land sales were opened by the colonial government in 1854, Backhaus quickly established himself as a frequent buyer of town lots. He also joined the early sales of country lots and then turned his attention to farming blocks north of the goldfields in the parishes of Axedale, Muskerry, and Strathfieldsaye. Backhaus soon became a gentleman farmer with an extensive rent roll of tenants.[17] He also acquired a quarry and a brewery in the centre of the emerging township of Sandhurst. Dobson suggests that knowledge of these purchases was withheld from clerical authorities in Melbourne and were all in his own name. Indeed, they were purchased from his own funds, not from church or parish funds. Backhaus, however, 'considered it all to be the one thing; his own and woe betide any Bishop or Vicar General who tried to tell him differently.'[18]

17 For the land purchases and estate of Henry Backhaus, see Nolan, *The Enterprising life*, 119–127. In 1882, Backhaus left an estate of £76,771 for estate duty. This placed him in the top one per cent of estates probated. In this year, only 25% of deceased adults left an estate that was probated. He was clearly among the wealthy elite of Victoria.

18 Dobson, 'Cloth of Gold,' 47.

Backhaus also had an interest in local affairs as a man of property. He became involved in the formation of the Bendigo Hospital and the Bendigo Benevolent Asylum. In both his purchase of land and the conduct of local affairs, Backhaus lent heavily on a number of Irishmen in his congregation who were also 'on the make' in this rough community. These civic affairs drew Backhaus into unseemly sectarian disputes, doing little credit to himself and his loyal Catholic allies, nor the Protestant clergy, particularly the Presbyterian Rev. James Nish and his supporters in the *Bendigo Advertiser* owned by Angus Mackay.[19]

Backhaus enjoyed considerable popularity with his congregation, as evident in the numbers he married, baptised and buried (Figure 6.1). Parishioners gave very generously at Easter and Christmas services. An examination of the marriage registers makes obvious the reasons for this. Coming to Bendigo, Backhaus found a congregation that was largely Irish, but he neglected the strictures against mixed marriages and was prepared to sanction unions between Catholics and non-Catholics. As noted above, the majority of goldrush settlers were single men: around one quarter came as married men with families, and there were substantial numbers of single women who travelled alone or with male siblings and other relations. In the second half of the 1850s, the colonial government attempted to redress the extremely unequal ratio of men to women in the colony by sponsoring the immigration of single female settlers.[20] Valiant as this attempt was, it could not overcome the high proportion of male settlers. Due to this imbalance, many men crossed sectarian and national lines to marry. At St Kilian's, between 1856 and 1863, one in five Irish women married men born in England and Scotland. Some of these men may have been Catholic, but it is likely that they were a minority. The demographic realities of the goldfields thus informed the 'rational and humane decisions' made by Backhaus.[21]

The demographics of the Irish men and women moving to the goldfields reflected national trends. They came from across Ireland, but one in four derived from the north, ensuring a strong Protestant presence. Despite this diverse spread, several areas stood out, including Galway in the west, the

19 For these public disputes, see Dobson, 'Cloth of Gold,' 57–93.

20 For the official policy towards the high male to female ratios in Victoria, see David Goodman, *Gold Seeking: Victoria and California in the 1850s* (Allen & Unwin, 1994), 149–187.

21 Calculated from the Baptismal, Marriage and Burial Registers at St Kilian's, Sandhurst Diocesan Archives. For the demography of the gold rushes, see Charles Fahey, 'Peopling the Victorian Goldfields: From Boom To Bust, 1851–1901' in *Australian Economic History Review* 50, no. 2 (2010): 148–161, doi.org/10.1111/j.1467-8446.2010.00298.x.

southwestern counties of Clare, Limerick, Cork and Kerry, and Tipperary in the midlands. Clare and Tipperary together accounted for 51 per cent of the Irish grooms and 57.4 per cent of Irish brides. Most were rural in origin, with many fathers of brides and grooms on St Kilian's marriage certificate citing their occupation as 'farmer'. Unfortunately, there is no way to determine whether these men and women were children of prosperous tenant farmers, very small landholders or merely conacre labourers. The geographical origins suggest the latter, supporting Chris McConville's argument that the Australian Irish were post-famine emigrants.[22] This is given more weight by death certificate evidence, which places the dates of departure from Ireland in the second half of the 1850s. Perhaps the most convincing evidence that the Bendigo Irish were not desperate victims of famine is their subsequent post-famine incorporation into the colonial economy and, particularly, the rural economy.

Backhaus found a coterie of upwardly mobile Irishmen whom he befriended while pursuing his secular ambitions. While these men were mostly Catholic, Backhaus had few compunctions in mixing in non-Catholic society. This was probably necessary for a man deeply involved in public affairs. In the 1850s, he worked closely with James Forster Sullivan and John Joseph Casey, becoming involved in machinations to run the hospital and benevolent asylum. Casey was a Catholic, but Sullivan was probably brought up a Methodist, although Backhaus believed he was Jewish by birth and a non-believer. Both came from prosperous backgrounds, had experience in the United States and were trained in the law. In the colony, they were drawn to democratic politics and at various times held local seats in the legislature. Backhaus was also close to several of the emerging city's more prominent publicans – John Crowley and William Heffernan, proprietors of the Shamrock hotel.[23]

Although there is extensive evidence that Backhaus mixed freely with the Catholic and Irish elite, it is harder to assess his interaction with the general Catholic community. Most had some interactions with him, as he married

22 McConville, 'Emigrant Irish and Suburban Catholics'.

23 For more information about the relationship between Backhaus, Casey and Sullivan, see Dobson, 'Cloth of Gold,' 94–119. John C. Oldmeadow, 'Casey, James Joseph (1831–1913),' in *Australian Dictionary of Biography*, National Centre of Biography, The Australian National University, published first in the *Australian Dictionary of Biography, Volume 3*, 1969, published online 2006, adb.anu.edu.au/biography/casey-james-joseph-3176/text4757; G. R. Quaife, 'Sullivan, James Forester (1817–1876),' *Australian Dictionary of Biography*, National Centre of Biography, The Australian National University, published first in *Australian Dictionary of Biography, Volume 6*, 1976, published online 2006, adb.anu.edu.au/biography/sullivan-james-forester-4666/text7715.

almost all Catholics. For those who formed families or baptised their children, it is difficult to determine whether the contact went beyond such rites of passage, but the actions of William Purcell suggest that Backhaus was held in some esteem. Purcell, the son of an Irish miner in Heathcote, left the town to become a casual labourer for the Victorian railways in Melbourne. It is significant that one of the first duties he performed in Melbourne was to visit Backhaus, who had retired to Brighton. When Backhaus died a few years later, his funeral procession was the largest ever seen in Bendigo.[24]

Backhaus married and baptised many Catholics, almost single-handedly ministering to the Bendigo Catholics from 1852 to 1863, because he discouraged any support from other clergy. His decision to leave Bendigo (from 1863 to 1866 to tour Europe, financed by his shrewd investments) was precipitated by Archbishop Goold's announcement that Backhaus should have assistance. But Bishop Goold experienced difficulties staffing St Kilian's. Sandhurst in the early to mid-1860s was a hostile environment. Water was scarce in summer, even in good years. As noted in Chapter Five, in 1866, the community was brought to a virtual standstill by drought. The horse-driven puddling machines that washed the alluvial gold of Bendigo could not operate without water. To add to the burden, the nascent quartz reefing industry had yet to prove that it was a profitable and viable industry. These enormously rich quartz reefs were opened by company mines in the early 1870s, supporting the local economy until the Great War. In the early 1870s, much of the commercial heart of the city was rebuilt; permanent timber and brick houses replaced tents and slab huts, and a reliable water supply was secured. Local government undertook extensive beautification of Sandhurst, which was gazetted as a city in 1871.[25] But Backhaus remained obdurate in his dealings with fellow clergy and was difficult to work with on his return. His strong personality ensured that he ruled St Kilian's until a new diocese was formed in 1874.[26]

24 For more information about Purcell's visit, see John Lack and Charles Fahey, '"I feel it dreadful to be out of work": Tom Purcell and William Farrell and the Melbourne Labour Market 1875–1908,' *Victorian Historical Journal* 87, no. 2 (2016), 201. For more information about the funeral of Backhaus, see 'Funeral of the Late Very Rev. Dr. Backhaus,' *Bendigo Advertiser*, September 12, 1882, p. 3, nla.gov.au/nla.news-article88575880.

25 For changes to the city in the 1870s, see Michael Roper, 'Inventing Traditions in Goldfields Society: Public Rituals and Townbuilding in Sandhurst, 1867–1885' (MA thesis, Monash University, 1986), see especially pages 33–98.

26 The fullest account of Backhaus and his relationship with fellow priests is in Dobson, 'Cloth of Gold,' 160–174.

Reflecting on the twenty-two years Backhaus spent in Bendigo, Monsignor Byrne wrote, in a *History of the Catholic Church in South Australia*, that Backhaus:

> did very little for the material advancement of religion though abundant means were at his disposal. He built, indeed, a large plain church which was not only unadorned, but even bare. He had no community of nuns or Christian Brothers to conduct Catholic Schools, and if the system of education was not denominational [state subsidised] it is doubtful if he would have gone to the expense of providing religious education for the children under his charge.[27]

Over a hundred and fifty years on, it is impossible to determine whether this rather intemperate assessment was motivated by personal animus towards Backhaus. Nonetheless, there is truth in this assessment. For all his wealth, Backhaus was not a renowned builder nor a promoter of Catholic education.

The building of the first St Kilian's church illustrates Byrne's charges. Unlike earlier settled colonies such as New South Wales and Tasmania, the introduction of self-government in Victoria did not privilege the Anglican Church in the provision of public land. All denominations could apply to the Lands Department for a Crown grant to build churches. Visiting Bendigo in late 1853, Bishop Goold described the place where he celebrated mass as a 'miserable slab affair covered with canvas' that could not accommodate many.[28] In April 1854, Backhaus made use of new land regulations to petition for a church grant. In typical fashion, he precipitately fenced in land before the Crown grant was issued, creating some public outrage. The construction of the church was also handled ineptly. Backhaus fell out with the first contractor, and prolonged legal disputes ensued before another contractor was engaged. Although the church was opened in 1857, it was barely furnished internally, as Byrne suggested. More alarmingly, it was built of inferior stone and on unstable ground. The church was demolished in 1887.

Few issues aroused more heated public dispute in nineteenth century Victoria than the issue of state aid to religion. Some called for state funding of denominational schools. Others were Liberals who were opposed

27 This quotation is reproduced by Rev W. Ebsworth in an article on the Catholic Church in Bendigo. This was one of a series he wrote on the history of the Catholic Church. 'Early History of the Church in Victoria-No. 29', *Advocate*, March 12, 1947, p. 7, nla.gov.au/nla.news-article172486095.

28 Brian Condon and Ian Waters, eds., *The Diary of James Alipius Goold OSA, The First Catholic Bishop of Melbourne, 1848–1886*, Melbourne Diocesan Historical Commission, Catholic Archdiocese of Melbourne (2009), entry for 10 December 1853.

to segregated religious education and argued for a state system that was free, secular and compulsory. In Ireland, under the guidance of Cullen, education was denominational, and Catholics were educated separately from Protestants. Irish clerics bought this desire to Victoria, and Goold was a staunch proponent of state aid to denominational schools. From the discovery of gold until 1862, there were two boards overseeing education: the denominational and national. Local communities could petition for a grant of Crown Land and state support to supplement local funding for a school building, and the state provided funding for the teachers' salaries. Both had to teach prescribed subjects from a specified range of texts and pass inspection. Teachers were chosen locally, and 'each admitted religious instruction, freely in the case of the Denominational school, circumspectly in the case of the National'.[29] While the two boards were reduced to one in 1862, religious instruction was permitted. In 1872, advanced Liberals managed to pass a bill that abolished state aid to religious schools and legislated for free, secular and compulsory education. Attendance at religious schools met the condition of compulsory attendance, but funding was no longer available to them. This was a divisive issue in Australian politics well into the 1960s.[30]

For most of his time in Bendigo, Backhaus favoured state aid for churches; he did little, however, to promote schools for his Catholic parishioners. The first Catholic school in Bendigo was opened in March 1853 in the tent used as Backhaus's chapel. Parishioners raised a tidy sum of £240, and the Denominational Board made two grants of £100 and £166. In the second half of the 1850s, alluvial mining moved north along the Bendigo Creek to Epsom, and an application for a school grant was initially turned down. Backhaus turned to Goold for a loan of £100, on which he promised to pay the existing interest rate. This school was subsequently approved by the board, and schools were opened at Axedale in 1859 and Myers Flat in 1860. These three schools reflected the spread of Irish people on the rural edges of the city and, to some extent, locations where Backhaus had purchased rural land, which he let out. In 1872, a school was opened at Eaglehawk. From the very beginning, Backhaus had difficulties in holding staff, and resignations of teachers unsettled the schools. There was even a dispute over the payment fees to a carpenter contracted by a teacher. Moreover, Backhaus

29 Stuart Macintyre, *A Colonial Liberalism: The Lost Worlds of Three Victorian Visionaries* (Oxford University Press, 1991), 132. For the debate on education, see 128–141.

30 On the *Education Act 1872*, see Denis Grundy, *'Secular, Compulsory and Free': The Education Act of 1872* (Melbourne University Press, 1972).

was lax in his paperwork with the Denominational Board, he neglected the teaching of religion at White Hills (Epsom), and complaints were made by inspectors to the Catholic Schools Committee. In 1863, Backhaus answered the criticism of the inspector, stating that he was 'not a man for schools' and was shortly about to leave the district. On the eve of the passing of the 1872 Act, just over 1,000 children were educated in five local schools; most of the young Catholics attended non-Catholic schools, and there was no formal provision for secondary education.[31]

The Diocese of Sandhurst

When Backhaus left Bendigo on his European sojourn in 1863, the Bendigo goldfield was at a critical juncture. Puddling mills worked a rapidly diminishing resource, and quartz reefing had still to prove its long-term potential. Drought in 1865–1866 was a terminal blow for puddling. In the year Backhaus left Bendigo, the goldfield was linked to Melbourne by rail, and in 1865, this was extended through to Echuca on the Murray. From the mid-1860s, Bendigo opened rich quartz reefs, and this gave a fillip to local industries – most importantly engineering – and encouraged extensive building for both domestic and commercial purposes. The completion of the Coliban water scheme brought water from south of the divide and made domestic life bearable in dry summer months. After 1865, and particularly after 1869, land bills opened the plains of the north and the high country of the north-east to agricultural settlement. With little experience in hard-rock mining, Irish settlers willingly moved in large numbers to the farming frontier. The town to which Backhaus returned in 1866 was soon to be an important regional service centre to these outlying communities.

It is clear from his scrupulously maintained registers that Dr Backhaus returned assiduously to his priestly duties. But he had lost none of his difficult temperament, and working with his fellow clergy continued to end in fractious disputes. He made little improvement to local church buildings and, as ever, there were concerns about his acquisition of property. Meanwhile, the growth of a bustling regional city and, more importantly, the growth of rural industries and population in the north reduced the ability of ecclesiastical authorities to run affairs from Melbourne. In answer, a new diocese of Sandhurst was established by Rome in 1874. This new diocese

31 For Backhaus and education, see Dobson, 'Cloth of Gold,' 189–98.

covered a vast area, extending from Wedderburn in the west, south to Heathcote and east through the counties of Gladstone, Gunbower, Bendigo and Moira into the high country in the counties of Delatite and Bogong. The Irish influence in Rome ensured that Backhaus, even putting aside his difficult personality and large fortune, had little chance of becoming the inaugural bishop. The new clerical authorities typified the influence of Cardinal Cullen.[32]

Martin Crane, the first Bishop of Sandhurst, was born into a prosperous farming family in Barrystown, Parish of Bannow, County Wexford. His four brothers were ordained as priests, and his only sister was a nun in a Carmelite monastery. After his early education in Wexford, he joined the Augustinian order at Grantstown. Like Cardinal Cullen, Martin Crane had strong links to Rome. He completed his ecclesiastical studies in Rome and was ordained at Perugia in 1841. He spent six years at Grantstown in Tipperary before returning to Rome, where he was head of the Augustinian convent. On his return to Ireland, he was head of the Augustinian convent in Dublin. Like many of his fellow senior clerics, he was a church builder, and one of his significant achievements was erecting the church of St Augustine in Dublin. He was in the United States canvassing for funds to complete this church when he was appointed the first Bishop of Sandhurst. A potent symbol of the interlocking connections of Irish Bishops in Australia was that future Cardinal Patrick Moran of Sydney officiated at his consecration service.[33]

On being appointed to Sandhurst, Crane sought permission for his relative, also an Augustinian priest, Father Stephen Reville, to accompany him to Australia. Reville was born in Wexford in May 1844. At age 14, like Crane, he entered St Peter's College in Wexford for religious and general education. Marked by the head of St Peter's as a highly capable student, Reville was encouraged to enrol at St Patrick's College at Hagworth in the Diocese of Ferms. Instead, he entered the Augustinian Novitiate at Callan, and at 19 undertook studies in Ghent in Belgium. Study here exposed him to a broad range of students from Ireland, America, France, the Netherlands and Belgium. At 23, he graduated as a Master in Philosophy and then in Theology and was ordained as a priest. He studied for a further 12 months before returning to Ireland in 1868. Reville was appointed by Martin Crane,

32 For the reach of Cullen across the anglophone world, see Colin Barr, '"Imperium in Imperio"', 627–31.

33 A. E. Owens, 'Martin Crane (1818–1901),' *Australian Dictionary of Biography*, National Centre of Biography, The Australian National University, published first in *Australian Dictionary of Biography, Volume 3*, 1969, published online 2006, adb.anu.edu.au/biography/crane-martin-3284/text4987.

then the Augustinian Provincial, to the St Lawrence O'Toole's seminary in Dublin, where he worked for almost seven years before moving to Sandhurst in 1875.[34]

Crane and Reville arrived in Victoria in the wake of two major legislative acts that were fundamental in determining the character of the local Catholic Church: an Act introducing free, secular and compulsory education (1872) and Grant's *Land Act 1869*. The *Land Act 1869* was the culmination of almost a decade of legislative experimentation to place settlers on the land, a process examined in Chapter Two. Earlier legislation resulted in extensive tracts of Crown Land passing into the hands of former pastoral tenants in the Western District. In February 1870, the vast area of the Wimmera Plains, the Northern Plains, the high country of the north-east and the forests of Gippsland were opened to selection before survey. The new Diocese of Sandhurst, which straddled the Northern Plains into the high country, proved attractive to Irish migrants. Their demand for land recalled the famine and post-famine agricultural adjustments of Ireland. Backhaus had understood this intense desire for land and had purchased agricultural land near Sandhurst under auction – always an expensive form of land transfer from the Crown – and let out farms to Irish settlers. Successful Irish diggers were also assiduous purchasers of small freehold blocks around the goldfields. In addition, the 42nd section of the *Land Act 1865* permitted unsuccessful diggers to obtain licenses for small agricultural areas, which eventually increased to up to 180 acres. On the eve of the northward movement initiated by the 1869 Act, Irish settlers had proven themselves to be tenacious acquirers of land. They and their children eagerly turned to the prospect of acquiring more land north of the Great Dividing Range and in the high country of the north-east. Crane and Reville arrived in Victoria as these settlers were establishing homesteads.[35]

In the years before the arrival of Crane and Reville, Backhaus allowed mixed marriages and, despite the occasional sectarian dispute, maintained good relations with the Bendigo Protestant elite. When Bishop Goold issued a Pastoral Admonition in June 1872 against the education Act, Backhaus fell into line. On two successive St Patrick's days in 1873 and 1874, he inflamed

34 For Reville, see his obituary: 'Death of Bishop Reville,' *Bendigo Advertiser*, September 20, 1916, p. 3, nla.gov.au/nla.news-article90029176.

35 Charles Fahey, 'A Fine Country for the Irish,' *Australian Journal of Irish Studies* 4 (2004): 190–201. For the effect of selection, see, Charles Fahey, 'The Free Selector's Landscape: Moulding Victorian Farming Districts, 1870–1915,' *Studies in the History of Gardens & Designed Landscapes* 31, no. 2 (2011): 97–108, doi.org/10.1080/14601176.2011.556370.

sectarian tensions by toasting the Pope before the Queen. Backhaus also opposed the construction of a new state school in the Upper Reserve. The political heat over the new education bill may also have pushed him to address Catholic education with more determination. In September 1871, Backhaus announced at Sunday Mass that a new building would be erected for St Kilian's School. The total cost of this was to be £1,500, with £300 donated by Backhaus, and the remainder was to be subscribed to by parishioners.[36]

From his arrival in 1875, the new Bishop Martin Crane adopted a determined ultramontane position by paying particular attention to the supremacy of the church in providing education. In his Pastoral Letter of 1878, Crane exhorted his flock:

> with all our zeal for your salvation, and you parents especially, to send your children to those schools where they will be taught to respect their religion, to adore the name of the Deity, and to revere and love Jesus and Mary. If you neglect this duty, you become the persecutors of your own children, and the enemies of Jesus Christ.[37]

In August 1879, he, like Goold, sought to politicise the issue when he convened a public meeting attended by 1,500 to form the Catholic Education Defence Association. Here, he charged Catholics not to vote for parliamentary representatives who would not support state aid to Catholic schools. According to Kevin Peoples, this inflamed sectarian bitterness and managed to 'drive the Catholic community to the fringes of Bendigo society'.[38]

The issue of state aid to Catholic schools remained an ongoing source of antagonism well into the twentieth century. The education of children was only part of the Devotional Revolution, and in the last quarter of the nineteenth century, Crane, aided by his deputy Reville, who was elevated to coadjutor bishop when Crane returned to Europe in 1882, put in place a system of Catholicism that bore the imprint of Irish Catholicism.

36 'Catholic School, Sandhurst,' *The Advocate*, September 23, 1871, p. 4, nla.gov.au/nla.news-article 170154442. For an excellent account of sectarian disputes see Roper, 'Inventing Traditions,' 237–68.

37 Pastoral letter, Right Rev. Dr. Crane O.S.A. Bishop of Sandhurst to the Clergy & Laity of the Diocese of Sandhurst with the Regulations of Lent for 1878, Sandhurst Diocesan Archives. Only a handful of these survive in the Diocesan Archives. However, the pastoral letters of both Martin Crane and Stephen Reville were published in the *Bendigo Independent* owned by a Catholic layman.

38 Kevin Peoples, 'The Great War And The Churches in Bendigo,' (MA thesis, University of Melbourne, 1979), 4–5.

In undertaking this enormous task across a vast geographical area, Crane and Reville were fortunate to find a new middle class of successful farmers emerging in their diocese.[39]

One of their first tasks was to organise priests for new areas farmed on the vast Northern Plains and in the higher grazing country of the north-east. When recruiting priests, they turned naturally to their homeland, and well into the twentieth century, almost all the clergy were trained in Ireland. There was also a sprinkling of Australian-born priests raised in pious rural households and educated in Sydney towards the end of the century.[40] Crane and Reville also recruited nuns to migrate to Australia and take up teaching duties. There were also plans to bring Christian Brothers to the diocese. While they did not achieve this aim, Reville's experience in Belgium may have encouraged the Marist Brothers from France to come to Bendigo.

Within five years of Crane's arrival, enormous changes had been wrought in the landscape of Catholicism in Northern Victoria. In 1880, the Catholic Registry recorded the personnel of the Sandhurst Diocese as one bishop, 15 priests and one convent (the number of nuns was not recorded). With the spread of settlement, there were now 57 churches (20 erected since Crane's arrival) and 34 schools educating 3,822 pupils. In 1882, Crane, on a visit to Europe for an audience with the Pope, consulted a London specialist to find relief for cataracts. The operation was unsuccessful and resulted in permanent blindness. Much of his administrative duties then fell on Reville. But progress continued to be impressive.[41] For the 1899 edition of the Catholic Registry, the Sandhurst Diocese reported two bishops, 37 priests, six brothers and 87 nuns. By the end of the century, 102 schools had been built in 17 districts for the education of young Catholics, and there were 7 boarding schools for girls, one college for boys, 31 primary schools and eight 'superior' day schools. Across the diocese, 4,500 children were in Catholic primary schools, and 1,000 children were educated by the Sisters of Mercy and the Marist Brothers in secondary schools. While in Dublin, Crane had built a magnificent church; he continued as a builder in Australia, and in September 1901, a cathedral was consecrated in Bendigo

39 For more about the changing wealth of northern farmers, see Charles Fahey, 'The Wealth Of Farmers: A Victorian Regional Study, 1879–1901,' *Australian Historical Studies* 21, no. 82 (1984): 29–51, doi.org/10.1080/10314618408595691.

40 Based on an Excel spreadsheet of priests provided by Donna Bailey, Sandhurst Diocese Archives. For more on the ordination of Australian priest Denis J Grogan, see *Benalla Standard*, April 5, 1900, p. 3. Denis Grogan, a Redemptorist priest, was the son of Martin Grogan, a successful farmer from Devenish.

41 Catholic Registry, 1880, Sandhurst Diocese Archives.

in a ceremony attended by many of the senior Catholic clergy of the newly federated nation, including Cardinal Moran from Sydney and Archbishop Carr from Melbourne.[42]

Lived religion

In his influential study, *The Madonna of 115th Street*, Robert Orsi sought to understand the lived experience of religion among Italian migrants to New York in the twentieth century.[43] Orsi had available rich testimony gathered by observers in the mid-twentieth century, and he undertook numerous interviews. Although we lack such rich evidence for the early Sandhurst Diocese, glimpses of the meaning of religion can be gained from newspaper and other written sources. The success of Crane and Reville in establishing their new diocese undoubtedly owed much to successful agricultural settlement of Northern Victoria, and changes in the social composition of urban Catholics in late nineteenth century Bendigo created a proud community of urban Catholics. While urban Catholics actively celebrated religious services, they frequently demurred from their clergy on political matters, most importantly in support of the Labor Party.

As we have seen, the first Irish arrivals to the Bendigo goldfield were overwhelmingly from rural districts. Few had experience in rock mining, and in the 1870s, they moved out of mining. Initially, they dominated unskilled urban occupations in the centre of the city and on its fringes. By the second generation, unskilled work was still a popular avenue for the Catholics. However, by the late 1880s, a quarter of the Catholics marrying at St Kilian's were skilled manual workers, and a further quarter plied white-collar, professional or business careers. Particularly important was government employment, and the railways were a safe sinecure.[44]

42 Catholic Registry, 1899, Sandhurst Diocese Archives. For the opening of the Cathedral, see 'Opening the New Cathedral,' *Bendigo Independent*, September 30, 1901, nla.gov.au/nla.news-page19061839.

43 Robert A. Orsi, *The Madonna of 115th Street: Faith and Community in Italian Harlem, 1880–1950*, 2nd ed. (Yale University Press, 2002).

44 Marriage Certificates, St Kilian's, 1886–1891, Sandhurst Diocese Archives. In these years, 17.6% of grooms were labourers, 10.5% other unskilled manual workers (largely carters and railway employees), 15.6% miners, 23.6% skilled manual workers, 25.6% white collar employees, business owners and professionals, and 7.0% were farmers. Occupations of parents at St Kilian's school show a similar pattern.

In November 1914, the *Bendigo Independent* celebrated the 77th birthday of Mr Patrick Mitchell, a staunch lay member of St Kilian's parish. At the age of 26, Pat Mitchell, 'harassed by the treatment meted out to the country tenantry in County Leitrim, as well as in other parts of the Emerald Isle', migrated to Victoria and joined the clerical staff of the Railway Department in Castlemaine. Here, he met and married Miss Bridget Williams, a domestic servant, who was also a newcomer to Victoria from County Limerick. From Castlemaine, Pat moved to Rochester in 1874, where land selection had developed heavy traffic for wheat. After four years at Rochester, he transferred to Bendigo so his children could be educated in the schools opened by Crane and Reville. He worked first as a ticket collector, and, in the early 1880s, he was appointed head porter. He retired in 1890. As early as 1870, Mitchell joined the Hibernian Australasian Catholic Benefit Society (HACBS), taking active involvement in 1878 and eventually becoming chair of the St Kilian's branch. In 1914, he was Senior Vice-President of the St Patrick's Day Sports Committee, president of the St Kilian's Conference of the St Vincent de Paul Society (a Catholic welfare group) and one of the promoters of the Sacred Heart Sodality. The Mitchells raised five sons and two daughters, all of whom received 'their whole education from the Sisters of Mercy and from the Marist Brothers'. One son was ordained a priest in Belgium and, in 1914, was a missionary in Ireland.[45]

Pat Mitchell was clearly a hard-working Catholic layman. Others may not have had his zeal yet were prepared to publicly support the church. The *Bendigo Independent*, which was owned by Catholic laymen, ran numerous accounts of well-attended parish activities. In March 1904, after Bishop Reville had returned from twelve months abroad, 700 men attended mass in his honour at St Kilian's and joined him for a communion breakfast in the parish hall. The following year was less well attended, yet some 300 to 400 men sat down to the communion breakfast after mass.[46] While the HACBS was made up of men, women could show their faith by joining sodalities such as the Sodality of the Children of Mary. As members, they met regularly under the direction of a priest, prayed and attended religious services. On the sad occasions of funerals, members of the Children of Mary joined in requiem masses for deceased members. Regular mission

45 'A Veteran Hibernian,' *Bendigo Independent*, November 11, 1914, nla.gov.au/nla.news-article22765 0589.

46 'H.A.C.B.S. Welcome to Bishop Reville,' *Bendigo Independent*, March 14, 1904, nla.gov.au/nla.news-article226998834; 'The Hibernian Society. The Annual Communion Breakfast,' *Bendigo Independent*, March 27, 1905, nla.gov.au/nla.news-article227775949.

services were well attended. In April 1911, for example, Prior Devlin from the Carmelite order in Middle Park ran a retreat for members of the men's branch of the Sodality of the Sacred Heart. With services running for a week, the cathedral was packed with such 'a number of persons that could fill every seat and leave a few standing'.[47] On special occasions, religious ceremonies could become large-scale outdoor festivals. In December 1916, the Annual Procession of the Most Holy Sacrament at St Aidan's Orphanage was estimated to have drawn an attendance of 2,000.[48]

Religious devotion did not preclude disagreeing with clerical authorities over politics. In the decade before the war, Bishop Reville became a strident voice calling for the reintroduction of state aid to Catholic schools. This cause was also taken up by Daniel Mannix, the new coadjutor Bishop of Melbourne, when he arrived in Australia in 1913. At both Federal and State elections, Catholic voters were called upon to support candidates who were in favour of state aid. Yet the decade before the Great War also witnessed an increasing focus on class issues, most importantly, the regulation of the labour market through wages boards and arbitration courts. In Sandhurst, Bishop Reville tacitly supported non-Labor candidates. Lay Catholics, it would appear from the high Labor vote in the eastern side of the city, nonetheless threw their support behind Labor. They voted for Protestant members of parliament and joined Methodist miners in supporting Labor.[49]

Catholic laymen, coming from rural backgrounds, were particularly successful in the rural parishes of the diocese, both on the edges of goldfields urban communities and in more isolated agricultural districts settled under the selection acts. Irish Catholic farmers were overrepresented in probate valuations among successful farmers.[50] Rural Victoria proved particularly propitious for a community of devout Catholics.

47 'Sacred Heart Cathedra. Mission Service,' *Bendigo Independent*, April 24, 1911, nla.gov.au/nla.news-article227807651.

48 'Procession at St Aidan's,' *Bendigonian*, December 7, 1916, nla.gov.au/nla.news-article91380327.

49 Peoples, 'The Great War And The Churches in Bendigo,' 24–40. There was no Catholic quarter in Bendigo. Catholics were over-represented in the centre of the city and on its eastern side. Methodists were over-represented among miners and lived disproportionately on the western side of the city. Both east and west of the city returned majorities for Labor after 1905.

50 The average size of estates probated by Irish Catholic farmers in the counties of Bendigo, Rodney and Gunbower between 1897 and 1899 was £1,575.

John Sweeney was a rare example of an Irish Australian Catholic who left a detailed account of his life as a land selector at Baulkamaugh on the Northern Plains. Catholicism was a critical part of his life and the life of his family. He wrote in his journal:

> We lost our mother on the 5th April 1893 after only 3 days of illness. Mother was at Holy Communion on Holy Thursday and then at Chaple [*sic*] on Easter Sunday, and died the next Wednesday night. The Priest came here Tuesday morning, Mother was always a great lover of her Church, and when we were in Castlemaine would never miss a Sunday, summer or winter out here of course there were years we only had Chapel once a month, and often less than that but of late years we have a Priest stationed in Numurkah and [for the] last four years about we have two Priests.[51]

This diary entry was a rare personal expression of belief. Catholics also expressed their faith in their wills by leaving bequests for their parish priest to celebrate masses for the 'repose of the soul'. Walter Quinn of Elmore, with an estate of £3,261 in 1898, left £10 to the parish priest at Rochester. More generous was John Tehan of Nanneella, who left the same parish priest the substantial sum of £300 in 1897. This was more than two years' salary for a Melbourne clerk or skilled tradesman. In addition to leaving £10 to the well-endowed parish priest of Rochester, Henry Shean left £25 for an altar at the smaller church at Corop.[52]

The lived religion of Catholic settlers was demonstrated regularly in the rural press by the lengths they undertook to build churches. Finance for new churches was raised by local parishioners. Settlers usually donated land. As a community, they cleared this land and frequently supplied the materials to erect the churches, as well as giving their labour for actual construction. Women were also actively involved, and they catered for dances and ran bazars to raise money. Building churches was not a one-off activity. As the community became more settled and farmhouses, outbuildings and fences passed from the rough early days to more prosperous purchased materials, communities built new and more substantial churches. Prosperous parishes

51 John Sweeney, Diary, c. 1977 – c. 1909, Box 332/6 MS 6668, entry for 1893, State Library of Victoria. For more on Sweeney, see Charles Fahey, 'John Sweeney and the Making of an Australian Farming Landscape: A Micro-Level Study of Baulkamaugh and Katunga, 1877–1955,' *Provenance* 10 (2011): 66–78.

52 156/305 Robert Quin: Will; Grant of Probate, VPRS 7591/P0002, Public Record Office Victoria; 64/735 John Tehan: Will; Grant of Probate, VPRS 7591, P0002, Public Record Office Victoria; 65/256 Henry Sheahan: Will; Grant of Probate, VPRS 7591, P0002, Public Record Office Victoria.

also built halls that could double as local Catholic schools.[53] In the early twentieth century, Jack Fahey helped to rebuild St Joseph's Church at Dederang. The first wave of settlers built a rough church with a shingle roof in 1883. In 1913, the community decided a more substantial structure was needed. Tim and Pat Arundel carted lime, cement and timber from the Yackandandah railway station – an overnight trip on rough roads. Bricks for the church were burnt on the property. Thomas Goonan and his brother Bill Goonan cut the firewood to fire the brick kiln. 'Well organized' balls, dances and race meetings were staged to raise money, and the church was opened 'free of debt' on 8 November 1914. By the date of the opening, Mick Fahey had moved his family to East Malvern in Melbourne and joined the local congregation at St Mary's. Jack Fahey continued to support St Joseph's, and he later rode his bicycle from Melbourne to Dederang and helped re-paint the church. Jack and his wife Ella lived to see their children express their faith in Melbourne, and one son, John, joined the Jesuits while their daughter Eileen joined the Presentation Congregation.[54]

Conclusion

Even before the arrival of incoming Bishop Martin Crane and his assistant Father Stephen Reville, frictions arose with the incumbent Henry Backhaus over travel funds from Ireland to Victoria. Despite uneasy relations with Crane, Backhaus continued as a priest in Sandhurst Diocese until 1881, when he retired to Brighton. He died in 1882 and left a Victorian estate assessed at £76,771. The bulk of this sum (essentially the real estate) was left to three trustees and was accumulated for 20 years, after which an annual income would be made available to the 'clergyman of St Kilian's church', provided he was a secular priest. But Crane and Reville eventually gained control of the estate.[55] In the interim, they borrowed from the mining magnate George Lansell to finance the construction of a cathedral. Building of the cathedral commenced in 1896, and, although only partially completed, it was consecrated in 1901, the year Crane died. Becoming

53 The Sandhurst Diocese Archives has files on most churches in the diocese. These files have drawn extensively on the files of rural newspapers. A particularly revealing folder is that of the former Devenish church.

54 Jack Goonan and Edna Arundel, 'Centenary St Joseph's Dederang, 1883-1903,' unpublished typescript on the history of St Joseph's, Sandhurst Diocese Archives. This manuscript contains a wealth of information on Irish Catholic settlers in the Gundowring and Tawonga region of North-East Victoria.

55 For the curious history of the Backhaus estate, see Nolan, *The Enterprising Life*, 87–118.

a builder in Australia, Crane continued a practice he had already developed in Dublin, and one that was shared generally by the Irish Catholic Church between 1850 and 1880. Building was integral to the 'Devotional Revolution'. While the cathedral was a magnificent legacy, it was only a minor part of the enormous impact of Crane and Reville. Together, the first and second Bishops of the Sandhurst Diocese imprinted on Bendigo and Northern Victoria a very Irish, and Roman, model of Catholicism. Across the Northern Plains and into the high country, Irish Catholics and their children willingly donated to church and school building and devotedly practised their faith in a way scarcely different from the brothers, sisters and cousins who remained in Ireland. The groundwork laid by Crane and Reville also placed the Catholic Church on a firm foundation to survive after gold. And while many Catholics, like Jack Fahey, migrated to the metropolis, they carried their Irish-Roman faith with them.

Popout Three: Interfaith marriage and Jewish familial identity on the Central Victorian Goldfields: The Herman family experience

The development of secular marriage laws and the rise of companionate unions meant love and matrimony increasingly crossed faith boundaries during the nineteenth century. The ethnic and cultural diversity of goldrush immigration also led to interactions and relationships between various groups, resulting in interfaith romances on the goldfields.

As a result, married couples found themselves positioned between two faiths and religious communities, thereby complicating the religious identification of their families and children. Even for families who clearly favoured one faith identity above the other, the dual religious and communal links of partners continued to complicate their belonging.

This was the case for Solomon Herman and Elizabeth Oxlade in Ballarat. Solomon Herman was born in Russia in 1836 and first arrived in the Victorian colony sometime in 1854. This colonial sojourn was short lived, as Herman soon sailed to England to undertake rabbinical studies.[1] Upon completion, Herman sailed back to Ballarat, where some of his immediate family had settled, including his father Samuel, who was officiating as the minister for the Ballarat Hebrew congregation. In 1861, thirteen-year-old

1 Australian Jewish Historical Society to Professor Geoffrey Bolton, File 1758, Australian Jewish Historical Society, Sydney Archive.

Elizabeth Oxlade, who was baptised at Lambeth St John the Evangelist, England in 1848, arrived in the Victorian colony with her parents and first settled in Woodend before relocating to Ballarat.[2] Oxlade and Herman soon became intimately acquainted. Whether Samuel knew of his son's choice was unclear, though later efforts suggest the couple tried to keep their relationship, including their marriage, a secret from Solomon's family. Solomon and Elizabeth's civil intermarriage shaped the religious and social identity of their family, as the pair made active decisions concerning their family's Jewish religiosity and communal belonging. This did not necessarily mean movement away from Judaism, but rather a renegotiation of the margins, markers and meanings of a Jewish identity. Such negotiations were not, however, unique to the Herman family.

In the middle of the century, marriages between persons of different faiths or nationalities were common in the Victorian colony. For the years 1855 to 1860, an estimated 43.5 per cent of marriages in Victoria were between persons of different national or religious backgrounds; for 1866 to 1871, this number increased to 51.6 per cent.[3] Such marriages were mostly between white colonialists of different Christian denominations, for instance, between Protestant Englishmen and Irish Catholic women; however, unions also occurred between white and Chinese or Indigenous persons. Relationships between white settlers and Indigenous people were viewed through an assimilationist lens, whereas unions between Chinese and white colonialists were often portrayed as 'degrading'.[4] Despite the degree of suspicion and at times contempt shown towards such unions, they remained relatively common and were generally accepted. As Kate Bagnall has noted, recent research has shown that relationships between white women and Chinese men occurred with surprising frequency.[5] Such interfaith unions were relatively uncommon for the Jewish community. In Bendigo and Ballarat, intermarriages were most likely to be between Jewish men and

2 'A Pioneer of the 'Sixties,' *The Daily News*, November 3, 1933, p. 8, nla.gov.au/nla.news-article 84998193.

3 Pauline Rule, 'Women and Marriage in the Irish Diaspora in Nineteenth-century Victoria,' *The Australasian Journal of Irish Studies* 8, (2008/2009): 51.

4 Katherine Ellinghaus, 'Absorbing the "Aboriginal Problem": Controlling Interracial Marriages in Australia in the late 19th and early 20th Centuries,' *Aboriginal History* 27, (2003): 203, doi.org/10.22459/AH.27.2011; Kate Bagnall, 'Rewriting the History of Chinese Families in Nineteenth-Century Australia,' *Australian Historical Studies* 42, no.1 (2011): 63, doi.org/10.1080/1031461X.2010.538419.

5 Bagnall, 'Rewriting,' 77.

Christian women who later converted to Judaism.[6] Marriage to Jewish partners on the early goldfields required a degree of mobility, access to resources and familial connections. Jewish men may have sought wives in the larger British Christian population because of the huge imbalance of the sexes on the goldfields. It is significant that the partners they chose were white, British Christians. There are no recorded indications that goldfield Jewish people married to any other group, religion, or race. Jewish men may have felt that they had more in common with white British women. Similarities in culture, a white colonial settler status and a shared social class may have provided the basis for marriage, rather than their religious identity. Indeed, this history of strong identification and 'almost complete acceptance' by non-Jews contributed significantly to Jewish intermarriage and assimilation.[7] As such, these interfaith unions had likely been founded upon compatibility and affinity.

Shifting ideas about marriage and spouse selection influenced the choices made by Jewish people regarding their partner and family. From the mid-eighteenth century, individuals increasingly selected their partners based on 'love', at times against parental and communal opinion.[8] This evolving form of marriage selection affected Jewish unions slightly later than more dominant Christian groups, becoming more noticeable after Jewish political liberties increased at the end of the eighteenth and early nineteenth centuries.[9] The rising availability of civil law marriages across much of the Western world from the nineteenth century allowed intermarriages to occur without conversion.[10] This provided individuals with an even greater choice in partners. On the Central Victorian Goldfields, such ideologies influenced Jewish intermarriages, as they did for Solomon Herman and Elizabeth Oxlade.

6 See 'Family Notices,' *Bendigo Advertiser*, December 11, 1879, p. 2, nla.gov.au/nla.news-article88209253; 'Lawlessness,' *Jewish Herald*, April 9, 1880, p. 6, nla.gov.au/nla.news-article149433912; Nathan Spielvogel, *Annals of the Ballarat Hebrew Congregation* (item box number AB175), B44 Australian Jewish Historical Society Institutional Archives, collections.ajhs.com.au/Detail/objects/7416. When Elizabeth Oxlade converted, her name was changed to Leah.

7 Lazarus Morris Goldman, 'The Early Jewish Settlers in Victoria and Their Problems (Part I),' *Jewish Historical Society Journal* 4, part 7 (1958): 335; Suzanne D. Rutland, 'The Jewish Community in New South Wales, 1914–1939,' (MA thesis, University of Sydney, 1978), 75.

8 Egon Mayer, *Love and Tradition: Marriage Between Jews and Christians* (Plenum, 1985), 75.

9 Ibid., 64.

10 Ibid., 43.

Expecting their first child when Miss Oxlade was eighteen, the couple decided to marry. They travelled to Geelong in 1869 to be wed by civil law rather than by Jewish or Anglican church rites.[11] On the marriage register, Herman used a false name: Isidore Hamburger.[12] This was likely a deliberate strategy employed by Herman to evade recognition and prevent news of his intermarriage from reaching his family. It was unlikely to be a means to hide his Jewish identity, as the pseudonym was like other well-known Jewish names in the colony. As a result, the first few children born to the couple were given Hamburger as a last name, not Herman. This meant that they could still identify with a Jewish name. The couple moved to Bendigo in 1872, and Elizabeth converted to Judaism, changing her name to Leah. Solomon and Leah were then married again, this time under Jewish law.

Once settled in Bendigo, Solomon and Leah raised a large family. They were heavily involved in the local Jewish community, with their children attending the Hebrew school and celebrating Jewish coming-of-age ceremonies in the local synagogue.[13] Solomon Herman acted for a time as president of the local Hebrew congregation committee and the community's *mohel*, a person trained to perform circumcision ceremonies.[14] Herman's marriage to a convert did not diminish his religious standing within the Bendigo community, nor his faith. Herman occupied one of the highest lay committee positions available and was woven into the religious institutional framework of the community. Solomon and Leah Herman established a Jewish family despite strict rabbinic law that marked their marriage void and their children as non-Jews. This reveals the complications that infused colonial interfaith marriages and familial identities.

11 Marriage Register of Isidore Hamburger (Solomon Herman) and Elizabeth Oxlade, File 1758, Australian Jewish Historical Society, Sydney Archive.

12 Ibid.

13 See 'Sandhurst Hebrew School,' *Jewish Herald*, June 17, 1881, p. 6, nla.gov.au/nla.news-article149434092; 'Sandhurst Hebrew School,' *Jewish Herald*, December 29, 1882, p. 4, nla.gov.au/nla.news-article149433598; 'Sandhurst,' *Jewish Herald*, March 1, 1889, p. 9, nla.gov.au/nla.news-article149550739; 'The Bendigo Advertiser,' *Bendigo Advertiser*, December 24, 1883, p. 2, nla.gov.au/nla.news-article88524611; 'The Rifle Clubs,' *Bendigo Advertiser*, May 6, 1885, p. 2, nla.gov.au/nla.news-article88536097; 'The Synagogue,' *Bendigo Advertiser*, November 24, 1886, p. 2, nla.gov.au/nla.news-article88917404.

14 'Sandhurst,' *Jewish Herald*, June 6, 1890, p. 4, nla.gov.au/nla.news-article149548811; 'A Possible Compromise,' *Bendigo Advertiser*, July 29, 1882, p. 2, nla.gov.au/nla.news-article88628860; 'Advertising,' *Bendigo Advertiser*, December 22, 1883, p. 3, nla.gov.au/nla.news-page9067242.

The Herman family navigated Leah's non-Jewish status and potential disapproval from Solomon's family to form a Jewish family based upon their felt identity and self-presentation. The religiously observant Herman family relied on expanding understandings of Jewish familial identity to rework personal and organisational limits of belonging. These familial identities, developed through and against religious law, were not without contention and conflict as couples navigated communal censure and battled institutional denials. On the Central Victorian Goldfields, the formation of a Jewish family and their identity did not become a binary choice between the rejection of or commitment to rabbinic law and Judaism. Rather, it became one of deep personal, familial and religious negotiation. Jewish families continued to form despite the many challenges of interfaith marriage, demonstrating the growing power of personal choice and self-identification that is central to modern identity.

7

Militant Protestant sectarianism in a religiously plural community: Why Bendigo failed to become a 'Protestant city'

The Reverend Henry Worrall was a Methodist minister who carried his religious mission directly into the political arena.[1] While commemorating the 'Battle of the Boyne' in July 1906, he addressed members of the Orange Lodge at Eaglehawk and asserted that since Federation, there had been 'an organised political effort … in Australia to turn the whole of the Commonwealth into a great Irish Roman Catholic State'.[2] Here, Worrall drew upon a familiar discourse of 'embattled Protestantism', a religious and cultural perception imported to the Australian colonies along with British organisations like the Loyal Orange Institution (LOI).[3] Worrall's speech adhered to three themes identified by historian Andrew Gill as characteristic of the 'Battle of the Boyne' sermon genre.[4] Worrall first stirred anxiety about Catholic conspiracy and the supposed threat that Catholic influence in the

1 The Methodist denomination of the Protestant Church began as a revival movement within the Church of England under the leadership of the Reverend John Wesley.

2 'Sectarian Savagery,' *Bendigo Independent*, July 9, 1906, p. 3, trove.nla.gov.au/newspaper/article/227761135.

3 Linda Colley, 'Britishness and Otherness: An Argument,' *Journal of British Studies* 31, no. 4 (1992): 320, doi.org/10.1086/386013.

4 Andrew Gill, '"To the Glorious, Pious and Immortal Memory of the Great and Good King William": The 12th of July in Western Australia, 1887-1930,' *Studies in Western Australian History* 10 (1989): 79.

Australian Labor Party posed to Australian democracy. He then articulated 'a view of history' that affirmed the Protestant character of Britishness and the British Empire.[5] His reference to a third familiar theme gained the hearty laughter of the audience. Worrall declared, by way of conclusion, 'Thank God Bendigo is a Protestant city, despite that we are sectarian savages'.[6] Orange Lodge members like Worrall often denied accusations of LOI bigotry or provocation in their speeches. They claimed that their views and actions safeguarded social values of 'toleration and liberty'.[7] The applause of this invested crowd, however, did not represent the success of the militant Protestantism in the context of religiously plural Bendigo.

This 1906 speech tried to affirm Protestant ascendancy and to stir local sectarian tensions, not by denying LOI intolerance, but by illustrating the apparent prejudice of Bendigo's Roman Catholic Lord Mayor, Luke Murphy. Worrall referred to a public address given by Murphy on 3 June 1906, where Bendigo's Protestant majority were apparently vilified by his reference to 'sectarian savages'. As Lord Mayor, Murphy had received a delegation advancing Irish Home Rule in June 1906. At the conclusion of a colourful procession to the Town Hall, led by Hibernian Society members in full regalia, the mayor told the cheering crowd that:

> as the son of Irish parents he felt deep sympathy with the object of the delegates' mission and was convinced that as long as sectarian savagery was suppressed and truth and reason allowed to prevail, the day was not far distant when Home Rule would be an accomplished fact.[8]

This 'inopportune expression', according to Reverend Worrall, demonstrated 'bad taste' and slandered the majority of Bendigo's citizenry when used by 'the civic head of the Protestant city of Bendigo'.[9] The LOI fraternity at Eaglehawk concurred with Worrall's complaint because militant opposition

5 LOI members interpret the Battle of the Boyne as pivotal to British national development because Protestant Prince William of Orange defeated the Catholic forces of King James II of England and VII of Scotland, leading to his ascension to the British throne. Worrall's recount affirmed the story's importance to the LOI some 217 years later. Andrew Mycock, James W. McAuley, and Jonathan Tonge, 'Loyalism, Orangeism and Britishness: Contemporary Synergies and Tensions,' in *Ulster Loyalism after the Good Friday Agreement: History, Identity and Change*, ed. J. McAuley and G. Spencer (Palgrave Macmillan, 2011), 116; Warwick Frost and Jennifer Laing, *Commemorative Events Memory, Identities, Conflict* (Taylor and Francis, 2013), 39.

6 'Sectarian Savagery,' *Bendigo Independent*, July 9, 1906, p. 3, trove.nla.gov.au/newspaper/article/227761135.

7 Gill, '"To the Glorious,"' 79.

8 'The Irish Delegates,' *The Argus*, June 4, 1906, p. 6, nla.gov.au/nla.news-article10035475.

9 'The Irish Delegates,' *The Argus*, June 11, 1906, p. 6, nla.gov.au/nla.news-article10039927.

to Irish Home Rule was a central object of the Orange movement. Murphy later asserted that when using the term, he referred to both Irish Catholics and Protestants. He also explained that it did not apply to 'respectable members of the Protestant community' in Bendigo.[10] Despite Murphy's claims to the contrary, it is apparent that both the Protestant LOI and the Roman Catholic Hibernian Society of Bendigo nurtured cultural memories of conflict under the auspices of fraternity. Yet this drive by certain clerics and community leaders to maintain imported sectarian agendas and distinctions was not always successful.

The transfer of religious views and practices from the metropole to the colonies was a dynamic process. Churches and societies were required to alter their religious expectations and adapt their observances to meet local Australian conditions. In this chapter, we argue that despite efforts to the contrary, the unique conditions of the Central Victorian Goldfields compromised the direct exportability of Irish sectarianism in the period 1890 to 1914. This is remarkable given that sectarian hostilities flared during the introduction of state-based secular education in late nineteenth century Victoria, becoming an electoral issue in all state elections from 1900 to 1914, as we note in Chapter Eight.[11] In the same period, sectarian questions and the spectre of a Catholic block vote influenced federation debates and, during the early twentieth century, the development of the two-party political system in Australia.[12] Nevertheless, defensive cultural Protestantism that prevailed in metropolitan centres did not consistently appear in the regional centre of Bendigo.

Understanding the local industrial context of the time, including the prevalence of mining-related illness and controversies over 'gold stealing' by mine employees, provides insight into local discontent with religious movements that ranked imported politics above tangible local needs. These case studies explain why sectarian Protestant religious fraternities encountered resistance in Bendigo during the period, regardless of the Protestant denominational adherence of most settlers.

10 'The Irish Envoys,' *Bendigo Independent*, June 23, 1906, p. 8, trove.nla.gov.au/newspaper/article/226929420.

11 Gregory Melleuish, 'Religion and Politics in Australia,' *Political Theology* 11, no. 6 (2010): 909–27, doi.org/10.1558/poth.v11i6.909.

12 See Scott Denis McCarthy, 'Federation, Sectarianism, and the Catholic Middle Class in Australia,' *Journal of the Australian Catholic Historical Society* 44 (2023): 50; Richard Broome, *Treasure in Earthen Vessels: Protestant Christianity in New South Wales Society, 1900-1914* (University of Queensland Press, 1980); Walter Phillips, *Defending 'A Christian Country': Churchmen and Society in New South Wales in the 1880s and After* (University of Queensland Press, 1981).

Gold digging, faith and the British Empire

Gold diggers of British descent who enthusiastically upturned the creeks and gullies of Bendigo drew upon the values and systems of the British Empire to support and justify their activities. Their shared ideals included the value of hard work, support for private enterprise and belief in social progress, all of which drew upon and strengthened Britain's ambition to lead the world in trade and politics.[13] Colonial acquisitions also supported Britain's expansionist aims by providing a forum for the visible exercise of power (through British law and order) and for the display of British moral superiority. The swift transplantation of Christian religious institutions and other national cultural organisations supported this process. Christian churches of all denominations recognised the empire as creating 'opportunities for the construction of transnational spiritual networks' that extended their geographical reach and influence.[14] Yet Hilary Carey notes that by 1851, when gold diggers descended upon Central Victoria, the forms of religion actively endorsed by colonial governments as celebrating British virtues of imperial loyalty, freedom, tolerance, justice and civic duty were 'assumed to be a "generic" Protestantism'.[15] As Linda Colley observes, since the 1700s, British nation-building efforts had supported the growth of Protestantism and systematically opposed Catholicism. Common sentiment included perpetual enmity towards Catholic states abroad and hyper vigilance for the 'conspiratorial menace' of Catholics within.[16] The reign of Queen Victoria also saw the rise of the 'cult of the monarch', a new forum for anti-Catholic sentiment that became a unifying force in the empire. Loyalists perpetuated the notion that Catholics were a constant threat to the British monarchy and the 'Protestant empire'.[17] As Australian colonies approached Federation in the 1890s, many citizens understood civic and religious liberties from this standpoint. They sought to extend Protestant influence into the new Australian state despite the absence of an established church in British

13 Philippa Levine, *The British Empire: Sunrise to Sunset* (Taylor & Francis Group, 2013), 94.

14 Hilary M. Carey, *God's Empire: Religion and Colonialism in the British World, c.1801–1908* (Cambridge University Press, 2011), 4.

15 Although, as Elizabeth Offer has argued, non-Christian settlers including Jews upheld these values and aspired to full social inclusion in settler society. See Elizabeth Offer, 'The Formation of Goldfields Anglo-Jewry: How Jewish Settlers Negotiated Judaism, Class, and Britishness on the Central Victorian Goldfields, 1851–1901' (PhD thesis, La Trobe University, 2021). Carey, *God's Empire*, 5.

16 Colley, 'Britishness and Otherness,' 317.

17 Levine, *The British Empire*, 12; Colley, 'Britishness and Otherness,' 318.

settler colonies and regardless of the secular underpinnings of Federation.[18] The moral and social advancement of Australia, in their view, would be best served if the constitution acknowledged Divine Providence and guaranteed religious freedom within a framework of ascendant civic Protestantism.[19] In the context of Bendigo's goldfields, such convictions found expression in Worrall's claim that demographic dominance of Protestants made Bendigo a 'Protestant City'. Below, we consider why the assertion of this civic identity by Protestant activists garnered local opposition. We do so by examining a devastating industrial crisis in the period of 1890 to 1914 and the apparent neglect of victims by Protestant organisations. These conditions reduced the appeal of sectarianism locally despite the resurgence of support for Protestant 'Greater Britain' in Bendigo just prior to and during the First World War. This enthusiasm for empire has been recognised as occasioning 'a vigorous and largely unified civic Protestant proclamation'.[20]

The establishment of Christian religion on the Bendigo goldfield

New alluvial mining communities are characterised by transience and dispersed settlement, with infrastructure designed to meet immediate needs at minimum expense.[21] Such was the case on the Bendigo goldfield, where worship services were initially conducted in the open air and under canvas. Methodist lay preacher James Jeffrey, a Cornish miner, apparently preached the first Methodist sermon from a tree stump in Golden Square in 1852.[22] 'Cornish Methodism' was then known for its demonstrative exuberance. One observer recounted a 'Cornish conversion' at a White Hills revival meeting in 1853, where a tall, strongly built miner came forward in the meeting:

18 A. E. Cahill, 'Catholics and Australian Federation,' *Journal of the Australian Catholic Historical Society* 22 (2001): 9–30; Stephen A. Chavura, John Gascoigne, and Ian Tregenza, 'A Secular Constitution? The Federation Debates,' chap. 6 in *Reason, Religion, and the Australian Polity: A Secular State?* (Routledge, 2019).

19 Richard Ely, 'The Forgotten Nationalism: Australian Civic Protestantism in the Second World War,' *Journal of Australian Studies* 11, no. 20 (1987): 59–67, doi.org/10.1080/14443058709386944.

20 Ely, 'The Forgotten Nationalism,' 60.

21 Peter Bell, 'Social Approaches to an Industrial Past: The Fabric and Structure of Australian Mining Settlements,' in *The Archaeology and Anthropology of Mining*, ed. A. Bernard Knapp, Vincent C. Pigott, and Eugenia W. Herbert (Routledge, 1998).

22 Clarence Irving Benson, *A Century of Victorian Methodism* (Spectator Publishing Co., 1935), 148.

> and fell flat on the gravel floor as if he had been shot. He groaned through the disquietude of his soul but soon found the Divine peace, and then jumped up and leaped over seats, and kissed and shouted as to frighten some of us who had never seen it after this fashion.[23]

Methodist revivalist outreach meetings burgeoned on the Bendigo goldfields, encouraging the erection of five tent chapels in Bendigo's mining localities during 1852. By December 1852, the first slab church had been erected in Golden Point.[24] Reverend William Butters reported in late 1853 that the Central Victorian Goldfields (including Ballarat, Bendigo and Castlemaine) boasted ten canvas and two wooden places of worship, with 72 local preachers conducting 100 weekly services for more than 3,000 people.[25] Yet Butters lamented the 'migratory habits of the diggers' which hampered the smooth function of societies and church organisation.[26]

As the population of Bendigo stabilised, citizens constructed permanent public institutions. Eaglehawk, Long Gully and Golden Square became noteworthy for the concentration of nonconformist places of worship. These churches and chapels were most frequently built by Methodist 'connexions'; the Wesleyan Methodists (est 1852), Primitive Methodists (est 1854), Bible Christian fellowships (est 1864) and United Free Methodists (est 1866).[27] The predominance of Methodist connexions in Bendigo reflected both the historic incidence of schism within the Methodist denomination and the cultural backgrounds of the mining workforce.[28] As we will see in Chapter Eight, when alluvial prospecting gave way to company-based quartz mining between 1861 and 1871, it attracted wage-earning migrants who had developed skills for deeper mining in their home country. Travis McHarg attests that half the workforce in Bendigo mines had Cornish heritage by 1881.[29] Although doctrinal disagreement fostered the development of these different expressions of Methodism, nationalistic sensibilities also

23 Blamires and Smith, quoted in Travis McHarg, *The Bible Christian Church in Victoria 1850s–1902* (Mercia Press, 2011), 117.

24 Frank Cusack, *Bendigo: A History* (Heinemann, 1973), 53.

25 Benson, *A Century of Victorian Methodism*, 100.

26 Ibid.

27 Ibid., 457.

28 Benson, *A Century of Victorian Methodism*, 293. Connexionalism refers to the circle of Methodist churches connected to one another in a supportive network. The term signifies a relationship between persons and groups and was used to describe the 'principle and pattern of church life' among Methodists, *Dictionary of Methodism in Britain and Ireland*, 'Connexionalism,' dmbi.online/index.php?do=app.entry&id=684; Charles Fahey, 'Peopling the Victorian Goldfields: From Boom to Bust, 1851–1901,' *Australian Economic History Review* 50, no. 2 (2010): 157, doi.org/10.1111/j.1467-8446.2010.00298.x.

29 McHarg, *The Bible Christian Church*.

informed their ability to attract worshippers. The highly fissiparous nature of Protestant non-conformity, as Jackson notes, also 'supplied the basis for limited … differentiation from England' as evident among the religious adherence of 'Scots, Irish, Welsh, Cornish and Breton peoples'.[30] Such was the case in colonial Bendigo, where Cornish distinctiveness was closely interrelated with religious identity. Congregants in the Primitive Methodists and Bible Christian churches on the goldfields, for example, were primarily from Cornwall and also Devon.[31] Cornish mine workers thus established ethnic enclaves with familiar religious infrastructure to serve the needs of their communities.[32]

The same industrial shift that consolidated the long-term residency of miners with Southwestern English heritage also saw other ethnic groups leave Bendigo to seek opportunities outside the mining sector. This included a large minority of Irish Catholic alluvial miners. Many Catholics settled in nearby agricultural districts with the aid of Father Henry Backhaus, the Catholic priest whose financial schemes encouraged the formation of 'a right staunch and respectable catholic yeomanry in this country'.[33] Backhaus, discussed in Chapter Six, hoped to entrench the Catholic faith in the district, irrespective of the fortunes of mining. The Methodist connexions thus became less culturally distinct as Bendigo advanced as a city.

Social mobility and Methodist unification

Social mobility, we suggest, also reduced the cultural differences that had distinguished the various Methodist congregations on the goldfields. These included the Wesleyan Methodist, Primitive Methodists and Bible Christians. Anticipating reunification in 1876, the Australian Methodist connexions optimistically commented that doctrinal accord had been reached 'in all

30 Alvin Jackson, 'Ireland, Scotland, Wales, Britishness and the UK, 1800–1925,' in *Nordic Experiences in Pan-Nationalisms: A Reappraisal and Comparison, 1840–1940*, ed. Ruth Hemstad and Peter Stadius (Routledge, 2023), 222.

31 Renata Howe, 'Methodism in Victoria and Tasmania, 1855–1902,' in *Methodism in Australia: A History*, ed. Glen O'Brien and Hilary M. Carey (Routledge, 2015), 48.

32 Fahey, 'Peopling the Victorian Goldfields,' 156; '"Foreign to Their Feelings as Freemen": Liberal Politics in a Goldfields Community, Bendigo 1853–1883,' *Journal of Australian Colonial History* 10, no. 1 (2008), 166.

33 Charles Fahey, 'Happy Valley Road and the Victoria Hill District: A Microhistory of a Victorian Gold-Mining Community, 1854–1913,' *Victorian Historical Journal* 90, no. 2 (2019): 289; Malachy J. Nolan, 'Henry Backhaus - A Different Type of Pioneer Priest,' *The Australasian Catholic Record* 85, no. 1 (2008), 64.

essentials', but nevertheless, their 'present divisions' took another twenty-five years to resolve.[34] Wesleyan Methodists were numerically the larger and wealthier of the Methodist congregations in Australia. Their worship was arguably styled after London's urban-middle-class Wesleyan congregations.[35] Primitive Methodists and Bible Christians were characterised as working people or were identified with Cornish ethnicity. Primitive Methodism in mining areas of Central Victoria also became associated with the Labor movement and trade unionism.[36] As these congregations became more affluent in Bendigo, and as their churches and chapels 'became more comfortable', the distinct 'emotional warmth and enthusiasm' of Cornish evangelicalism waned, apparently losing its 'sharp edge'.[37] This gentrification process can be attributed in part to Methodist emphasis upon self-help and the formation of Mutual Improvement Associations.[38] These bodies fostered the intellectual interests of congregants and created networks that boosted social and employment opportunities. As members gained skills through 'leadership and administration in the church', they also developed qualities 'suitable for success in business' and experienced social mobility.[39]

Beneficial associations were forged in the pews, for example, between mine managers responsible for recruiting workers and working-class congregants like Cornish miner and diarist Richard Pope, who rose to become a manager.[40] When Pope moved to Bendigo, he found a Cornish enclave in the 'economically and culturally cohesive St Just Point-Long Gully community'.[41] Pope worshipped at the Long Gully Bible Christian chapel and took membership with their Mutual Improvement Association. This association was formed in 1869 to address want among workers and to deliver social advancement. Newspaper advertisements noted that mutual self-help was necessary because 'the wealthy and well to do tradesmen, mining managers, and others do not contribute according to their means

34 Benson, *A Century of Victorian Methodism*, 307.

35 McHarg, *The Bible Christian Church*; Julie-Ann Ellis, '"Cross-Firing over the Gulf": The Rift Between Methodism and the Labour Movement in South Australia in the 1890s,' *Labour History* 64 (1993): 89–102.

36 Howe, 'Methodism in Victoria and Tasmania.'

37 McHarg, *The Bible Christian Church*, 119–120.

38 Howe, 'Methodism in Victoria and Tasmania,' 50.

39 Renate Howe, 'Social Composition of the Wesleyan Church in Victoria During the Nineteenth Century,' *Journal of Religious History* 4, no. 3 (1967), 212, doi.org/10.1111/j.1467-9809.1967.tb00289.x.

40 Fahey, 'Happy Valley Road,' 292.

41 Charles Fahey, 'Richard Pope: A Miner's Life in the Inland Corridor,' in *Outside Country: Histories of Inland Australia*, ed. Alan Mayne and Stephen Atkinson (Wakefield Press, 2011), 144.

towards so desirable an object'.[42] Uplift strategies benefited members of the Bible Christian and Primitive Methodist connexions, which increasingly reflected aspirational middle-class values. A letter to the editor of the *Bendigo Advertiser*, penned by the pseudonymous 'Willing to join', complained in May 1871 that Young Men's Mutual Improvement Associations had become so exclusive that 'many an humble youth' were discouraged 'from either joining or continuing as a member'.[43] The author concluded that the attractions of the 'billiard room' and the 'young lady behind the bar' would therefore 'allure away many who otherwise would be WILLING TO JOIN'.[44] Social justice activism, which had fostered these improvement associations within Methodism, now dwindled in some congregations.[45] Methodism attracted increasing critique for moralising temperance and anti-gambling campaigns that targeted so-called 'working-class' vices.[46]

By 1901, Methodists represented a large Bendigo demographic, at 27 per cent of the total population. This was nearly double that of Methodists in the general population of Victoria, which stood at 15.2 per cent.[47] When amalgamation between the four major Methodist denominations was effected in 1902, the Bendigo circuit (including outlying rural areas) boasted 36 church buildings and 1,318 voting adult members.[48] The demographic dominance and middle-class orientation of Methodist churchgoers impacted the character and aims of other Protestant organisations that drew upon Methodist membership, including the Orange fraternities.

42 'Mutual Improvement Association,' *Bendigo Advertiser*, February 27, 1869, p. 1, nla.gov.au/nla.news-article87917724.

43 'Young Men's Mutual Improvement Society,' *Bendigo Advertiser*, May 23, 1871, p. 2, nla.gov.au/nla.news-article87969750.

44 Ibid.

45 Ellis, '"Cross-Firing over the Gulf,"' 94.

46 Ibid.

47 Kevin Peoples notes that Bendigo's Methodist population was 27% in 1901. The state average population of Methodists was 15.2%, according to the 1901 census, Australian Bureau of Statistics, '1301.2 – Victorian Yearbook, 1902', 33, www.abs.gov.au/AUSSTATS/abs@.nsf/DetailsPage/1301.21902; Kevin Peoples, 'The Great War and the Churches in Bendigo' (PhD diss., University of Melbourne, 1979), V.

48 The number of 'cultural' Methodists who align for census purposes is distinct from involved or voting members. Methodist Union vote of 1,896 recorded adult members 781 Wesleyans, 249 Primitive Methodists, 203 Bible Christians, 85 United Free Methodists (Total 1,318). 'Methodist Union Vote,' *Bendigo Advertiser*, September 5, 1896, p. 5, nla.gov.au/nla.news-article88990799; 'Methodist Union,' *Bendigo Independent*, January 8, 1902, p. 3, nla.gov.au/nla.news-article227554568.

Friendly societies and fraternities in Australia

Social vulnerability motivated Bendigo miners to join friendly societies and fraternities. Gaining access to the resources, networks and influence of these associations assisted the material, political and religious aspirations of mining families. Members paid into these funds to mitigate future risk. Sick and injured members of friendly societies, or their bereaved dependents, could access 'formalized reciprocity' via financial support from pooled contributions.[49] In 1882, Sandhurst miners invested in more than forty friendly societies, as Frank Cusack notes. The most affluent and influential of the friendly societies in Bendigo was the Independent Order of Rechabites, which drew upon the religious loyalties of Bendigo's Cornish population. Historic connections with the British temperance movement also encouraged trust in the sober intentions of the organisation and hence in their investments.[50] Retailer Fletcher Jones, whose father worked in Bendigo's gold mines, recalls family privations caused by industrial injury and illness:

> The concept of sick pay did not exist. We belonged to a Friendly Society, but there were still some charges to see the doctor. [In times of need] Every morning there would be a plucked chicken under cover on the back verandah, and we never never knew who put it there. 'Known only unto God,' Dad would say; we suspected that the Cornish miners were the good Samaritans.[51]

Jones observes that the 'milk of human kindness' saw needed commodities 'handed over the fences of the workers.' Such action was more common 'amongst the poor than in the average affluent home', according to Jones.[52] Many workers also joined fraternities including the Masonic Lodge to augment these informal support systems.

49 Daniel Weinbren, 'Fraternal Networks of Victorian Norfolk,' *Family & Community History* 24, no. 1 (2021): 25, doi.org/10.1080/14631180.2021.1924457.

50 Cusack, *Bendigo: A History*, 170.

51 Fletcher Jones, *Not by Myself: The Fletcher Jones Story*, 2nd ed. (Kingfisher, 1984), 5.

52 Jones, *Not By Myself*, 5.

The doctrine of 'universal brotherhood' motivated fraternities to dispense 'hospitality and charity [and] material benefits' to members.[53] Freemasonry, for example, was based upon principles of exchange and trust. It offered intangible benefits of mutuality, including access to networks of credit, commerce and information, which diminished social stratification and even mitigated sectarianism and antisemitism.[54] As a non-proselytising society, Bendigo's Freemasons formally held that their 'principles and practices' would require them to admit 'any honourable true and good man, whatever his creed or country, who voluntarily seeks admission', including Catholics.[55] The Masters and past Masters of Bendigo's Golden, Corinthian and Zenith lodges publicly defended their non-sectarian admissions record in 1891. This was following public accusations to the contrary by the Catholic Bishop of Sandhurst. Sectarian discord, the Freemasons argued, neither advanced nor damaged the interests of either group, but rather caused 'strained relations to usurp the place of peace and amity which should prevail amongst all the classes'.[56] Australian Catholics and Protestants had 'for the most part' coexisted peacefully, according to Jeff Kildea:

> It was mostly charismatic individuals, on both sides, who stirred up trouble. As against the headline-grabbing rantings of these sectarian warriors, there are many stories of interdenominational cooperation, particularly in rural areas.[57]

Orange fraternities provided welcoming stages for the performances of these 'sectarian warriors.' The LOI, whose activities we outlined in the introduction, had been modelled on the success of the Masonic Lodge. They replicated Freemasonry's structures and developed similar ritual and regalia, but their bold championing of anti-Catholic exclusivity made them distinctive.[58] Local studies have shown that the benefits of associationalism

53 David Fitzpatrick, 'Exporting Brotherhood: Orangeism in South Australia,' *Folk Life* 45, no. 1 (2006): 77–102, doi.org/10.1179/flk.2006.45.1.77.

54 Daniel Weinbren, 'The World in 1913: Friendly Societies,' *The Historian: The Magazine of the Historical Association*, no. 120 (February 6, 2014), 12–16, www.history.org.uk/publications/resource/7082/the-world-in-1913-friendly-societies; Jessica Harland-Jacobs, 'All in the Family: Freemasonry and the British Empire in the Mid–Nineteenth Century,' *Journal of British Studies* 42, no. 4 (2003): 466, doi.org/10.1086/376462.

55 'The Bishop of Sandhurst and Freemasonry,' *Bendigo Advertiser*, February 28, 1891, p. 5, nla.gov.au/nla.news-article88958686.

56 Ibid.

57 Jeff Kildea, 'Absence or Amnesia: Was the Golden West Really Free of the Noxious Weed of Sectarianism that Blighted Early Twentieth-Century Australia?' *Journal of the Australian Catholic Historical Society* 40 (2019), 134.

58 Fitzpatrick, 'Exporting Brotherhood.'

drew a wide range of non-conformists into Orange lodges in Australia, including people without family ties to Ireland.[59] But as Diane Hall persuasively argues, such members necessarily consented to the 'Protestant libertarian vision' that formed an essential component of group symbolism, rhetoric and public action.[60] Orange leaders proclaimed this overarching focus as the strength of the movement. At Bendigo's annual Battle of the Boyne address of 1889, Reverend J. T. Kearns noted that:

> The Orange Lodge was not a club, it was not a friendly society; there was no benefit to be gained by it in that sense, but they gained by it in intellectuality, in loyalty, in real devotion to the Empire and the Constitution under which they lived.[61]

This esoteric and sectarian focus, however, strained the good will of Bendigo's citizens towards the LOI, particularly as a long-entrenched industrial problem gained increasing public recognition. The experience of mining-related disability and death was shared across religious divides, fostering empathy and willingness to maintain good social relations. But as Reverend Kearns noted, the Orange Lodge was not a society formed for mutual material advantage. The defence of Protestantism was the LOI's primary and most public goal. This focus annoyed onlookers who were aggrieved that strident ultra-Protestant voices emanated from increasingly comfortable Methodist pulpits. Newspaper correspondents suggested that the mission to the needy had faltered in these churches. Yet Orangeism flourished in the city. Kevin Peoples records that the movement in Bendigo grew from one lodge in 1900 to four in 1904 and seven in 1907. Five of these lodges were found in 'the heart of Methodist territory', and all were 'serviced by Methodist clergy from Methodist buildings'.[62] Religious and political controversialists from within these ranks wrote incessant 'letters to the editor' to promulgate their views locally.

A prominent public voice defending Protestant ascendancy in the Federation period was Andrew N. Collier, a painting contractor from Long Gully. Public responses to Collier's extreme minority views provide important

59 Ibid.; Dianne Hall, 'Defending the Faith: Orangeism and Ulster Protestant Identities in Colonial New South Wales,' *Journal of Religious History* 38, no. 2 (2014): 211, doi.org/10.1111/1467-9809.12007.
60 Hall, 'Defending the Faith,' 211.
61 'Commemoration of the Battle of the Boyne,' *Bendigo Advertiser*, July 13, 1889, p. 5, nla.gov.au/nla.news-article88588926.
62 Peoples, 'The Great War,' 30.

historical insight into debates over sectarianism.[63] The following debate reveals the entanglement of religious, political and class issues in Bendigo. A local resident wrote numerous letters to the *Bendigo Independent* in 1903, contesting the views of Andrew Collier. Using the pseudonym 'Respect for Your Neighbour's Religion', the correspondent made a link between declining church attendance, anti-Catholic sentiment and lack of social justice action in Protestant churches:

> The people are so disgusted with having Rome and the evils of Rome continually drummed into their ears that they stay away … Can [ultra-Protestants] point to any refuge for the fallen supported by their section. No; and yet they are insidiously endeavouring to destroy Catholic institutions … Have they a charitable institution of any description? No … My humble advice is to act up to the teachings of the Bible, love God and your neighbour, and respect his religion.[64]

A condition known colloquially as the 'miners' complaint' strained the resources of charitable institutions in 1903. Associated with the debilitating symptoms of tuberculosis, the condition resulted in chronic poor health and early death.

The miners' complaint

Miners' complaint, also known as miner's phthisis, is caused by the inhalation of sharp particles of silica dust that become embedded in the lungs following exposure to underground drilling and blasting. Local physicians first recognised this silicosis-related lung condition as an industrial disease in 1889. They instigated a public campaign for mitigation via ventilation and other improvements to underground working conditions. Physicians formed this view in the early 1870s, but because gold mining was an important local industry, successive governments 'ignored recommendations of their own commissions … and passed legislation that did not protect miners from

63 Although Andrew Collier asserted that he was not associated with the Orange Institution, he consistently articulated Orangeist, anti-Catholic and ultra-Protestant principles. His critics, who represented both moderates within the Protestant community and the Roman Catholic sector, often presumed a connection.

64 'Reply to A. N. Collier,' *Bendigo Independent*, September 19, 1903, p. 5, nla.gov.au/nla.news-article223414771.

silica dust exposure'.[65] Ambivalence towards industrial lung disease was then common. The tone adopted by officials in the Victorian Yearbook of 1902 reflects these views. The writer notes that although tubercular mortality in Melbourne had fallen 'from 27.8 per 10,000 of the population in 1888 to 19.8 in 1901 and 18 in 1902', cases in Bendigo and its suburbs were much higher:

> The average yearly rate per 10,000 of the population during the 13 years prior to 1902 was 24.8 … the excess of these rates being no doubt attributable in part to mining operations … and to the selection of that city as a place of residence by consumptives.[66]

Lung disease was acknowledged as a common feature of Bendigo life during the Federation era. Fletcher Jones (b1895) recalls hearing miners 'coughing up their lungs' as he walked to school. Even as a child, he was aware that 'every third miner's cottage had a sheet fixed between the verandah posts, hiding a poor man with "miner's complaint"'. These invalids were 'seemingly abandoned to their fate', because the disease was associated with negligent occupational behaviour and with family predisposition to tuberculosis.[67] But as the role of occupational hazards gained credence, the unmet needs of invalid miners gained increasing attention.[68] Tom Mann, Labor leader in Great Britain, criticised the Bendigo Council of Churches as showing 'a want of sympathy for the oppressed and poverty-stricken' in 1894.[69] When Mann visited Bendigo in 1903, he reiterated his call for churches to support 'righteous distribution of wealth'.[70] Amid such suffering, the high-profile involvement of Protestant clergy in the Orange Lodge became the target of public criticism. In 1905, one correspondent recalled that 'Catholic and Protestant could hold out the "hand" of friendship to each other' until social relations were soured by sectarian extremists. Their views had:

65 Beris Penrose, 'The State and Gold Miners Health in Victoria, 1870–1910,' *Labour History*, no. 101 (2011): 35–36.

66 Australian Bureau of Statistics, '1301.2 – Victorian Yearbook 1902', 196, www.abs.gov.au/AUSSTATS/abs@.nsf/DetailsPage/1301.21902?OpenDocument.

67 Jones, *Not By Myself*, 5.

68 Sandra Kippen and Yolande Collins, 'Radical Reformers: The Role of Medical Men in Improving Working Conditions in the Bendigo Goldmines, 1890–1910,' *Journal of Australasian Mining History* 2 (2004): 75-89.

69 'The Council of Churches,' *Bendigo Advertiser*, November 24, 1894, p. 4, trove.nla.gov.au/newspaper/article/88937130/9080321.

70 'Rousing the Workers,' *Bendigo Independent*, September 28, 1903, p. 3, trove.nla.gov.au/newspaper/article/223406351.

> emptied the churches and starved the ministers and forced them into all sorts of devices and un-Christian tactics to try and collect a congregation for the sake of a living. But respectable Protestants say they hear enough of that sort of thing the six days of the week and think they can serve God better in their own homes than go to church on Sunday to hear their neighbours or perhaps their customers belied and scandalised.[71]

Reverend Henry Worrall was prominent among the Methodist clergy liable to the accusation of using sectarianism and political controversy to 'collect a congregation' in this period of population decline in the city. Arriving in Bendigo in 1906, 16 years after his ordination to the Wesleyan ministry and 25 years before he became the Grand Master of the Loyal Orange Institution of Victoria (1931–1933), Worrall was known as a 'crusader who pulled no punches from his church pulpit'.[72] Renowned for 'pack[ing] to the doors any building in which he was a speaker', Worrell was surprised to observe that of the 1,200 members of his Bendigo congregation, only 20 were working miners.[73] Worrall ascertained that only five per cent of all Bendigo miners were then churchgoers, yet in the recent past, 'the miner of Bendigo was a man who went to church and loved God and made the darkness of the mines ring with the praise of God'. He attributed the change to 'a low moral tone – a false conception of ethics.'[74] The common but unauthorised mining practice of gold theft, Worrall determined, had caused the decline in church attendance.[75] He sought to reverse the trend in 1908 to 1909 by preaching a series of sermons on the text 'Thou Shall not Steal'. His lectures drew raucous crowds and prompted angry responses from the Miners Association. While denying that 'those who dropped out of the church were all thieves', Worrall suggested that underground codes of

71 'Mr. A. N. Collier and the Councillors,' *Bendigo Independent*, November 1, 1905, p. 4, nla.gov.au/nla.news-article223518602.

72 Tas Vertigan, *The Orange Order in Victoria: Origins, Events, Achievements, Aspirations and Personalities* (Loyal Orange Institution of Victoria, 1979), 105.

73 Vertigan, *The Orange Order*, 105; Worrell was a divisive figure whose temperance and anti-gambling campaigning saw him dubbed 'wowser Worrall' and 'Worry-all, the meddling minister' by his critics. John Lack, 'Worrall, Henry (1862–1940),' *Australian Dictionary of Biography*, National Centre of Biography, The Australian National University, published first in the *Australian Dictionary of Biography, Volume 12*, 1990, published online 2006, accessed August 25, 2021, adb.anu.edu.au/biography/worrall-henry-9191/text16233.

74 'The Rev. Henry Worrall and the Miners,' *Bendigo Independent*, January 6, 1908, p. 3, nla.gov.au/nla.news-article227891677; 'Gold-stealing. National conscience wanted,' *The Argus*, March 8, 1909, p. 7, nla.gov.au/nla.news-article10706526.

75 'Gold-stealing,' p. 7.

brotherhood, including unionism, pressured miners to tolerate dishonesty: 'There seems to be a kind of freemasonry underground by which a man was ostracised who would dare to tell his master of an infringement of the law.'[76]

Miners 'dropped out of the church', according to Worrell, 'because men who steal gold do not like to listen to the Gospel of God, but only to the Gospel that appeals to certain sentiments of theirs'.[77] Worrall alludes here to contemporary debates on socialism and its relationship to Christianity. Christian Socialism or 'Social Christianity' emerged in 1890s Britain and the USA as a respectable, welfare-oriented expression of socialism that attempted to apply the principles of Christianity to the realities of modern industrial life. Advocates sought to achieve social unity and improve the lives of the working classes through education and housing initiatives.[78] Christian Socialism was prevalent in the newly united Methodist church, especially among Primitive Methodists in industrial towns like Newcastle (New South Wales) and Creswick (Victoria). But in Bendigo, the cause was taken up by Anglicans.[79]

The formation of a 'Christian Social Union' (CSU) at Bendigo in 1909 was contemporaneous to Worrall's gold-stealing controversy and reflective of efforts among Anglican clergy to secure pluralist church practice under the leadership of evangelical bishops. The new Bendigo Diocese of the Church of England was formed in 1901, and the first two bishops, Henry Archdall Langley (1901–1906) and his brother John Douse Langley (1906–1917), were both conservative evangelical Anglicans. The brothers, who trained in Sydney, were both known as 'uncompromising in their loyalty to the Evangelical revival' and pietistic in their rigid moral standards.[80] Conservative evangelicalism often prioritised transcendent values, like gospel-focused mission and conversion, ahead of material concerns, like social action. Humanitarianism drew the attention of liberal Anglicans (both liberal evangelical and Anglo-Catholics), as it represented a 'practical manifestation of the Kingdom of God on earth'.[81] The actions

76 'The Rev. Henry Worrall and the Miners,' *Bendigo Independent*, January 6, 1908, p. 3, nla.gov.au/nla.news-article227891677.

77 Ibid.

78 Guy Featherstone, 'Co-Workers with Christ: George A. Brown and Christian Socialism in Victoria 1885-1894,' *Victorian Historical Journal* 77, no. 1 (2006): 16–33; Chavura, Gascoigne, and Tregenza, *Reason*, 146–147.

79 Howe, 'Methodism in Victoria and Tasmania.'

80 Stuart Piggin and Robert D. Linder, *The Fountain of Public Prosperity: Evangelical Christians in Australian History, 1740-1914* (Monash University Publishing, 2018), 332.

81 Piggin and Linder, *The Fountain*, xxviii, 316.

of the Bendigo CSU exemplify these different priorities and approaches to Christian mission. The CSU sought to investigate the 'conditions under which the miners of Bendigo are working' and to ameliorate their material circumstances.[82] Trade unionists supported the new Anglican committee, suggesting that 'it was evident that some good was trying to be done for the miner and not preaching on gold stealing'. One supportive miner noted that ministers of religion:

> had been branded in Bendigo as small-hearted clergymen … It came as a relief to find that the miners still had somebody who was willing and able to take up their side [adopting] a commonsense view of helping [the miners] instead of branding them as a class.[83]

One outcome of this new connection between Bendigo clergy and miners was a delegation of CSU members to the Minister for Mines on 5 May 1909. Led by the Venerable Dean McCullagh, the delegation sought improved working hours and conditions for miners who gave their 'time, labour and lives' to their employment. Under such circumstances, McCullagh suggested:

> Some miners doubtlessly argued that they would die at a comparatively early age and their widows and children would be left destitute. The temptation to steal gold was very strong … [because] in some of the mines it was impossible to labour without becoming afflicted with disease.[84]

While McCullagh stressed that he understood but did not condone gold stealing, he highlighted the tragic context of the practice. In the previous three months, one local priest had buried three miners aged under forty years, leaving destitute widows and orphans. Another concluded that if miners did not receive good wages, 'the temptation placed before them grew even greater'.[85] The Minister for Mines noted the empathy of the Bendigo clergy and 'cordially endorsed' the Dean's remarks, repudiating earlier accusations

82 'Miners and the Churches,' *Bendigo Advertiser*, March 5, 1909, p. 3, nla.gov.au/nla.news-article 89405675.

83 Ibid.

84 'Mining Conditions of Bendigo,' *Bendigo Independent*, May 6, 1909, p. 4, nla.gov.au/nla.news-article227897611.

85 Ibid.

of 'small heartedness'. The CSU later hosted lectures on 'unemployment relief systems in Germany', 'Socialism and poverty' and proposed a new venture to assist unemployment relief.[86]

Conclusion

Contrasting standpoints over the 'gold stealing' adopted by ultra-Protestant Methodist ministers and Christian Socialist clergy drew fresh attention to the class-related failures of Protestant denominations in Bendigo. Prior to the advent of the Bendigo CSU, Protestant churches had not adequately addressed the impacts of debilitating industrial disease nor the waning employment opportunities that threatened mining families. This neglect saw the Methodist churches of Bendigo become less relevant to the working classes during the period 1890 to 1910. The loudest Methodist voices then emanated from comfortable middle-class pulpits. Drawing upon imported hatred, these Methodist preachers advocated sectarian division in Bendigo, where the pressures of industrial illness and decline in the mining sector had dampened community enthusiasm for Irish sectarianism. This harmony prevailed for a brief period just prior to the advent of the First World War, when support for the British Empire and assumed civic Protestantism again soared.

86 'Christian Social Union. Helping the Miners,' *Bendigo Advertiser*, June 24, 1910, p. 3, nla.gov.au/nla.news-article100528067.

8

Faith after the gold rush: Demographic and religious change

The formation of churches in nineteenth century Bendigo was borne out of the patterns of migration to both the alluvial rushes of the 1850s and the later phase of quartz reef mining. While migrants brought with them adherence to the major Christian denominations of the United Kingdom – Scottish Presbyterians and Irish Catholics, for example – hard-rock mining required special skills and technology, and this industry fostered distinctive migration patterns. Methodists – drawn in large numbers from Cornwall – gave Bendigo and the goldfields a distinctively nonconformist character. Moreover, the various divisions of Methodism that flourished in Cornwall and in the industrial north of England – Bible Christians and Primitive Methodists – were strongly represented on the goldfields. Migration of Germans, often from the Harz Mountains where hard-rock mining was undertaken, helped to establish a small but strong Lutheran community on the goldfields. Finally, gold brought Christians into contact, frequently for the first time, with migrants from South and East Asia and their diverse religious practices. Gold led, therefore, to a rich engagement between religious faiths (see Figure 8.1).

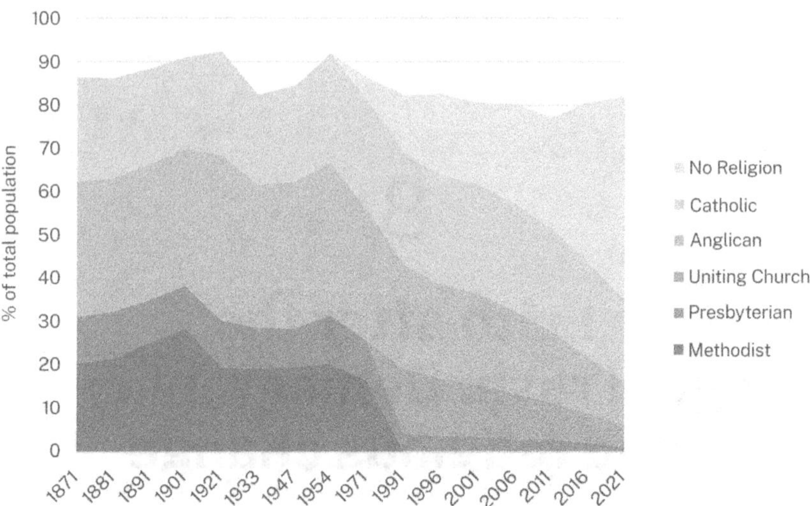

Figure 8.1: Major Christian religions in Bendigo, 1871–1921

Source: Compiled by the authors.

This diversity and intercultural engagement was built on gold. Gold, however, was a wasting asset. The rapid demographic shifts and outward migration precipitated by the decline of the gold industry created significant organisational challenges for most of Bendigo's churches, some more than others. As we have seen, church buildings and infrastructure were resource intensive. They were expensive to establish in the first instance and could not easily move to match population shifts. With the collapse of mining during the First World War, the population of Bendigo declined, and local churches faced a severe loss of members. In the latter twentieth century, Bendigonians also left institutional religion in larger numbers than elsewhere in the country. By the time of the 2021 census, Bendigo was significantly less religious than Australia as a whole, with 48.6 per cent of people identifying with 'no religion' compared with 38.9 per cent nationally. It was also half as religiously diverse, with 4.3 per cent of people nominating a non-Christian religious identity versus 8.3 per cent nationally. The proportion identifying with Christianity, however, remains closer to national statistics (40 per cent v 43.9 per cent).[1]

1 For an overview of religion from the 2021 census, see: 'Religious affiliation in Australia: Exploration of the Changes in Reported Religion in the 2021 Census,' Australian Bureau of Statistics, July 4, 2022, www.abs.gov.au/articles/religious-affiliation-australia.

This chapter will chart these shifts in religious demographics and institutions as Bendigo's gold industry declined by first establishing the religious patterns that gold migration implanted. It will look at the impact of the collapse of mining and how religious congregations adapted to the changing economy of the city until the late twentieth century. The chapter will explore the major trends of religious observance by comparing the histories of two significant Protestant churches, the Golden Square Methodist Church and the All Saints' Anglican Church, with the Catholic Church. It concludes by reflecting on the contemporary census returns on religious affiliation. Using population statistics and the physical infrastructure of different churches enables us to represent broad shifts in religious affiliation over the twentieth century. This facilitates a comparison to the more intimate sources in earlier chapters, which provide a window into Bendigonians' inner spiritual lives.

Religion and the socio-economic structure of Bendigo

It is difficult to obtain good data on religious affiliation from nineteenth century census returns. These published limited information regarding places of birth and religious affiliation. Places of birth were aggregated into countries, and there was no cross-tabulation of place of birth and occupation, nor religion and occupation. A more nuanced picture can be obtained by looking at the records of births, deaths and marriages. Although conclusions drawn from these are often not precise – religion has to be determined by church of marriage or celebrant presiding over interment at death – they do outline general trends.

After 1870, Bendigo became known for its industrial mining. From the early 1870s, a small group of mine owners and investors controlled the mining industry. The more successful of these 'quartz kings', George Lansell and John Boyd Watson, for example, could mix on equal terms with the wealthy mercantile elite of Melbourne and the squattocracy of the Western District. The local wealthy elite, men with £10,000 or more of property in 1891, numbered fewer than a few dozen. More numerous were the men who turned to small-scale mining investment and combined this with property owning, building, commercial enterprises or manufacturing. After 1870, the City of Sandhurst (Bendigo from 1891), the Borough of Eaglehawk and the adjacent rural shires gave employment to a small minority of professionals (lawyers and doctors) and white-collar employees (clerks in commercial or government employment).[2] Men with property of £1,000 or more were fewer than 650 in 1891, or around 4 per cent of men aged 15 and above. Women almost invariably achieved this level of property owning through inheritance. From the late 1870s, the typical Bendigo resident had settled into a life of wage earning. Mining was the dominant form of employment until the First World War; the mining city also offered employment to a range of artisans, building workers, those engaged in transport and the common labourer. In 1891, 33 per cent of male householders in the City of Bendigo and the Borough of Eaglehawk were miners, 29 per cent were skilled tradesmen, and 26 per cent were labourers and other unskilled working men. On the fringes of the city, in the rural shires of Huntly, Marong and Strathfieldsaye, settler farmers were the predominant propertied group.[3]

The human capital that migrants brought to the goldfield had an important impact on how they adjusted to the world of industrial mining. The Irish, who came from the least industrialised regions of the United Kingdom, faced the most testing challenges: less than 2 per cent of the male Irish came from mining families, while almost 60 per cent were the sons of farmers or, more accurately, rural labourers and cottagers. The English (largely because the Cornish were counted as English) in more than a third of cases came from mining families, and just over one in ten originated from farming or agricultural labouring backgrounds. A very small proportion of Scots migrants came from mining backgrounds, and one in ten from farming families. Around a quarter of both the Scottish and English male migrants were the sons of skilled artisans.[4]

In his history of the Bendigo Churches during the First World War, Kevin Peoples argued that the city was divided bitterly by religion from the nineteenth century through to the first decade of the twentieth century.[5] Our discussion of sectarian divisions in Chapter Seven reveals a distinct

2 Since 1992, the City of Bendigo and the Borough of Eaglehawk have been merged with a large rural district to become the City of Greater Bendigo. To approximate this for earlier years, the City of Bendigo (Sandhurst 1871–1891) and the Borough of Eaglehawk have been combined with the rural shires of Huntly, Marong and Strathfieldsaye. The contemporary City of Greater Bendigo is somewhat larger than this area.

3 This picture of wealth is drawn by linking probate records to death certificates and using 'inverse mortality multipliers' to estimate wealth among the living population at the census of 1891. Manuscript Death Certificates were made available by the Registry of Births, Death and Marriages. Probate inventories are available at Victoria Public Record Office, VPRS 28/P0001 and VPRS 28/P0002. This analysis of the occupational structure is drawn from Rate Assessment Books for Bendigo VPRS 16267/P0001, 1891 and Eaglehawk Rate Assessment Books VPRS 16263/P0001, 1885-1891.

4 The background of migrants is drawn from manuscript Death Certificates.

5 Kevin Peoples, 'The Great War and the Churches in Bendigo,' (MA thesis, University of Melbourne, 1979), 18–23.

pattern of class and religious affiliation that nuances Peoples' sectarian thesis, which we expand upon here. Records from the official Registry of Births, Deaths and Marriages, and adopting a broader geographical perspective, show a more comprehensive picture of interreligious relations that reflects the opportunities used by different settler groups. Among the first generation of settlers in Bendigo, the Catholics were clearly the largest group among unskilled labourers. Yet, as a group, they also sought out rural land adjoining the defined urban areas of Bendigo and were over-represented among rural landholders. Peoples was correct in identifying the Presbyterians and Anglicans as dominating the wealthy elite of Bendigo. Together, they made up perhaps 59 per cent of those with assets of £1,000 or more in 1891. This needs qualification. Undoubtedly, the superior educational background provided to Scottish children enabled them to seize business opportunities in their new country, and they were over-represented among the wealthy elite. By force of their sheer numbers in Bendigo, nominal Anglicans dominated the wealthy elite. There were fewer Methodists among the elite, but they made up a high proportion of the working class. Rural Catholics provided a propertied group who gave solid support to their church.[6] They were joined by local Catholic businessmen, including publicans, contractors and provision merchants. Many of these Catholic middle-class individuals shared the values of private morality and public respectability that served as 'subjective class markers' for the Protestant bourgeois.[7] These patterns indicate that individuals from various Christian church traditions navigated opportunities based on subjective class distinctions and established socio-cultural spaces within Australia's predominantly Protestant power structures that drew upon and innovated their original positioning.

To further understand the socio-economic structure of Bendigo, we must acknowledge that the local class character was structured by mining, the major industry. Mining was the largest employer throughout the nineteenth century, and its dominance ensured that among all religious denominations, working men predominated. And, unquestionably, one of the more distinct characteristics of the Greater Bendigo working class was the high proportion of Methodists – Wesleyans, Bible Christians, Primitive Methodists and United Methodist Free Church followers – employed in mining. This facet

6 This is an estimate based on probate records linked to religions listed on death certificates. Among this group with assets of £1,000 or more, 15 per cent were Methodist and 20 per cent were Catholic.

7 Scott Denis McCarthy, 'Federation, Sectarianism, and the Catholic Middle Class in Australia,' *Journal of the Australian Catholic Historical Society* 44 (2023): 53.

of the city endured into the late nineteenth and early twentieth centuries. This factor also shaped the religious and social character of post-industrial Bendigo, as those Methodists who chose to stay in Bendigo after the gold rush had limited avenues for employment. From 1896 to 1899, 39 per cent of grooms marrying in Bendigo gave their occupation as 'miner'. Among miners, half of these grooms were Methodists. The Cornish, Methodist character of the Bendigo mining workforce gave Bendigo its distinctive Protestant feel, and it was this group that experienced the collapse of mining most bitterly.[8]

Nineteenth century church building and sectarian tensions

The extent and size of church buildings in nineteenth century Bendigo indicate the significance of religious community and religious social infrastructure. While the government made land grants to the various churches, church buildings were funded through donations of local congregants. In 1878, the Forest St Wesleyan Church completed extensions to its church that accommodated an average of 650 worshippers at Sunday morning services and 850 to 1,000 for evening services. The neighbouring Congregational Church built seating spaces for 450 and welcomed an average attendance of 250. Even the small congregation of Lutherans had 250 communicants and 125 Sunday school scholars. The geographical reach of religion was also impressive. In 1881, the Anglican Church offered its adherents services at two inner city churches, All Saints' and St Paul's, and smaller churches at Golden Square, Kangaroo Flat, White Hills, Long Gully and Eaglehawk. All congregations, as we have seen, relied on working-class adherents, none more so than the Methodist Bible Christians. Because their ministry relied largely on lay preachers, the Bible Christians were able to hold services at McKenzie St, Long Gully, Sailors Gully, California Gully, Sheepwash, Emu Creek, St Mungo, Redesdale and Horseshoe Bend.[9]

8 This is based on an analysis of manuscript marriage certificates for Bendigo and Eaglehawk, 1896–1899.

9 Churches are listed in G. Stevens and J. W. Burrows, Sandhurst and Echuca districts' residence, trade and mining directory for 3 February 1881, 119–23.

In the nineteenth century, sectarian tensions surfaced on several occasions, at least between religious authorities and local politicians. As early as 1856, Father Henry Backhaus, the leader of the Catholic Church, and the Reverend James Nish, a Presbyterian minister, clashed over the management of the Bendigo Hospital.[10] In 1871, the management of the Bendigo Benevolent Asylum descended into turmoil over the religious affiliation of teachers instructing pauper children at the Industrial School attached to the asylum.[11] Backhaus's opposition to the introduction of free, secular and compulsory education in 1872 was unquestionably the most divisive sectarian issue of nineteenth century Bendigo, and this opposition was maintained with the arrival of Martin Crane as the inaugural Bishop of the Sandhurst Diocese in 1875. Yet, it is likely that these disputes were more the concern of the clergy than the laity.

After 1875, the Catholic hierarchy regularly denounced mixed marriages in shrill pastoral letters at Easter. Catholic parishioners often paid little heed to these strictures, and the demography of immigration undoubtedly softened sectarian differences among the laity. In the early 1850s, patterns of migration saw the arrival of three men for every woman. While government initiatives to bring single women to the colony under assisted migration reduced the imbalance, such efforts went only part of the way to ameliorate the gender imbalance. To avoid bachelorhood, men had little choice but to cross religious divides in search of partners. Father Backhaus, unlike his successors, did not prohibit mixed marriages, and many Irish Catholic women married Protestants. There was a tendency for Cornish migrants to reside on the west side of the city and Catholics on the east side. Nonetheless, these two areas were never single ethnicity districts. And the workplace, even in the mines, saw Catholics working alongside Protestants. The realities of daily life diminished sectarian differences for ordinary working families.[12]

10 William T Dobson, 'Cloth of Gold,' unpublished manuscript, Sandhurst Diocese Archives, 81–89. This unpublished manuscript recounts the part played by Henry Backhaus in the formation of the Catholic Church in Bendigo.

11 See Peoples, 'The Great War,' 1–12. See also Michael Roper, 'Inventing Tradition in Goldfields Society: Public Rituals and Town Building in Sandhurst, 1867-1885,' (Master's thesis, Monash University, 1986), 239–68.

12 Analysis of marriage and birth certificates demonstrates considerable intermarriage across ethnic boundaries. Birth certificates clearly show that, despite some concentration of national groups, all nationalities were dispersed across the city. For the social structure of Bendigo and other gold towns, see Charles Fahey and Alan Mayne, '"All that Glitters ..." The Hidden History of Victoria's Central Goldfields Region,' in *Gold Tailings: Forgotten Histories of Family and Community on the Central Victoria Goldfields* (Australian Scholarly Press, 2010), 1–61.

Religion and declining gold production

In the early twentieth century, religious leaders again brought sectarian tensions to the fore. Both the Catholic and Protestant clergy shared their belief in religious education. As we noted in Chapter Seven, they had differences over how religious education should be developed. With the passing of the *Education Act 1872*, free, compulsory and secular education was established in the colony. The system was designed to replace segregated religious schools in the interest of improving social cohesion and access to education.[13] It needed to be secular, not to exclude faith, but to ensure religious inclusivity: that the teaching of any particular faith wasn't privileged over another. Careful rules were established for the provision of voluntary religious education on state school campuses outside of regular school hours.[14] This became an electoral issue in all state elections from 1900 to 1914. Bishop Reville, the Catholic bishop, opposed this, stating that it would undermine Catholic faith among children in state schools. This was itself a tacit admission that the drive for Catholics to attend non-government schools was often not completely successful, and that in small rural areas, separate Catholic education was difficult.[15] The Catholic clergy called on their faithful to vote against the Labor Party for its failure to support state aid. Senior Protestant clergy were also not friendly towards Labor. The working-class Protestants and Catholics, however, turned to the Labor Party in both state and federal elections in the years leading up to the First World War.

The war itself tore open sectarian strains. Protestant clergy threw themselves wholeheartedly into promoting the war, declaring it to be almost a holy crusade. Bishop Reville was more reticent in his support for the war. When the first conscription plebiscite was called by the Prime Minister Billy Hughes in 1916, the Protestant clergy were strong supporters of the Yes case. In one of his last pronouncements, Bishop Reville stated his objection to conscription. He died in September 1916, however, and his successor Bishop McCarthy was silent on the issue. This undoubtedly soothed sectarian tensions at the clerical level.[16]

13 Marion Maddox, *Taking God to School: The End of Australia's Egalitarian Education?* (Allen and Unwin, 2014), 29–55.

14 Ibid., 39.

15 For the issue in the early twentieth century, see Peoples, 'The Great War,' 31–40.

16 The issue of the conscription plebiscites is recounted excellently in Peoples, 'The Great War,' chapters 2 and 3.

These differences between Catholic and Protestant clergy came at a particularly difficult time for their working-class congregations. From the rise of quartz reefing in the 1870s, outwards migration had been a rite of passage for many of the young men of Bendigo. As mines went deeper in search of more difficult and lower-yielding gold, unemployment rose. From the 1880s, hundreds of young men left the Bendigo goldfields for the Barrier Ranges in New South Wales. In the 1890s, the copper deposits of the Tasmanian West Coast were another means of escape. More important were the great gold mines of the west. By the turn of the century, new mining communities such as Boulder (Western Australia) were familiar to the households of Long Gully. While mostly young men migrated, many families also uprooted themselves to the west. In the early twentieth century, Melbourne emerged from a long depression, and new manufacturing industries and better wages were a powerful lure. For young women, Bendigo was an extremely inhospitable labour market. In Melbourne, new factories in food production, clothing and other consumer needs offered employment on a scale that dwarfed Bendigo and other declining mining communities.[17]

In the late nineteenth and early twentieth centuries, the focus of Bendigo mining moved north into the Eaglehawk district with the rise of the New Moon series of mines. These mines were on an extension of the Garden Gully line reef. In the 1870s, mines on the Garden Gully reef produced fabulous returns for speculators and were the best employers of labour. In the decade before the war, the Garden Gully United mine, the most profitable mine on the Bendigo field, faltered and declared its last dividend in 1908. This was just a precursor to the general malaise that struck the field during the Great War. As mines closed, pumping machinery was turned off, and the rising water table increased the costs of pumping for those mines that struggled on. During the war, the Commonwealth Government banned the export of gold, and the cost of mining materials rose. This led to further closures, and mass unemployment confronted miners and their families.[18]

The ability of churches to withstand the collapse of the mining industry was directly proportional to their wealth and the share of their adherents in mining employment. The impact of the decline of mining and the general drift out of Bendigo was clearly evident in the census of 1921. Between 1901

17 See Charles Fahey, 'Peopling the Victorian Goldfields: From Boom to Bust, 1851–1901,' *Australian Economic History Review* 50, no. 2 (2010): 148–61, doi.org/10.1111/j.1467-8446.2010.00298.x.

18 For a brief account of the failure of the mines, see Ralph W. Birrell and James A. Lerk, *Bendigo's Gold Story* (J. A. & R. S. Lerk, 2001), 86 and 97.

and 1921, the population of Bendigo, Eaglehawk and their adjacent rural shires dropped by 30 per cent from 53,862 to 38,029. Between 1901 and 1921, all religious groups lost population in Greater Bendigo proportionate to their congregation's employment in mining. The Anglican Church lost 14.6 per cent of its nominal adherents, and the figures for the Presbyterians and Catholics were respectively 23.2 per cent and 19.8 per cent. The number of Methodists decreased by half between 1901 and 192, reflecting their demographic presence among working-class miners. This precipitous decline in the Methodist population was further complicated by the 1902 merger of the Wesleyan Methodist Church, the Primitive Methodists, the Bible Christians, the United Methodist Free and the New Connection churches. Undoubtedly, this amalgamation and migration placed strains on smaller chapels, some of which were built adjacent to mines; virtually all households depended on mining breadwinners.[19]

The archives of the Golden Square Methodist Church illustrate the pressure that these demographic shifts placed on both congregations and clergy. They also reveal successful strategies that enabled some parish churches to be resilient in contexts of demographic and financial pressure. In the period of the gold industry's decline, from 1910 to 1930, the Golden Square church saw a high turnover of pastors. In the nineteenth century, leadership had changed every 5 to 7 years; from 1905, this was shortened to around 1 to 3 years before lengthening again by 1930. An anniversary service and fair to raise funds was a vital part of the community life of Golden Square Methodists. In April 1912, they celebrated their diamond jubilee with the return of Reverend William Shaw of Moonta, who had been pastor during the golden jubilee celebrations of 1902, with a congregation of 515 at the Sunday morning service, 780 in the afternoon and 1,031 in the evening.[20] These were record attendances for a church anniversary, with many former members returning for the celebration. During the month of April 1912, a total of 2,300 subscriptions were recorded, which brought in £114. Yet, by 1920, the church was still in a poor financial position. A publication for the 1912 diamond jubilee celebration noted that the 'golden period' of the 'palmy days of Bendigo' was short lived and left a legacy of debt. With

19 For the decline in population, see '2112.0 – Census of the Commonwealth of Australia, 1911,' *Australian Bureau of Statistics*, 1911, www.abs.gov.au/AUSSTATS/abs@.nsf/mf/2112.0; '2111.0 – Census of the Commonwealth of Australia, 1921,' Australian Bureau of Statistics, 1921, www.abs.gov.au/AUSSTATS/abs@.nsf/productsbyCatalogue/7F4430C75D27EA86CA25783A00112DA2?OpenDocument.

20 *Golden Square Methodist Church: Centenary, 1852–1952* (Bolton Bros., 1952), MCL CHU 487, nla.gov.au/nla.obj-44036041.

the continued loss of members by 'removal and a heavy upkeep', averaging £200 per year, this jubilee was seen as a last chance to remove debt. Through the 'indomitable will' of Treasurer G. A. Pethard, the celebrations of 1912 cleared the debt.[21]

Concerns highlighted during the First World War led congregants to make critical evaluations of their church. The Annual Report of 1917 regretted that attendances were way down due to 'removals from the district', mostly to Melbourne, while 'Several of Our Scholars' were still 'fighting for God and Empire'. The Honour Roll for the church contained over a hundred names, with 'great and heroic sacrifices being made in the cause of freedom and righteousness'. Sunday School attendance grew slightly, ladies' and men's bible classes continued throughout the war, while the Girl Guilds was suspended by 1916. While declining attendance could be linked to demographic change, the cause of the decline in religious attendance was attributed to the war and the resulting questioning of faith. One article commented in 1915:

> We are not wanting in earnestness and activity in relation to some aspects of the war, but we are wanting, lamentable wanting, in depth and strength of religious feeling, and in devout and fervent engagement in religious observances.[22]

Historians debate how much the experiences of the First World War shaped people's religiosity, with most scholars now being critical of claims that the war accelerated secularisation.[23]

Perhaps surprisingly, given its more elite profile, the Church of England in Bendigo faced even greater challenges as gold declined. Although the Church of England had established a diocese in Ballarat in 1875, the Bendigo diocese was not created until 1902. The delay came down to two major reasons: divisions over the financing of the Bendigo diocese from lands granted to the Anglican Church in Melbourne, and whether the new bishop was to be the local Archdeacon J. C. MacCullagh or H. A. Langley

21 This paragraph has been compiled from notes and newspaper cuttings collected by James Henry Crump from 1914 to the early 1930s. Crump was Secretary of the Golden Square Methodist Church and Sunday School, Uniting Church Archives, Golden Square Methodist Church, 0168/Box3/Files 6 and 7. See also, *Bendigo Independent*, April 29, 1912, p. 6.

22 Undated newspaper cutting from the *Bendigo Advertiser*, in Crump newspaper cuttings, Uniting Church Archives, Golden Square Methodist Church, 0168/Box 3/ File 6.

23 Philip Jenkins, *The Great and Holy War: How World War I Changed Religion For Ever* (Lion Books, 2014).

from Melbourne. A decision to make funds available for the creation of three dioceses in Wangaratta and Gippsland, as well as Bendigo, settled the issue, and H. A. Langley was appointed the first bishop. All Saints' was chosen as the cathedral church over St Paul's. While the latter possessed a superior building, sentiment favoured All Saints' as the foundation Anglican Church in Bendigo.[24]

This tardiness in establishing a local diocese found the Anglican Church setting up administrative structures during years of declining mining and stringent financial conditions. In February 1912, Wilfred Percival, the Dean of All Saints', reminded his parishioners of their religious duties. He observed:

> We need more whole-hearted devotion to God. This is proved by (a) irregular attendance at Public Worship and at Holy Communion of so many both old and young communicants; (b) the neglect of Sunday Morning Service; (c) the inadequate financial support of our church; (d) scarcity of Sunday School teachers … We need more loyalty to our Church … We need the spirit of obedience to the teaching of our Church.[25]

It is difficult to tell from Percival's lament if he was aware of the financial hardship and emigration of many of his parishioners with the decline of mining, or if he experienced this, too, as a spiritual adversity. It is possible too that Anglicans struggled to adjust to the requirements of voluntary funding, not receiving the level of state support that they had received in England as the established church.

For the Catholic Church, the loss of population was a severe blow, yet the church did not face the same financial struggles as its neighbouring Protestants. In December 1925, the Bishop of Sandhurst saw population loss as a problem facing Australia generally, and he lamented the drift to the capital cities. In Bendigo, the Catholic Church was insulated to a considerable degree against the loss of population from the proceeds of the estate of Catholic priest Father Henry Backhaus, as seen in Chapter Six. In November, opening the new church St Monica's in Kangaroo Flat, Bishop McCarthy, forgetting much of the controversy that had accompanied the terms of Backhaus' will, claimed that the estate paid for practically all the churches in Bendigo, including the Cathedral of the Sacred Heart, of which

24 Keith Cole, *A History of All Saints' Church Bendigo: The Rise and Demise of a Cathedral* (Keith Cole Publications, 1990), 46–48.

25 Cole, *A History of All Saints' Church*, 49.

there was 'no more beautiful example of Gothic art in Australia'.[26] The insistence of the Catholic clergy that children attend Catholic schools, while a significant factor in the formation of resilient Catholic identities, placed a burden on the Catholic laity to pay school fees and donate to school building programs. With the issue of state aid virtually a dead letter, fundraising remained a major activity for Catholic lay groups. In Bendigo, many threw themselves into this endeavour with great fervour, and the annual St Patrick's Day festival in 1921 raised £2,308 for primary Catholic schools.[27] Like their city confreres, rural Catholics raised considerable sums for their church.[28] The first two decades of the twentieth century were generally prosperous years for Australian agriculture, and Bishop McCarthy could count on firm support in the rural districts of his diocese, where attendance at church was high. The financial stability of the Sandhurst Catholic Diocese during this period significantly contrasted with that of Bendigo's dissenting congregations.

A religious revival?

As Bendigo came to terms with the decline of mining, population losses were stemmed to some degree with the development of new industries. Local parliamentary members lobbied for the construction of railway works; land was acquired in 1912, and the workshops opened in 1917. In December 1920, the workshops employed 250. In the 1920s, the state government also expended considerable sums in pursuit of closer settlement on the land. Large properties north of Bendigo were purchased and subdivided into smaller farms – some irrigated and others dryland only – and settlement in the Mallee was encouraged. While these schemes were poorly devised and resulted in financial losses to the state government, they did underpin the role Bendigo played as a service centre. State Government functions in the provision of water, forestry, land settlement and agriculture were located in Bendigo, and private enterprise offered services such as law, medicine and retailing. There was also an attempt to tie local manufacturing to agriculture, most significantly with

26 'St. Monica's Church, Kangaroo Flat,' *Advocate*, November 11, 1926, p. 19, nla.gov.au/nla.news-article171427319; see also 'Holy Rosary Parish, Kensington: Bazaar Opened by McCarthy,' *Advocate*, December 3, 1925, p. 9, nla.gov.au/nla.news-article171411263.

27 'St Patrick's Sports, Bendigo Credit Balance of £2308,' *Advocate*, December 15, 1921, p. 29, nla.gov.au/nla.news-article171244280.

28 See for example a fete in Tatura in aid of the local convent school, 'Garden Fete at Tatura,' *Advocate*, November 4, 1920, p. 27, nla.gov.au/nla.news-article171052435, and 'St Joseph's School, Benalla,' *Advocate*, December 21, 1922, p. 17, nla.gov.au/nla.news-article176525641.

H. M. Leggo's jam factory.[29] From 1921 to 1933, Anglicans, Catholics and Presbyterians lost numbers but less severely than from 1901 to 1921. In the same years, the Methodists slightly increased their numbers.[30]

In the 1920s, the financial position of the All Saints' Anglican Church improved, with local wealthy families donating land and funds for renovating various church assets. By 1924, a committee was formed to consider the 'provision of a Cathedral with … capacity and dignity befitting a provincial city' on the existing site. The architectural design they proposed left the original church's nave intact, while the choir, vestries and Episcopal throne at the front of the church would be rebuilt for a grand total of £80,000. With much debate ensuing over the appropriateness of the existing site, discussions considered the ongoing financial capacity of the church to build a cathedral, but no action was taken to redevelop the church into a grander cathedral.[31] Following several bequests from wealthy congregants, in 1934, new plans were drawn with a 'tapering central spire of 300 feet … [and an] overall length 186 feet, with lofty windows'.[32] The aim of the architects was:

> to conceive a building combining in both plan and design a sense of height and an offering of space ... a free treatment of Gothic has been favoured by the architects, avoiding a copy of period work.[33]

While this was a novel and inspiring design, the plans for the cathedral came during a period of prolonged economic depression, when rural industries were at their lowest ebb since European settlement, and the state government practised a policy of extreme fiscal stringency. In response to high unemployment, birth rates had collapsed, and there were few positive signs that Bendigo would grow. It was, perhaps, naïve optimism to plan an ambitious building project in this climate of economic and demographic decline.[34]

29 Henry Madren Leggo was the son of Cornish Methodist immigrants who developed a successful condiments, preserves and canned foods business. See: australianfoodtimeline.com.au/leggos-founded/; For the development of Bendigo in the pre- and immediate post-war years, see Central Planning Authority, *Resources Survey: Loddon Region* (Melbourne: Government Printer, 1952). For a very brief account of Bendigo between the wars, see Frank Cusack, *Bendigo: A History* (Revised Edition) (Lerk and McClure, 2002), 241–6.

30 Census of the Commonwealth of Australia, 1921; '2110.0 – Census of the Commonwealth of Australia, 1933,' *Australian Bureau of Statistics*, 1933 www.abs.gov.au/AUSSTATS/abs@.nsf/mf/2110.0.

31 Cole, *A History of All Saints' Church*, 58–60.

32 Cole, *A History of All Saints' Church*, 70.

33 Cole, *A History of All Saints' Church*, 70.

34 There is no adequate overview of regional economic development in the 1930s. The Census of the Commonwealth of Australia taken in June 1933 gave an unemployment rate of 31.05 per cent for men of wage and salary earners and 18.72 per cent for women in the combined area of Bendigo and Eaglehawk.

The Presbyterians also had to take concerted action with the collapse of mining to maintain members and meet financial needs. In 1912, St Andrew's, the leading Presbyterian church, recorded 350 communicants on its rolls, with average attendance at 185 each week. Regular attendance fell during the war years, and, according to the church historian, men returned from the war 'nervy and unsettled and had moved away from the church'.[35] By the war's end, the fabric of the church and the caretaker's cottage were in severe disrepair, and stones frequently dropped out of the walls. Church rebuilding was seen as a means of reviving the congregation. A house-to-house drive was undertaken. There was an uptake in attendance and an improvement in finances. In November 1930, the foundation stone of a new St Andrew's was dedicated. To reach a wider audience, the church launched a quarterly magazine, built a kindergarten, and shorter sermons on topical notes were given. These gains were consolidated during and after the Second World War.

Although the Catholic Church lost numbers at each census with the declining population until 1933, Catholics were strong in the practice of their faith. By adhering faithfully to their own educational system, the Catholic hierarchy maintained close contact with children until they left primary school. Strictures against mixed marriages ensured that, nominally at least, both parents were Catholic. Local parish priests visited families, and the bishop closely monitored religious adherence. Unlike the other churches, the Catholics kept detailed censuses of local participation. These demonstrate a very strong participation in the services of the church and its schools. Although it is difficult to accurately align the boundaries of the Catholic Census with the official Commonwealth Census, the local clergy were particularly assiduous in undertaking home visits compared to clergy in capital cities. They kept track of nominal Catholics, and their own count was almost 95 per cent of the number acknowledged in the official count. At this date, almost all the young Catholics of Bendigo and its adjoining shires attended Catholic schools, and the census claimed that 5,743 Catholics took Easter Communion, and there were only 833 who 'failed' in their duty.[36] Priests in Bendigo and its adjoining shires were more successful in reaching Catholics and encouraging participation than their colleagues in the more heavily populated Melbourne Diocese. In his analysis of the parish censuses from inner Melbourne in the early 1930s,

35 Margaret Temple, *The Story of St. Andrew's Church Bendigo, 1854–1965: The Which Has No Past, Has No Future* (Neptune Press, 1984).

36 Diocese Census, 1933, Sandhurst Diocese Archives.

Chris McConville found that priests only made contact 'with perhaps one in three nominal Catholics' and even 'among those with some nominal link with their local church, almost as many failed to meet clerical estimations of practical Catholicity'. This contrasted with the active connections the clergy maintained in Bendigo and its surrounding rural areas.

War and post-war recovery

Throughout Australia, the 1930s was a decade of economic stagnation. In much of rural Australia, superimposed on this was a period of extremely dry weather extending from the late 1930s to a particularly dry year in 1944–1945. The pressures of the threat of invasion forced Australia to increase its industrial capacity, and almost a million service personnel had to be clothed, armed and fed. The arrival of US troops to fight the Pacific War provided a market for significant volumes of food. The war provided opportunities for Bendigo's consumer manufacturing industries, and the Commonwealth Government joined the State Government in providing employment in the engineering sector with the establishment of a Commonwealth Arms Factory. With the coming of peace, pent-up demand – a product of pre-war unemployment and wartime restrictions on consumers – kept wartime manufacturing buoyant. Returning soldiers were keen to establish families. Bendigo joined Australia in the long boom of the 1950s and 1960s. The city's population grew throughout these decades, and the city's domestic architecture moved into the former rural suburbs on the fringes of Bendigo and Eaglehawk. Much of the post-war housing development was located in the new suburbs of Kensington and Strathdale, and in Golden Square and Kangaroo Flat.[37]

Fortunately for Bendigo, there was also significant growth in service industries in this period. During the war, the Commonwealth Government established a cartographic unit in Fortuna, the old mansion of George Lansell, the Quartz King. In the 1950s and 1960s, employment in education expanded with the growth of secondary schools and tertiary training provided by the Bendigo Technical College and a teachers' college. These eventually grew to become part of La Trobe University. In the post-war years, health became a major employer and education for health professionals was provided

37 This overview of the post-war development is drawn from the City of Bendigo Newspaper Cuttings Books. When examined, these were held in the Council Archives. They have been transferred to the Bendigo Regional Archives and are currently not open for access.

by La Trobe University. Bendigo also benefited from mass ownership of automobiles, and better transportation helped local retailing, with the city acting as a regional centre. The strength of this service sector permitted Bendigo to withstand the demise of much manufacturing in the 1980s. In the past 30 years, since the establishment of the City of Greater Bendigo, the city has continued with steady, if not spectacular, growth.

Except for the Catholic Church, the churches of goldrush Bendigo did not grow in line with general population growth. In 1947, in the early years of the long boom, the numbers declaring themselves as Methodists, Anglicans or Presbyterians in the census simply held ground over the numbers recorded in the 1933 census. Over the next quarter of the century, there was some modest growth in nominal allegiance revealed to the census taker. Nominal allegiance, however, did not translate into regular attendance at services. And in the post-war years, many parishes and chapels struggled to remain viable.

One of the major issues confronting the churches was the simple demographic changes in the city. Mining left deep scars on the environment, particularly in areas such as Long Gully, and housing rapidly put up in the 1870s and 1880s did not meet modern standards. Housing schemes developed by the federal government, such as cheap loans to returned servicemen, encouraged the construction of new housing. In the 1950s and 1960s, Bendigo witnessed a minor version of what historian Graeme Davison labelled the 'Cream Brick Frontier'. Just as Melbournians moved to new suburbs and built modern weatherboard or the more popular brick veneer house, Bendigo spread into the adjoining rural shires. Kennington became the dream destination for many young families in the 1950s and 1960s, and today contains a significant stock of post-war housing. Here, they found large blocks and escaped the scars of mine tailing heaps. At the same time, commercial uses began to impinge on the residential areas of the inner city. Churches in the inner city and old mining suburbs faced declining populations, while new churches were established in these 'greenfields' suburbs.[38]

Bendigo's oldest churches, Golden Square Methodist Church and All Saints' Anglican Church, illustrate the problems encountered by inner city churches due to demographic shifts and secularisation. While All Saints'

38 Graeme Davison, Tony Dingle and Seamus O'Hanlon, *The Cream Brick Frontier: Histories of Australian Suburbia* (Monash University Department of History, 1995). For developments in Bendigo, see the Council Newspaper Cutting Books.

had a prime location in the heart of the city, it never took advantage of this architecturally. Its building was often considered unfitting for a cathedral, yet plans to build a new cathedral were overly ambitious and never realised. Only modest additions were made in the late 1930s. In the nineteenth century, All Saints' had the advantage of being the church of several of the city's leading families, such as the Lansells and the Dyasons. In the twentieth century, the influence of these families declined, and many left Bendigo. With the population moving out of the inner city, attendance at All Saints' did not sustain its immediate post-war boom. To manage falling numbers, affiliated women's guilds and groups, an integral part of church life, were amalgamated in 1962 to become the All Saints' Cathedral Guild.

These trends continued in the 1970s and 1980s. Businesses replaced houses in the inner city, resident numbers declined, and those remaining were an older age group. Younger families were being drawn to the peripheral areas of Bendigo, and the city could no longer support two city parishes. The church made several studies into the changing ministry of the church in Bendigo, deciding to merge the two city parishes in 1980.[39] Maintaining one parish across two buildings proved expensive, and in 1989, the All Saints' Cathedral was closed. With the closing of All Saints', St Paul's became the new cathedral, and the Anglican Church strengthened its presence in the new suburbs with a new church, Holy Trinity, in Kennington. By the end of the 1980s, communicants at these churches were under ten per cent of the nominal Anglicans recorded in the census.[40]

The Golden Square Methodist Church experienced a modest revival with post-war suburbanisation in the south of the city. Their optimism for the future is represented in their costly restoration of the church's magnificent organ for the congregation's 100 year anniversary in 1952. Yet the 1950s and 1960s were both a high point of evangelical Christianity in Australia and the beginning of a sustained crisis. Revivalism, epitomised by Billy Graham's popular tours (1959–1979), transformed many people's lives. Yet the affluence of the post-war boom also provided distractions from the church and chapel as social hubs. The advent of things as banal as television proved stiff competition for the entertainments of Sunday sermons. Socially engaged churches like the Methodists endeavoured to renew and

39 Cole, *A History of All Saints' Church*, 118–19.

40 Cole, *A History of All Saints' Church*, 122–28. For statistics on Communion, see page 133. The proportion taking Communion is estimated from the Commonwealth Census. '2101.0 – Census of Population and Housing, 1986,' *Australian Bureau of Statistics*, 1986 www.abs.gov.au/AUSSTATS/abs@.nsf/DetailsPage/2102.01986.

revive their message for modern Australia. But the connections between Christianity and national identity weakened during this time, and many Evangelicals were confused about how to maintain their congregations and their relevance.[41] As elsewhere in Australia, Bendigo's Protestant churches experienced a sustained decline in church membership and in nominal affiliation in the late twentieth century.

In 1967, Golden Square and Quarry Hill Methodist churches were combined, and in 1971 became designated 'Bendigo South'. In 1977, the Uniting Church of Australia was formed through the union of the Congregational, Presbyterian and Methodist churches. The new denomination had a broad and inclusive Protestant theology with a pronounced commitment to social justice. In the late 1980s, the congregation of Bendigo South formed part of 22 parishes in the Presbytery and 1 of 13 Presbyteries in Victoria. Centrally, the new Uniting Church sustained many programs of 'witness and service', including TV and radio, ministerial education, mission activities, community services, ecumenical missions, field services, social justice and education. These services, however, did not translate into attendance at church on Sundays. By 1989, the average attendance had fallen to below 25, down from 80 to 30 over the previous 10 years. Reasons given by a task group set up to investigate were: ageing worshippers, limited interest of organ music to young worshippers and cold, hard seats in winter.[42] Interestingly, these reasons do not overlap with the reasons provided by contemporary theorists of secularisation, such as the failure of institutional religions to compete in modern 'marketplaces of ideas', or to face up to the moral challenges of feminism and civil rights.[43]

In 1994, the Bendigo South congregation commissioned a heritage study of the church and grounds and communicated with the City of Bendigo over their future. The sites were designated as having regional significance, and demolition was ruled out. A financial summary of the parish saw the church in deficit from 1989 to 1994 and existing on around $65,000 each year. As there were only around 150 people per week attending services at Kangaroo Flat, Lockwood and Golden Square, it was decided that the present offering was insufficient to pay for the minister, mission and service

41 Hugh Chilton, *Evangelicals and the End of Christendom: Religion, Australia and the Crises of The 1960s* (Taylor & Francis, 2020).

42 Golden Square Methodist Church Heritage Study, Uniting Church Archives, Golden Square Methodist Church, 0168/Box 4/File 5.

43 See the summary in Adam Possamai and David Tittensor, *Religion and Change in Australia* (Taylor & Francis Group, 2022), 73–90.

payments and property services and maintenance. In 1997, the church looked at its structure, relevance and mission once more. The elders needed to consider what the 'mission directions of each congregation' were whether the parishes should be linked. The Bendigo South parish was then without a minister and vacant for a year, as it was in 1991. A questionnaire was sent out in 1995 that asked whether the existing congregations should unite in Bendigo, including the more informal congregation at McKenzie Street that used 'much contemporary Christian music'. Results came back with around 50 responses, mostly supportive of the move.[44]

Despite the challenges of small active membership, these Uniting Church congregations continued to advance their mission for social justice and equality. Records from the early 2000s showed the Golden Square Uniting Church working with primary schools and demonstrating a desire to help local single mothers and those in the community who needed help due to de facto relationships, abuse, drugs and alcohol in the home. The church maintained an overseas mission, a youth committee, bible study groups, adventure groups, talks and Music at Midday. It was also being regularly used as a cultural centre for concerts, performances and exhibitions. At the 150 year anniversary in 2002, Golden Square held a service that recognised the church's long history in the area, bringing in a range of community groups, theatre groups and the secondary college ensemble to celebrate. In 2000, the Bendigo Community Theatre and Arts were granted control of the property for two years. However, by 2016, the congregation was no longer independently viable. It was closed, and the building sold.[45]

In 1947, the Catholic Church still commanded the firm adherence of nominal Bendigo Catholics. Between 1933 and 1947, the local church weathered the disruption of the war, and there was a slight growth in the number of nominal Catholics. Wartime mobility for military service or employment may have loosened or hindered the ability of the clergy to monitor their congregations. By 1949, the local clergy enumerated around 76 per cent of the nominal Catholics recorded in the Commonwealth Census. Among those with whom the clergy were in contact, there had been a decline in the proportion attending Easter services; in 1947, only 11 per cent 'failed' in meeting their duty of taking communion. Among children of identified Catholics, attendance at parochial schools also remained high at

44 Summary of unsorted papers, Uniting Church Archives, Golden Square Methodist Church, 0168/Box 4/File 5.
45 Ibid.

83 per cent. This highly organised Catholic pastoral attention and emphasis on Catholic education may go some way to explaining the persistence of Catholic affiliation, culture and identity in the latter twentieth century when Protestant, especially nonconformist, affiliation and identity declined.

With Catholics settling on the edges of the city in the nineteenth century, the Catholic Church was in a good position to extend services to the expanding urban frontier. In the old Strathfieldsay Shire, churches were well established at Axedale and Axe Creek. This area had been favoured by Father Backhaus with his land purchases in the late 1850s and 1860s, and land-hungry Irish migrants purchased land at auction or selected land in the area. In 1958, two rural churches were augmented by the construction of a new building for the parish of St Teresa's in the growing suburb of Kennington. Over the next thirty years, this parish grew from 1,090 Catholics in 1961 to 2,030 in 1971 and 3,400 in 1988. In this latter year, the parish priest, Father Frank Marriott, urged his superiors to establish a 'mass centre' at Strathdale, then emerging as a middle-class suburb of Bendigo. By the early 1960s, the Parish of Kennington had all the institutions of the nineteenth century Devotional Revolution. The Sodality of the Holy Name for men boasted 140 members; its female companion, the Confraternity of the Sacred Heart, welcomed 160 members, and 30 young women had joined the Children of Mary. Missions were a part of parish life, and the Franciscan Fathers visited the parish for a week in 1959. The largest lay organisation in the parish was the Propagation of Faith with 230 members. The sodalities maintained their numbers through the 1960s but had declined by the late 1980s. Catholic education remained a vital part of the work of the parish. After Vatican II, the laity played a greater part in mass, and Father Marriott observed that attempts were being made to involve parents in preparing their children for the Eucharist. Other devotional practices included Review in Lent, Special Rosary Effort in May and October and Advent Prayers on three days in that season. In the 1980s, however, weekly attendances at mass fell below half the estimated population of the parish. As an explanation, Father Marriot, who had only been in the parish for a year, acknowledged modern automobility and admitted he could not determine how many attended mass in other parishes.[46] Reliance on the car was emblematic of modern Australian suburban life; Kennington, however, lacked the other great defining feature of Australian post-war society, immigrants, who tended to

46 In the post-war years, informative surveys were made for Episcopal visits. See Episcopal Visitation of Parishes, Kennington 7 April 1963 and 30 August 1970, and Report of Episcopal Visitation, Kennington, 27 November 1988, Diocese of Sandhurst Archives.

bolster attendance at mass in urban parishes elsewhere in Australia. Asked what minority ethnic groups lived in his parish, Father Marriott wrote, 'none in real numbers'.[47] The diminishing diversity within Bendigo was not confined to the Catholic congregations, impacting social cohesion in the early twenty-first century, as examined in Chapter Nine.

Conclusion: Into the twenty-first century

The migration of Cornish miners and their families to the quartz mines of Bendigo from 1870 had given the city a distinctive Methodist character. In 1901, Methodists were almost as large as the majority Anglican denomination, almost three times the size of the Presbyterians and had over 4,000 more adherents than the Catholics. With the collapse of mining in the early twentieth century, the local population declined as people moved elsewhere for work. All churches lost adherents, but the Methodists, with their strong representation in mining, lost proportionally more adherents than other denominations. World War Two revived the economy of Bendigo, and prosperity continued through the long boom of the 1950s and 1960s. Bendigo weathered the collapse of manufacturing and developed a service economy. While the population grew through to the early 1990s, attendance at church services declined, and nominal affiliation in the census barely kept pace with population growth. Catholics were better able to withstand the dramatic population shifts associated with the end of the gold rush due to the legacy of Father Backhaus' early investments. As elsewhere in the world, Catholics' affiliation to their church identity was 'stickier' than Protestants; by the early 1990s, they had become the largest Christian denomination in the newly created city. However, as Wilkins-LaFlamme shows, those Protestants who remained affiliated with their churches were more active and enthusiastic about their religious observance.[48]

By 1991, Bendigonians were more prepared than ever before to state that they followed no religion. Largely untouched by the waves of post-war migration, Bendigo did not experience a substantial growth in non-Christian religions. In the first twenty years of the new century, all the traditional Christian denominations lost nominal adherents as people became more comfortable identifying with 'no religion'. There was a slight upswing in

47 Report of Episcopal Visitation, Kenington, 27 November 1988, Diocese of Sandhurst Archives, p. 3.
48 Sarah Wilkins-LaFlamme, 'Protestant and Catholic Distinctions in Secularisation,' *Journal of Contemporary Religion* 31, no. 2 (2016): 165–80, doi.org/10.1080/13537903.2016.1152660.

minor, but notably vigorous, Protestant denominations such as Pentecostals and Baptists. As elsewhere, Catholic identity and affiliation was more resilient than other Christian denominations. In 2021, more Bendigonians nominated Catholicism in the census than the combined members of the Uniting Church (former Methodists and a portion of the Presbyterians), the Presbyterian Church and the Anglican Church. By 2021, like other regional, post-industrial former goldrush towns such as Ballarat and Broken Hill, 'no religion' had become the largest category of 'religious' affiliation in the census. In these centres, no religious affiliation sits at just under 50 per cent, while nominal Christian affiliation sits at around 40 per cent. Recent research has shown that trends in religiosity are not easily captured by single concepts, such as secularisation or the 'postsecular' and suggests that we are living in an era of religious complexity.[49] Many nonreligious Australians, for example, still seek meaning, spiritual experience and care from diverse sources.[50] How this new population of nonreligious Bendigonians finds sources of community, meaning, belonging and, crucially, social cohesion and neighbourliness with people of diverse faiths remains to be seen.

49 Inger Furseth, 'Religious Complexity: Theorizing Multiple Religious Trends,' *Journal of Contemporary Religion* 36, no. 1, (2021): 1–18, doi.org/10.1080/13537903.2021.1889138.

50 Andrew Singleton, Mary Lou Rasmussen, Anna Halafoff and Gary Bouma, *Freedoms, Faiths and Futures: Teenage Australians on Religion, Sexuality and Diversity* (Bloomsbury Academic, 2021).

Popout Four: Completing the Sacred Heart Cathedral: Craft and tradition in Bendigo's faith-scape

A young Paul Copock stands strong and confident among the bare ceiling joists of the incomplete Sacred Heart Cathedral. It is the early 1970s, and Paul leans into his work with apparent indifference to the heat and to the photographer who recorded his toil. Just as Paul's nonchalant ease belies the sweat and artistry in motion, this image eschews his devotion to excellence and family tradition (see Figure P.2). Faith, family and duty were deeply interwoven in the life of Paul Copock, who worked diligently at 93 Myrtle Street to finish the world's third-tallest Catholic cathedral. Envisioned and funded by German-born Henry Backhaus, Bendigo's first Roman Catholic priest, the cathedral was built in two stages: 1896–1901 and 1953–1977. The second construction stage incorporated post-Vatican II reforms to Roman Catholic liturgical practices, representing a response of the church to 'the needs of our own times'.[1] Moving the main altar forward and relocating the bishop's throne, for example, enabled mass facing the people.[2] During this period, the Young Christian Workers (YCW) movement, rooted in Catholic Social Teaching and developed through the lay apostolate, fostered a social justice orientation in the daily lives of working-class Catholics. Established in the Sandhurst Diocese in 1944, this influential movement sought to transform young people's lives through its

1 'Constitution on the Sacred Liturgy *Sacrosanctum Concilium* Solemnly Promulgated by His Holiness Pope Paul VI on December 4, 1963,' Institutional Website of the Holy See, www.vatican.va/archive/hist_councils/ii_vatican_council/documents/vat-ii_const_19631204_sacrosanctum-concilium_en.html.

2 'Sacred Heart Cathedral,' Victorian Heritage Database, vhd.heritagecouncil.vic.gov.au/places/3311.

method of Christian reflection, judgment and action, and through sports and social activities, leadership training, apprenticeship schemes, cooperatives and credit unions.[3] Paul Copock and his father Frank, who oversaw much of the second stage of the Sacred Heart Cathedral's construction, were trained under this philosophy. Its influence is clear in Copock's management style and support for post-war migrant workers recruited for their building expertise. The design modifications made by the Copock team achieved an unexpected spaciousness for the cathedral, but the wider church aspirations and reforms did not fully meet societal expectations.

Figure P.2: Paul Copock on the roof of Sacred Heart Cathedral, 1973
Source: Catholic Diocese of Sandhurst, Paul Copock Collection.

3 Breda Phillips, *More Prophetic Than We Knew: A History of the JCW in the Diocese of Sandhurst* (Richard Cambridge Printers, 1999).

The grandeur of the Gothic-style cathedral mirrors the diversity and lofty aspirations of the gold miners who were originally drawn to the Bendigo fields; rising 'steeply from the gentler slopes beside the Melbourne Highway', the Sacred Heart Cathedral is Australia's largest provincial church. Its imposing spire 'tipped by a three-tonne bronze cross, rises 86 metres into the sky' and was designed to dominate the city skyline.[4] The interior furnishings include the fine gilded bishop's throne of Austrian oak, rare blackwood pews and chapels lined in marble from around the world. Cistercian monk Thomas Merton once said of the Shakers, a millennialist Christian sect that produced faultless craftwork, that 'making' represented a spiritual act.[5] The Shakers believed that their designs and innovations came directly from the Holy Spirit, which made their daily labour a hallowed activity.[6] The artisans who finished the Sacred Heart Cathedral also saw their work as answering a call to faith, duty and tradition. In this way, their craft materialised and manifested their beliefs.[7]

Paul Copock's story is enmeshed with that of his father Frank and the upkeep of standards in their carpentry trade. Returning from war service in 1945, Frank Copock was rushed through his apprenticeship with local business Hume and Iser by a government desperately short of skilled building and construction workers.[8] Frank was then apprenticed as a church carpenter by Monsignor Owens, spending many years building pews, doors and windows. When Frank's son Paul came of age and into his father's trade, regional Australia was again experiencing rapid change. Paul left school at fifteen after an altercation with a Marist brother and having failed shop class. In 1962, he was directly apprenticed to Bishop Stewart. Known as 'Bernie the Builder', Stewart supervised the post-war boom in school and church construction across the Diocese of Sandhurst that we traced in Chapter Eight. Paul hung a picture of the bishop over his workbench, materialising this oversight. Remembering this image and Bishop Stewart's influence on his life and craft, Paul said, 'I never thought much about it. It was just

4 Peter Staughton, 'Bendigo RC Cathedral,' *Architecture Australia* 66 (1977): 47–66; Brian Coman, 'Art and Culture: Beauty and the Beholder,' *News Weekly*, April 1, 2016, 15.

5 Thomas Merton, *Seeking Paradise: The Spirit of the Shakers* (Orbis Books, 2003), 60.

6 Edward Deming Andrews and Faith Andrews, *Work and Worship Among the Shakers: Their Craftsmanship and Economic Order* (Dover Publications, 1982).

7 Webb Keane, 'On the Materiality of Religion,' *Material Religion* 4, no. 2 (2008): 230–1, doi.org/10.2752/175183408X328343.

8 The celebrated timber family, originally Humme and Iser, had begun sawmilling in the gold rush and continue to this day. See 'Long running family business Hume & Iser part of Bendigo's history,' *Bendigo Advertiser*, November 2, 2019, updated November 4, 2019, www.bendigoadvertiser.com.au/story/6464487/building-citys-retail-history/.

something that had to be there with me. I thought that he was guiding me.'[9] This lifelong bond between cleric and worker also influenced the construction of the soaring Bendigo cathedral.[10] As a permanent landmark in a society that was founded by transient workers and characterised by interim measures, this building responded to the city's past, but did it convey a sufficiently ambitious trajectory?[11]

Phase Two architects for the Sacred Heart Cathedral, Bates Smart and McCutcheon, closely adhered to the 1895 design of their predecessors Reed, Smart and Tappin. This decision was critiqued by architectural commentators after completion of the building in 1977, viewed as a missed opportunity to showcase contemporary architectural advances and achievements.[12] Adherence to traditional cathedral design and building techniques, however, aligned with the ideals of a burgeoning movement within the Catholic Church. The YCW movement, which was brought from Europe to Australia by enthusiasts during the Second World War, sought to address the 'de-humanizing and de-Christianizing effects of industrialization' by leveraging the dignity of human labour.[13] The YCW, with strong clerical support in Victoria, aimed to cultivate an apostolic spirituality that engaged young people rather than isolating them 'from the deleterious effects of the culture'.[14] Now best remembered for sports competitions, the YCW also fostered housing cooperatives, delivered vocational training for apprentices and offered support for young leaders: initiatives thought to re-Christianise the wider social milieu.[15] Apprenticed to a bishop who enthusiastically supported the movement, these values undoubtedly influenced Paul Copock's vocational formation.[16] His later employment practices were also influenced by broader social and cultural changes occurring locally and globally.

9 Jennifer Jones, oral history interview with Paul Copock, 2015.

10 James C. Scott, *Seeing Like a State: How Certain Schemes to Improve the Human Condition Have Failed* (Yale University Press, 2020).

11 Ralph Ghoche, 'Erasing the Ketchaoua Mosque: Catholicism, Assimilation, and Civic Identity in France and Algeria,' in *Neocolonialism and Built Heritage: Echoes of Empire in Africa, Asia, and Europe*, ed. Daniel E. Coslett (Routledge 2020).

12 Staughton, 'Bendigo RC Cathedral,' 65.

13 Christopher Ryan, 'A Brief History of Australian Catholic Youth Ministry—Part I,' *Australasian Catholic Record* 96, no. 4 (2019): 440.

14 Christopher Ryan, 'A Brief History,'442.

15 Melissa Jean Walsh and Nicholas Thomas Shaw Marshall, '"Necessary Cessation from Toil and Work": Young Christian Workers and the Question of Sport on Sundays in Post-War Melbourne,' *The International Journal of the History of Sport* 35, no.1 (2018): 87–107, doi.org/10.1080/09523367.2018.1471063; Breda Phillips, *More Prophetic Than We Knew: A History of the YCW in the Diocese of Sandhurst* (Breda Phillips, 1999).

16 Breda Phillips, *More Prophetic.*

In 1960, Frank and Paul Copock began constructing the sanctuary roof on the Sacred Heart Cathedral. Then, in 1964, they established their own business, Copock's Joinery, to continue this painstaking work. The family firm produced the knaves, pews, roofs, transepts, crypts and delicate wood carvings that adorn the great church. As site manager, Paul Copock insisted on high-quality work that 'could last 500 years.'[17] The family business engaged up to a dozen employees at peak times, with a trusted core gang of multicultural tradesmen. The work ethic of these intergenerational families of Italian, Yugoslav and German stonemasons and carpenters aligned with Copock's values. Paul's recollections are marked by stories of cross-cultural mateship and solidarity derived from shared values, and of a revolving door of Aussie drifters who shirked work expectations who, he recalls, 'weren't really up for much … a lot of them were scallywags.'[18] Paul remembers some Anglo-Australians who were challenged by the behaviours and beliefs of a new wave of migrants. Their willingness to work was considered a 'grave industrial and political danger' because they competed with more reluctant 'native labour'.[19]

Forming part of the 'populate or perish' credo adopted by Prime Minister Joseph Chifley's government, southern European migrants were critical to the spatial and material making of Australia after wartime. This diverse workforce contributed to monumental industrial sites and infrastructure projects in manufacturing, farming, mining and commerce sectors that gave Australia's modernising programme a transnational texture.[20] Yet the relationship between white Australian settlers and newer migrants, particularly Italians, was characterised by systematic racism and suspicion in economic, social and cultural realms.

Paul's recollections address these themes and how religious identity, labour and communitarianism overcame such challenges during those years. He recalls how job seekers 'would say they was looking for a job [but] "we're not Catholics"'. His father's response was 'we don't care as long as you keep the beliefs to yourself and do your work'. Church hierarchies,

17 Staughton, 'Bendigo RC Cathedral,' 49.

18 Paul Copock interview with Jennifer Jones.

19 Rosario Lampugnani, 'Postwar Migration Policies with Particular Reference to Italian Migration to Australia,' *Australian Journal of Politics & History* 33, no. 3 (1987): 197–208, doi.org/10.1111/j.1467-8497.1987.tb00146.x.

20 Anoma Peiris, Mirjana Lozanovska, Alexandra Dellios et al., 'Forum: Industrial Sites and Immigrant Architectures. A Case Study Approach,' *Fabrications* 29, no. 2 (2019): 257–72, doi.org/10.1080/10331867.2019.1589917.

however, proved less accepting. When Italian workers married Protestant women, 'it was a "no no" really, and they got put off'. The completion of the Sacred Heart Cathedral thus charts the persistence of sectarianism at the intersection of love and labour, where expected performances of religious piety clashed with the realities of a pluralising society.[21]

In considering the erosion of dogmatic religious belief in post-war Australia, some discussions of secularisation have considered how labour and other forms of 'civil religion' replaced formal religious institutions as moral educators and practitioners. Richard Ely points out that in the nineteenth century, use of the term 'sacred' was used largely in 'churchly circles' to set apart the objectives, instruments, locations and symbols of religious experience.[22] Through the twentieth century labour movement, 'sacred' also came to signify the inviolability of workers' rights, time and safety.

Paul Copock's oral history makes recurring reference to dangerous and unregulated working conditions that draw these realms together. He recalls working through summer 'right up against a slate. All I used to have on was a pair of football shorts and a nail bag and a pair of boots … sometimes working 80 or 90 feet off the ground.' Numerous accidents and near misses impress his memory:

> I was hoisting some timber up … slinging the beams up on the transept roof and the chap at the bottom didn't sling it right. I [was] just about to grab the beam and it slipped because the wood was oiled. There was an Italian standing underneath. I can still see the bald patch on his head, just there, and this beam come down and missed him by that much [indicates a tiny amount] … 12 foot of Oregon about 20 inches wide. It landed just beside him and flew into splinters. Of course, I yelled, and I could have been heard around Bendigo. Anyway, I took him over and set him down and he said to me 'You just try to kill me, Paulino?' They used to mostly call me Paulino. 'You try to kill me Paulino?'[23]

From monkey-poling up a scaffold to adjusting unworkable plans, Paul's expertise shaped the material surfaces of the church. Meanwhile, he gradually stopped attending services. Paul's story thereby mirrors the

21 Benjamin Edwards, 'Vatican II and the Dying Gasps of Australian Sectarianism,' *Journal of the Australian Catholic Historical Society* 33 (2012): 115–24.

22 Richard Ely, 'Secularisation and the Sacred in Australian History,' *Australian Historical Studies* 19, no. 77 (1981): 562–3, doi.org/10.1080/10314618108595659.

23 Paul Copock interview with Jennifer Jones.

increasing secularity of his generation. Recalling the waning influence of the YCW in parish life and as a mass movement, Pat Crudden suggests that its key impact can be seen 'in the lifestyle of those who had been trained in earlier times'.[24] Paul's fidelity to certain values in his religious heritage, such as community service and pride in excellence, represent this sustaining personal ethic.[25] Paul Copock's powerful connection to the Sacred Heart Cathedral suggests how religious symbols and identifications still shape identity in Australia's diverse society. Copock's craft practice clearly has a spiritual function – in terms of existential meaning, purpose and belonging.

Within Paul Copock's lifetime, familial craft traditions have faced similar challenges to accommodate change. The slow replacement of venerable traditions by commerce, globalisation and modern technology has left many looking for meaning and renewal. After deindustrialisation, gold cities like Bendigo needed drivers of regeneration. Attention turned to creativity, which facilitates 'a sense of "belonging" and "community" through fostering social relationships'.[26] Craft practitioners have long understood their art as 'woven into the ongoing social fabric of life.' Eda Gunaydin suggests that making can also offer spiritual transcendence.[27] Such was the case in 2020, when artisans from around Australia convened the first 'Lost Trades Fair' in Bendigo. Founder and director Lisa Rundell described Bendigo as the perfect venue for the fair, because of its 'strong arts culture and a natural connection to trades'.[28] This connection to the spiritual, through craft tradition, is central to the story of Paul Copock's family and to that of his post-war migrant staff. Together, their legacy is manifest in the very structure of the grand Sacred Heart Cathedral.

24 Breda Phillips, 'Robustly Australian, Deeply Spiritual, More Prophetic Than We Knew,' in *More Prophetic Than We Knew: A History of the YCW in the Diocese of Sandhurst* (Breda Phillips, 1999), 127.

25 Marian Burchardt, 'Becoming Secular: Biographies of Disenchantment, Generational Dynamics, and Why They Matter,' *Social Compass* 69, no. 2 (2022): 223–40, doi.org/10.1177/00377686221079699.

26 Gordon Waitt and Chris Gibson, 'Creative Small Cities: Rethinking the Creative Economy in Place,' *Urban Studies* 46, no. 5–6 (2009): 1223–46, doi.org/10.1177/0042098009103862.

27 Eda Gunaydin, 'Handmade Transcendence: On Fashioning Presence Through Process,' *Griffith Review*, no. 79 (February 2023), www.griffithreview.com/articles/handmade-transcendence/.

28 Julieanne Strachan, 'Bendigo Will Host the Lost Trades Fair Again in 2022,' *Bendigo Advertiser*, November 18, 2021, updated October 4, 2023, www.bendigoadvertiser.com.au/story/7516731/lost-trades-fair-back-again-in-2022/.

Popout Five: Emu Point Joss House: The spirit and architecture of faith

This book has shown how buildings reflected and supported the faith-scape of Bendigo: canvas tents and structures of brick, wood and stone all sheltered people in warm proximity while they worshipped. Chinese diasporic communities built 'joss houses' – or temples of god and ancestor worship – across the goldfields.[1] From its opening in 1871, the Emu Point Joss House has been at Bendigo's edge, but it is of no marginal importance to the city's religious history. It has been a centre of faith, tradition and politics for the communities of diverse faiths who have used it. First built to meet the needs of migrants from Southern Canton, it has since served as a place of worship and reflection for migrants from across Southeast Asia and China, including those from Vietnam.

Migration and adaptations of faith

The Emu Point Joss House (see Figure P.3) represents the material legacy of intra-Chinese adaptation and a spatial cohesion of religions. During the nineteenth century, around 52 historical joss houses were constructed in Victoria, many of which have been inclusive spaces of intra-Asian diversity.[2] Temples grew during the nineteenth century from small, minimally sheltered

1 'History,' Bendigo Joss House Temple, www.bendigojosshouse.com/history/; for histories of the wider landscape of Chinese temples in regional Victoria, see Hu Jin Kok and Golden Dragon Museum, *Chinese Temples in Castlemaine, Maryborough, Bairnsdale, Daylesford, Bright, Harrietville and Beechworth, all in Victoria: Studies* (Golden Dragon Museum, 2005).

2 Paul Macgregor, 'Joss Houses of Colonial Bendigo and Victoria,' in *An Angel on the Water*, ed. Mike Butcher (Holland House Publishing, 2015), 109.

shrines to more permanent structures. Hu Jin Kok writes that these permitted 'more extensive religious and secular activity', including the worship of ancestors and gods and political and social organisational meetings.[3] A brick temple at Ironbark Camp, writes historian Paul MacGregor, was called the All Nations Temple 'because all Chinese, regardless of their district of origin, were allowed to worship in it'.[4] The word 'joss' comes from the Portuguese *dios*, and it has a connection to a figure intelligible as 'God' in Western ontologies as Guan-di. Scholar Prasenjit Duara has written that Guan-di, the Chinese God of war, was 'superscribed' by various communities, who wrote their 'version of a myth or symbol over extant versions' without eliminating traditional versions.[5] The Emu Point Joss House has the words 'Chee Goon Tong (Cantonese transcription) above its entrance, usually translated into English as Chinese Masonic Society,[6] which promoted a faith in the importance and possibilities of brotherhood. 'It was believed', writes Macgregor, 'that appeals to the virtue of Guan-di would encourage co-operation within diverse mining communities'.[7]

Figure P.3: Postcard of Chinese Joss House

Source: Victorian Collections.

3 Kok & Golden Dragon Museum, *Chinese Temples*, 105.

4 Paul Macgregor, 'Joss Houses,' 115.

5 Prasenjit Duara, 'Superscribing Symbols: The Myth of Guandi, Chinese God of War,' *The Journal of Asian Studies* 47, no. 4 (1988): 778–95, doi.org/10.2307/2057852.

6 Paul Macgregor, 'Joss Houses,' 116.

7 Ibid., 107.

The struggle for space to meet and practice faith

People of Chinese descent practised diverse faiths: syncretic fusions of Buddhism, Taoism and Confucianism, as well as various denominations of Christianity.[8] One of the most important manifestations of Chinese community in Bendigo, writes Historian Valerie Lovejoy, 'were the temples or joss houses where Chinese worshippers gathered to pray to a pantheon of gods for justice, protection for their families, success in their work and peace for deceased relatives.'[9] The Emu Point temple is made from bricks sculpted from clay extracted from sacred Djaara lands and dedicated to the deity Guan Di, the god of war and prosperity. With its origin in the third century historical hero of the Three Kingdoms, the meanings of Guan Di changed over centuries and through migration. 'For rural communities', writes Duara, 'the image of a trustworthy protectors of temples yielded naturally to that of protector of communities and eventually to those of healer and provider.'[10]

The Bendigo Joss House Temple was built around 15 years after religiously diverse people of Chinese descent began making Bendigo home during a time when the city was informally racially segregated along spatial lines. The temple was positioned in the Ironbark Chinese Camp, the distant site where Europeans had pushed the Chinese miners.[11] Miners of Chinese descent were viewed by working-class Europeans 'as competition and the government basically segregated them from the rest of the community by putting them into camps', non-Chinese caretaker Mr Wright had recounted; the 'Joss House was built out of a need for protection against discrimination, with the Chinese in need of a deity that would look after them.'[12] The use of these temples, then, was shaped by the diasporic context of the faith and the intermittent violence of white settler racism. Numerous

8 See Valerie Lovejoy, 'Chinese in Late Nineteenth-Century Bendigo: Their Local and Translocal Lives In "This Strangers' Country",' *Australian Historical Studies*, 42, no. 1 (2011): 45–61, doi.org/10.1080/1031461X.2010.539239. See also 'One of Australia's Oldest Chinese Temples Brings Fortune and Family, Worshippers Say: The Bendigo Joss House Temple was Built to Protect Chinese Miners, and Almost 150 Years Later is Still Used as a Place of Worship,' *ABC News,* February 18, 2018, www.abc.net.au/news/2018-02-18/chinese-temple-brings-fortune-family-worshippers-say/9454664.

9 Lovejoy, 'Chinese in Late Nineteenth-Century Bendigo.'

10 Duara, 'Superscribing Symbols,' 783.

11 For more on the dynamics of inter-cultural relationships among informal segregation, see Lovejoy, 'Chinese in Late Nineteenth-Century Bendigo.'

12 Interview with Darren Wright by Nadia Rhook, Bendigo, May 20, 2017.

joss houses have been destroyed by fire, including a significant incident in 1887 when fire 'ravaged the Ironbark Camp', razing several joss houses and clan meeting places.[13]

Racial-religious hierarchies would also shape the temple's life in less violent albeit significant ways. An evidently racialised curiosity influenced the fusion of tourism with worship. Newspaper reports show how, from its beginnings, the Joss House attracted voyeurs of Chinese faith alongside worshippers.[14] In the early 1970s, the Joss House was restored by the National Trust of Victoria and formally became a tourist attraction, with the resident caretaker's room becoming the office for admission of tourists.[15]

Spirits awakened in stone

In early 2017, the Bendigo Joss House Temple celebrated Chinese New Year with a traditional lantern festival. Guests had 'the unique opportunity to see the Bendigo Chinese Association's three new lions and witness the culturally significant Hoi Gong Ceremony'.[16] The following interview was recorded with Dennis O'Hoy at his Bendigo residence. O'Hoy is a community leader whose grandfather, Louey O'Hoy, was a prominent herbalist whose work supported the health of Chinese and non-Chinese Victorians. Dennis O'Hoy is also a heritage activist. Since he played a major role in founding the Bendigo Trust in 1970, O'Hoy has been enormously and proudly influential in stopping the Bendigo council from tearing down the Town Hall, as well as saving the Bendigo trams and preserving the Chinese Joss House so that it continues to serve the community as a living temple today.[17] The interview details the active, intergenerational, and ongoing process of enlivening the Joss House as a space of cultural and spiritual meaning. O'Hoy tells a spirited story of the April 2017 Joss House Ceremony to bring to life the statue lions that would be placed at the front entrance:

13 Paul Macgregor, 'Joss Houses of Colonial Bendigo and Victoria,' in *An Angel on the Water: Essays in Honour of Reginald O'Hoy*, ed. Mike Butcher, 115.

14 'Opening of the New Chinese Joss House at Ironbark,' *Empire* (Sydney), August 4, 1859, p. 8, nla.gov.au/nla.news-article60402774.

15 'Bendigo's Joss House Gets Back its 1860s Glory,' *The Australian Women's Weekly*, June 13, 1973, p. 22.

16 'Lantern Festival to Welcome New Year,' *Bendigo Advertiser*, February 9, 2017.

17 'Bendigo Man Honoured for a Job Well Done,' *Bendigo Advertiser*, April 12, 2011, www.bendigoadvertiser.com.au/story/715946/bendigo-man-honoured-for-a-job-well-done/.

This is the Lantern festival we just had a couple of weeks ago ... Three new lions were purchased by the Bendigo Chinese Association, and of course we had to bring the lions to life by ceremoniously blessing them, and then dotting the eyes with dragon blood ... So the lion is ... paying homage to Guan Dong, and of course you've got the symbols going, the drums, and the gongs, and the whole atmosphere and the vibration. And the performers. They. Were. So. Good. It got so large that the crowds went out. Look, there must have been about four to five hundred people that came and the first time I did it I only had about sixty or seventy.

So now we all pray that this will be a fortuitous event. Notice the three lions here. They haven't been awoken yet. But, oh, look. To have this happen. Now, the covers come off the lion. The blessing takes place. Wei Tung(?) is blessing them. And now the most important thing is, I now have the dragon's blood. I have the brush and I dot the horn, the eyes, the whole line ... So you've got the drums going veeery silently because they are still not alive yet ...

Now. They are live. They're stirring. Their eyes open.

There is the brush with the dragon's blood. Look, the ceremony, it was just so perfect to think that these old customs have not died.

Now, the lions are awakening. Notice the lettuce there? Because they are hungry. And the next stage – this is again what I was taught 65 years ago, 70 years ago that I was taught this. They are now stirring, they are wakening up ... So now they are going to eat. And they get the vegetables. And the way they do it ... They are all starting to digest the lettuce.

Now, the last time I did that was in 1983. I tried to lift my son up and I tore the muscles in my right arm, and it was [laughing] two years of physiotherapy. That was it. That was the last time I did the lion dance. I was too old. They are all young.

The skill, and the balance. Notice? The lettuce is all gone.

All the young children now are being taught the art of dance, they range from 6, 7 years of age to teens ...

That is the peacock dance. And she was so graceful and beautiful miming the actions of the peacock ...

Look. All the trouble, and all the work. It was worth it.[18]

18 Dennis O'Hoy, interview by Nadia Rhook, Bendigo, April 5, 2017. Transcript available on request.

The Bendigo Joss House Temple is one of the few diasporic Chinese temples that remain standing in Victoria today. It continues to function as a space of tourism and of worship and living spirituality. Its presence serves as a reminder that preserving the autonomy to practice one's faith in an Anglo-Christian–dominated city has necessitated resistance and effort to maintain the building materials and statues, which have been enriched by spiritual practices.[19] After the dismantling of immigration restrictions in the late twentieth century, migrants from across Southeast Asia, including from Vietnam, Indonesia and Malaysia, as well as international students, would worship in this temple. It has a spiritual life that now far exceeds the desires of goldrush Chinese migrants.[20] In 2018, worshipper Wendy Tang described her relationship with the Joss House as one that continues a tradition laid by visitors before her: 'It's been blessed by the people before us. Those people were also migrants … I'm just following those steps.'[21] But in 2022, the Joss House was temporarily closed for security reasons after 'team members were subjected to verbal abuse & antisocial behaviour'. At this time, Dennis O'Hoy called for the Bendigo Trust and the Bendigo Chinese Association to become the caretakers of the site.[22]

Today, the Emu Point Joss House stands as visible evidence of continuity. It is a living space of culture-making and religious expression. Its rooms support the practice and expression of several diasporic faiths, including Buddhism and Confucianism.[23] Ceremonies that were in earlier decades poorly understood and denigrated by European observers are in contemporary times proudly observed by Bendigo residents of both Chinese and non-Chinese descent.

19 Paul Macgregor, 'Joss Houses,' 119.

20 Vanessa Murray, 'Homegrown: Bendigo, Vic,' SBS Food, June 6, 2013, www.sbs.com.au/food/article/homegrown-bendigo-vic/wc2y645bi.

21 Wendy Tang quoted in Larissa Romensky, 'One of Australia's Oldest Chinese Temples Brings Fortune and Family', *ABC News*.

22 Shannon Schubert, 'Bendigo's Chinese Community, Historian Saddened by Closure of Joss House Temple,' *ABC News*, October 11, 2022, www.abc.net.au/news/2022-10-12/joss-house-temple-in-bendigo-closed/101523466?utm_campaign=abc_news_web&utm_content=link&utm_medium=content_shared&utm_source=abc_news_web.

23 Romensky, 'One of Australia's Oldest Chinese Temples.'

Popout Six: Transforming 'Old Sandhurst Town' into the Great Stupa of Universal Compassion

When the author Helen Garner visited 'Old Sandhurst Town', a privately owned goldfields theme park in 1982, she contrasted the experience with her recent visit to Ballarat's 'Sovereign Hill'. Although tourists accessed an important and carefully re-purposed historic mine site at Sovereign Hill, Garner thought it 'offered a sanitised version of the past'. At Sandhurst Town, by contrast, visitors were administered 'a stiff dose of realism'.[1] This tourist attraction was situated on an isolated block of whipstick bush near Myers Flat, an agricultural district near Bendigo that had seen minor gold rushes in 1852 and 1867.[2] For Helen Garner, the authentic experience offered at Sandhurst Town did not depend on the conservation of built heritage assets (aka, Sovereign Hill). Rather, the 'huddle of miserable tents, brown with dirt and absolutely still in the brutal heat of midday', simulated authentic feelings about settler Australia and goldrush society.[3] Here, period-dressed characters presented a riotous historical pageant involving 'mining licences, guns, death in mine shafts, bribery of officials, gold panning, flogging and the like'. Most importantly, this fictional presentation of harsh goldfields living was 'extremely enjoyable', leaving adult visitors shaking with laughter and briefly oblivious to their own discomfort under the summer sun. Tourism theorists describe such experiences as evoking 'existential authenticity'.[4] Destinations use 'emotional design' and staged activity to

1 Helen Garner, 'Five Train Trips,' in *True Stories: Selected Non-Fiction* (Text Publishing, 1996).

2 'Myers Flat,' Victorian Places, www.victorianplaces.com.au/myers-flat.

3 Garner, 'Five Train Trips,' 209.

4 Xueyan Xu, Truc H. Le, Anna Kwek, and Ying Wang, 'Exploring Cultural Tourist Towns: Does Authenticity Matter?' *Tourism Management Perspectives* 41 (2022): 2, 100935, doi.org/10.1016/j.tmp.2021.100935.

Figure P.4: People circumambulating the Great Stupa of Universal Compassion, Bendigo, 2022

Source: Photo by Jiayuan Liang.

trigger appreciation of cultural memories, like camaraderie and laughter in the alien and unforgiving bush. This 'sense of authenticity' confirms a shared identity, strengthens appreciation of local heritage and develops favourable attitudes towards a site. Generations of Bendigonians and visitors loved the wry-spirited humour presented at Old Sandhurst Town, which opened in the early 1970s and operated until about 1995. When the proprietor Ed Green approached retirement, the high community profile of the location became the focus for succession planning and a completely different rendering of the site. The land was offered to his son, Ian Green, who envisaged building the Atisha Buddhist Centre and the Great Stupa of Universal Compassion at Sandhurst Town (See Figure P.4).

After an inspirational visit by spiritual teachers Lama Yeshe and Lama Zopa in the early 1980s, the raw structures at Sandhurst Town gradually made way for an enormous Buddhist sacred object. Modelled on the famous fifteenth-century Tibetan 'Great Stupa of Gyantse' (Kumbum), construction on the Stupa itself commenced in 2010.[5] In the meantime, the two operations coexisted on the Sandhurst Town site, and preparation for building included raising mainstream community awareness and acceptance of the religious architecture project. During this fifteen year transition, the Buddhist Centre successfully leveraged existing sentiment towards the goldfields tourist operation.

The transfer of this favourable community disposition to the Great Stupa of Universal Compassion may seem surprising given that in the 1980s, Bendigo was a big country town with a relatively narrow Anglo-Celtic culture. The newly arrived Buddhists and their ambitious building project appeared 'very odd and unconventional' in this context, but Lama Yeshe encouraged the founders not to retreat onto their isolated bush site. They were challenged to 'fit in and become part of the community'.[6] Here, the long-term status of the Green family as 'locals', and the public relations experience of co-founder (advertising executive) Ian Green proved valuable. Plans to reconceptualise an established rural tourist asset can challenge the place attachments and community ownership of established residents, especially when exotic newcomers initiate the change and seek the same

5 Judy Green, in discussion with Jennifer Jones, September 20, 2017, transcript available on request.; Ursula De Jong and David Beynon, 'Non-Christian Religious Architecture,' in *The Encyclopedia of Australian Architecture* (Cambridge University Press, 2011), 500.

6 Judy Green, in discussion with Jennifer Jones, September 20, 2017, transcript available on request.

rights as locals.[7] Co-founder Judy Green quickly gauged the degree of local attachment to Sandhurst Town by watching the responses of her own children, who revelled in their new environment:

> they remember that time as being full of great adventure, because Sandhurst Town actually operated every day and attracted a lot of tourists. There was a horse and cart that took rides, and a real working train. For them it was something like living in a wild-west town. They loved it. There was a street full of buildings including an old church [and] a large restaurant which we used for the teaching course when Lama Yeshe visited [and] railway carriages that we renovated and turned into accommodation in the first six months.[8]

The opportunity for adventure and self-creation at Sandhurst Town points to the cultural power of frontier myths, which also disposed the Bendigo community to accept the Stupa.[9] Judy Green recalls the process. Small changes taking place at Sandhurst Town prompted 'a certain amount of curiosity' among locals, which the centre capitalised upon by organising a festive day towards the end of Lama's visit in 1981. The open day included:

> all kinds of things such as street acts, stilt walkers, bands, and food stalls. We made it an open day for the people of Bendigo and 5,000 people came along. That was August 1981. We think this was significant in opening up the centre and showing people what we were about.[10]

In addition to the strategic open days, the Buddhist Centre offered regular meditation courses on the Sandhurst Town premises. Such resources fostered public awareness and acceptance of the Stupa as a site for self-improvement. Indeed, only minor opposition was apparent when council planning approval was obtained for the large structure in 1999. This contrasted vociferous opposition to similar 'visibly "foreign" religious architecture' in other regional centres, including Wollongong.[11] Sally McAra suggests that

7 Judith Mair and Michelle Duffy, 'Who Has the Right to the Rural? Place Framing and Negotiating the Dungog Festival, New South Wales, Australia,' *Journal of Sustainable Tourism* 29, no. 2–3 (2021): 176–92, doi.org/10.1080/09669582.2020.1747476.

8 Judy Green, in discussion with Jennifer Jones, September 20, 2017, transcript available on request.

9 Jane Lovell and Sam Hitchmough, 'Simulated Authenticity: Storytelling and Mythic Space on the Hyper-Frontier in Buffalo Bill's Wild West and Westworld,' *Tourist Studies* 20, no. 4 (2020): 409–28, doi.org/10.1177/1468797620937912.

10 Judy Green, in discussion with Jennifer Jones, September 20, 2017, transcript available on request.

11 Sally McAra, 'Buddhifying Australia: Multicultural Capital and Buddhist Material Culture in Rural Victoria,' in *Buddhism in Australia: Traditions in Change*, ed. Cristina Rocha and Michelle Barker (Taylor & Francis Group, 2011), 63.

the Stupa's proponents were advantaged by long-term ownership of the land at Bendigo and their relative privilege as members of Australia's dominant European stratum. McAra argues that highlighting the Stupa's cultural and economic benefits, including potential as a tourist drawcard, helped to attract the crucial support of Bendigo's local business and government sectors. Judy Green adds historic nuance to this view. She remembers that a degree of benevolent scepticism lingered after planning approval was gained:

> In the early days people would say to Ian and I that we were crazy, 'this is going to cost millions, how are you going to do this?' There was a feeling [locally] that they would [wait and] 'see what happens', because [the Stupa] looked like a very large thing. We just thought, 'One step at a time'.[12]

What predisposed locals (including decision-makers) to wait with supportive doubt rather than critical disinterest or vocal opposition? In addition to those benefits gained from the preparatory work of the Buddhist Centre and the 'ethics of care' associated with localism, we suggest that the built heritage of the site evoked cultural attachments to self-creation, risk taking and community building.[13] In this way, the co-founders also benefited from the transference of a form of 'religious capital' from Old Sandhurst Town to the Great Stupa that drew upon important goldfields myths. Religious capital is understood as a by-product of religious activity that explains behaviour. Michelle Barker notes that religious capital is generated as a consequence of attachment, usually to a spiritual tradition or a religiously associated site. This theory holds relevance for the Great Stupa. We argue that Old Sandhurst Town and the Great Stupa gained support because they were perceived as beneficial tourist offerings that affirmed culturally important foundation stories. Tourist sites that use enigmatic symbols in their storytelling have the capacity to help visitors to make sense of the world 'by providing opportunities beyond the mere gathering of information, by generating emotional and affective responses, by entertaining and by providing explanations'.[14] Although starkly disparate in form and envisioned purpose, the transformation of Old Sandhurst

12 Judy Green, in discussion with Jennifer Jones, September 20, 2017, transcript available on request.

13 E. Melanie DuPuis and David Goodman, 'Should We Go "Home" to Eat?: Toward a Reflexive Politics of Localism,' *Journal of Rural Studies* 21, no. 3 (2005): 359–71, doi.org/10.1016/j.jrurstud.2005.05.011.

14 Michael Fagence, 'Using Geographical and Semiotic Means to Establish Fixed Points of a Never-Ending Story: Searching for Parameters of Authenticity in a Case Study of Australian History,' *Journal of Heritage Tourism* 14, no. 5–6 (2019): 488, doi.org/10.1080/1743873X.2018.1551401.

Town into the Great Stupa of Universal Compassion was successful in part because both promised explanatory experiences in the same whipstick scrub. While this favourable perception of the Stupa does gesture to the primary spiritual purpose of the structure, to provide benefit through the power of holy objects, council prioritisation of tourist opportunities over inherent Buddhist meanings ultimately affirms hegemonic discourses and re-centres existing power relations.[15] As Judy Green observes, 'to the City, the Stupa is very much a draw card for tourists. But a Stupa is important for Buddhists'.[16] The legacy of Old Sandhurst Town, therefore, remains impactful long after the frontier-styled entertainments had closed and the laughter subsided.

15 Sally McAra, 'Buddhifying Australia,' 71.

16 Judy Green, in discussion with Jennifer Jones, September 20, 2017, transcript available on request.

9

Navigating faith and cultural diversity: The Bendigo Mosque controversy[1]

Muslims worshipped publicly in Bendigo over a century before the construction of the city's first mosque began. The distinctive features of Muslim prayer were noted by Christian settlers in the late nineteenth and early twentieth centuries. Religious observance of the most prominent holy days in the Islamic calendar was regularly reported in the local European settler press alongside the varied Christian churches in the region. Islamic rituals and practices were most often located in a common religious sensibility, described in the terms of commonalities between the Abrahamic traditions. Muslim religious leaders, for example, were recognised in the local newspapers, usually described as 'Mahommedan priests'.[2] Of particular note was the observation of Ramadan, the month of fasting that is one of the five pillars of Islam. Eid al-Fitr, the feast of the breaking of the fast marking the end of the month of Ramadan, was reported as the 'Mahommedan "Christmas"' or 'a kind of Mohammedan Feast of Tabernacles', referencing the Jewish feast, Sukkot.[3] Eid al-Adha, the other principal Islamic holiday, was similarly reported as 'Abraham's Day'.[4]

1 Thanks to Natasha Joyce and Bryn Jones for sharing their records of these events and consulting on historical details.

2 See Valait Shah in 'A Murderer Hanged,' *Bendigo Independent*, June 13, 1907, p. 4, nla.gov.au/nla.news-article226716332; also Munchee Goolan Mahomed is mentioned several times, including in the *Bendigo Independent*, December 12, 1904, p. 2, nla.gov.au/nla.news-page24135387.

3 *Bendigo Independent*, January 23, 1901, p. 2, nla.gov.au/nla.news-page19062427.

4 'Abraham's Day,' *Bendigo Independent*, March 22, 1902, p. 4, col. 4, nla.gov.au/nla.news-article22 7558112.

In nineteenth and early twentieth century Bendigo, Muslim prayers, the regular rhythm of devotion punctuating a faithful Muslim's day, often took place in the open air in public parks. Described in the newspapers through a colonial lens as 'oriental ritualistic methods', they were 'closely watched by a number of curious occidentals' (or Westerners).[5] This identification and interest continued into the early twentieth century, despite a shift in public policy.

In 1901, the White Australia Policy was formalised federally as the *Immigration Restriction Act 1901* (IRA), which inhibited the movements and livelihoods of people of South Asian descent.[6] The IRA was meant to make spaces imagined as 'Australia' absent of South Asian bodies, as well as their cultures. That same year, a group of South Asian Muslim hawkers applied to the Bendigo City Council for permission to celebrate Eid al-Fitr in Rosalind Park. These large public gardens were situated at the centre of the city, in the midst of Bendigo's civic buildings and a few blocks from the Roman Catholic Sacred Heart Cathedral, then under construction.[7] On the following Wednesday, 32 Muslims (probably all men) gathered in the park to pray together. Attired in distinctive white garments, they were observed by 'a good number of interested spectators', and later, 'the kindly disposed' Muslims treated the children in the vicinity with a distribution of lollies.[8] In 1907, an Eid feast of 'the favorie [*sic*] relish, mutton and macaroni' was again reported. At this time, the pattern of the rituals was familiar to locals. The *Bendigo Independent* reported that boys had been asking when and where the feast was going to be held, 'for they well know a bountiful supply of lollies accompanies it'.[9] The paper continued:

> Around the camping ground juveniles as thick as flies on tanglefoot awaited the conclusion of the ceremony … Tins of lollies were carried from their hiding place and for a quarter of an hour there was a rough and tumble, and much gleeful excitement, which was enjoyed as much by the Mahommedans … as by the boys themselves.

5 Ibid.

6 Kama Maclean, *British India, White Australia: Overseas Indians, Intercolonial Relations and the Empire* (NewSouth Publishing, 2020).

7 'A Novel Request,' *Bendigo Advertiser*, January 19, 1901, p. 4, col. 5, nla.gov.au/nla.news-article 88598125.

8 'Mahommedan Ceremonies,' *Bendigo Advertiser*, January 24, 1901, p. 2, col. 3, nla.gov.au/nla.news-article88598438.

9 'Mahommedan "Christmas": The Feast of Ramadan,' *Bendigo Independent*, November 9, 1907, p. 4, nla.gov.au/nla.news-article223262707. Also reported in *Bendigo Independent*, December 12, 1904, p. 2; *Bendigo Independent*, October 7, 1910, p. 4.

These light-hearted reports of Islamic worship taking place in public, at the civic heart of Bendigo, observed and joined by non-Muslim locals, give us a glimpse of religious diversity celebrated and welcomed. The pleasant tone of these reports contrasts markedly, however, with wider contemporary racial anxieties and attempts to create Australia as an exclusive 'White man's paradise' represented by the newly implemented IRA.[10] Indeed, it seems reasonable that this 'light-heartedness' might have partly been underwritten by white settlers feeling more in control and less threatened by Muslim presence and strength after the IRA was in force.[11] At the time that these Eids were reported, the population of inner urban Bendigo was contracting. Its population almost halved between 1901 and 1911, falling from 30,774 to 17,883.[12] In the decades that followed the IRA, the population of non-white migrants and sojourners fell even more precipitously.[13] It is interesting to note, however, that the 30 to 50 Muslims recorded in the Bendigo press as praying in public in the first decade of the twentieth century may represent a similar proportion of the local population as the 300 to 500 Muslims who today call Bendigo home.

In contrast to these reported joyful early twentieth century Eids, and many of the stories of religion and social cohesion examined in this book, the remainder of this chapter explores a moment of bitter and violent religious conflict: the reactions to the proposal to construct Bendigo's first mosque from 2014. Local and national groups opposed to the inclusion of Muslim faith and institutions in contemporary society mobilised to try to stop the mosque. Drawing on strategies deployed internationally by similar Islamophobic groups, they staged graphic and performative protests and made formal appeals against the council's approval of the development all the way to the High Court. The press and social media amplified this conflict, and it became a national and international controversy. The conflict over the Bendigo mosque is significant in this book's focus on material culture and the symbolic as well as physical inclusion of religious difference as a site of particular struggle for religious and social cohesion. The violent

10 Nadia Rhook, '"Turban-clad" British Subjects: Tracking the Circuits of Mobility, Visibility, and Sexuality in Settler Nation-Making,' *Transfers* 5, no. 3 (2015): 104–22, doi.org/10.3167/TRANS.2015.050308.

11 Andrew May, *Melbourne Street Life: The Itinerary of Our Days* (Australian Scholarly Publishing, 1998), 163, 177.

12 'Bendigo,' Victorian Places, accessed September 5, 2023, www.victorianplaces.com.au/bendigo.

13 Margaret Allen, 'Shadow Letters and the 'Karnana' Letter: Indians Negotiate the White Australia Policy, 1901–21,' *Life Writing*, 8, no. 2 (2011): 187–202, doi.org/10.1080/14484528.2011.559735; Alexander Yarwood, *Asian Migration to Australia* (Melbourne University Press, 1964), 163.

struggle over the mosque's approval, dominating media coverage of Islam in the contemporary goldfields, contrasts sharply with the longer and gentler history of Muslim worship in Bendigo. The materiality of the mosque and cultural centre's design purposively references this more peaceful history to tell a story and plot a future of social cohesion and religious diversity. The failure of authorities to resolve the conflict, however, points to limitations in their application of multicultural policy.

Figure 9.1: Bendigo Mosque
Source: Photographed by Natasha Joyce.

Building for the modern Bendigo Islamic community

The physical heritage of Islam that remains in present-day Australia from the colonial era is sparse relative to its significant place in Australian history. Southeast Asian Muslims have a trading history with First Nations people that long predates European invasion and settlement.[14] Muslims from Central and South Asia played a significant part in the colonisation of Country, managing the camel transport that was crucial to Europeans accessing and

14 Regina Ganter (with Julia Martinez, and Gary Lee), *Mixed Relations: Narratives of Asian-Aboriginal Contact in North Australia* (University of Western Australia Press, 2006).

transporting goods through the Australian inland.[15] In colonial Victoria, Muslims played a crucial role in facilitating commercial trade, being prominently remembered and recorded as merchants and hawkers. In South Australia and New South Wales, fixed places for Islamic worship were built from the 1860s.[16] Victorian Muslims did not build their first mosques until a hundred years later, worshipping in private or, as we have seen, praying in public to the apparently benign and curious interest of their neighbours.[17] Victoria's earliest mosques were built in Shepparton and Melbourne, and there are now over a hundred dedicated Muslim prayer spaces in Victoria, including over 45 mosques. While there have been occasional planning objections and social disquiet related to new Muslim planning approvals, the 2013 proposal for a mosque in Bendigo [see Figure 9.1] was unusual in that it faced sustained and violent opposition.

While contemporary Bendigo is home to Muslims from around the world, it has a small Muslim population compared with other parts of the state. The vast majority of Victoria's Muslims today live in Melbourne (94.7%), with significant regional populations in Shepparton and Geelong.[18] The Muslim population in Bendigo increased rapidly between 2011 and 2016, more than doubling. It is a diverse population, with members from over 27 different national, ethnic and language backgrounds and includes permanent residents, refugees and international students temporarily residing in Bendigo for their education.[19] Most were born in Australia, with significant numbers of people born in Afghanistan (16%), Pakistan (11%), Bangladesh (11%) and Iran (7%).[20] A large number are in professional employment, particularly in health and medicine. Regular prayer is a central pillar of Islam, but the closest mosques to Bendigo are more than

15 Peter Scriver, 'Mosques, Ghantowns and Cameleers in the Settlement History of Colonial Australia,' *Fabrications* 13, no. 2 (2003–2004): 19–41, doi.org/10.1080/10331867.2004.10525182; Hanifa Deen, *Ali Abdul vs the King* (University of Western Australia Press, 2011); Nahid Kabir, *Muslims in Australia: Immigration, Race Relations and Cultural History* (Kegan Paul, 2005); Samia Khatun, *Australianama: The South Asian Odyssey in Australia* (University of Queensland Press, 2019).

16 Katharine Bartsch, 'Building Identity in the Colonial City: The Case of the Adelaide Mosque,' *Contemporary Islam: Dynamics of Muslim Life* 9, no. 3 (2015): 247–70, doi.org/10.1007/s11562-015-0345-z.

17 James Barry and Ihsan Yilmaz, 'Liminality and Racial Hazing of Muslim Migrants: Media Framing of Albanians in Shepparton, Australia, 1930–1955,' *Ethnic and Racial Studies* 42, no. 7, (2019): 1168–85, doi.org/10.1080/01419870.2018.1484504.

18 Andrew Markus, *Division in Bendigo: Mainstream Public Opinion and Responses to Public Protest in Bendigo, 2014–2016* (Monash University, May 2018), iv.

19 Julie Rudner, *Social Cohesion in Bendigo: Understanding Community Attitudes to the Mosque in 2015* (Victorian Multicultural Commission, 2017), 26.

20 Markus, *Division in Bendigo*, iv.

100 kilometres away in Shepparton and Melbourne. La Trobe University made rooms available to the Muslim community for prayer in 1997, but these can only accommodate a fraction of the local Muslim community. They were quickly insufficient for Friday prayers and are particularly inadequate on Muslim holy days when many from the community want to pray together. The Bendigo Islamic Association (BIA) was formed in 1998 to support local Muslims, partly out of concern that the lack of religious facilities was leading Muslim families to move away to locations that were better supported with religious spaces, 'weakening the fabric of the local Islamic, and wider Bendigo, community'.[21]

Supported by the successful Sydney-based Australian Islamic Mission, the BIA made plans to build an Islamic community centre that could accommodate local worshippers and support them and the wider community with extra public facilities. Plans to build the centre were lodged with the City of Greater Bendigo in late 2013. The development was proposed for industrial land on Rowena St in East Bendigo. The mosque proposal included two prayer rooms, an education room, an office and a caretaker's dwelling.[22] The proposal also included facilities for the wider community, including a café and sports hall. Given Bendigo's celebration of religious and cultural diversity, epitomised in the Chinese Museum, the Emu Point Joss House and Great Stupa of Universal Compassion (the focus of Popouts Five and Six), members of the Muslim community hoped that the mosque would be 'welcomed as a valuable addition to the diversity of the town'.[23]

To the surprise of organisers, opposition to the mosque was organised soon after the plans were lodged. A 'Stop the Mosque' group formed on Facebook, and a campaign fund was established with Bendigo Bank.[24] National and internationally linked far-right groups, The Q Society and Restore Australia, advised local residents on strategies to oppose the mosque and provided

21 'Our Story,' Bendigo Islamic Community Centre, accessed March 2, 2022, bicc.org.au/about/our-story/, available web.archive.org/web/20220301080005/https://bicc.org.au/about/our-story/.

22 'Bendigo East – Mosque and Community Centre,' GKA Architects, 2016, gkaarchitects.com.au/community/160405_bendigo_east_mosque.

23 Markus, *Division in Bendigo*, v.

24 The bank later closed the account because of 'values differences'. Simon Lauder, 'Bendigo Bank Stands by Decision to Close Account of Anti-Mosque Group,' *ABC News*, April 8, 2014, www.abc.net.au/news/2014-04-08/bendigo-bank-stands-by-decision-to-close-account-of-anti-mosque/5375340.

significant funds for campaign material.[25] Funds were channelled to Stop the Mosque in Bendigo and to the Victorian chapter of the Patriot Defence League Australia (PDLA). The PDLA had recently been registered as an incorporated association in Queensland in January 2014, with the objective 'to raise awareness of women and childrens [*sic*] rights and domestic violence against women and children'.[26] In Bendigo, affiliates of this and similar groups began to tie up ominous black balloons in public spaces in May 2014.[27] At this time, the council had also received 179 formal objections and only six letters of support. In a decision that would later be critiqued as exacerbating social conflict, the council decided it would depart from normal procedure and not hold a consultation meeting with objectors, judging that 'meaningful mediation [was] impossible'.[28] A week before the council was due to vote on the mosque proposal, the *Bendigo Advertiser* received an anonymous email with the subject line, 'Mysterious black balloons revealed'. The email set out the intention behind the balloon campaign to oppose the mosque development. Mirroring the PDLA's putative objectives, the email asserted that accepting Islam into the community would be an endorsement of domestic and child abuse, linking Islam to child marriage, genital mutilation and the oppression of women.[29]

In the face of this concerted opposition, Bendigo council met to decide on the mosque plans on 18 June 2014. The gallery of the council chambers was packed on the day of the vote. Onlookers brandished placards and heckled speakers in favour of the development, including using racial epithets against Councillor Mark Weragoda, who has Sri Lankan heritage.[30] The debate went for more than two hours and was constantly interrupted by audience

25 Blair Thompson, 'Group Rallies Against Mosque Proposal,' *Bendigo Advertiser*, January 14, 2014, www.bendigoadvertiser.com.au/story/2023064/group-rallies-against-mosque-proposal/; Chris Johnston, 'Anti-Islam Lobby Group Funds Mosque Fight in Bendigo,' *The Age*, June 28, 2014, www.theage.com.au/national/victoria/antiislam-lobby-group-funds-mosque-fight-in-bendigo-20140627-3az6n.html; Sue Bolton, 'Right-wing Groups Unite To Fight Bendigo Mosque,' *Green Left*, July 4, 2014, www.greenleft.org.au/2014/1015/news/right-wing-groups-fight-bendigo-mosque.

26 Bianca Hall, 'Anti-Islam Group Deregistered for Masquerading as Domestic Violence Group,' *The Age*, July 2, 2015, www.theage.com.au/national/victoria/antiislam-group-deregistered-for-masquerading-as-domestic-violence-group-20150702-gi360o.html.

27 Chris Johnston, 'Bendigo Mosque a Cause Celebre for Right-Wing Outsiders,' *The Age*, June 27, 2014, www.theage.com.au/national/victoria/bendigo-mosque-a-cause-celebre-for-rightwing-outsiders-20140627-zsoft.html.

28 'Council Decides Against Consultation Meeting With Mosque Opponents,' *ABC News*, May 30, 2014, www.abc.net.au/news/2014-05-30/council-decides-against-consultation-meeting-with/5488904.

29 Johnston, 'Bendigo Mosque.'

30 Adam Holmes, 'A Mosque Two Years in the Making Has Dominated Bendigo Discussion,' *Bendigo Advertiser*, June 15, 2016, www.bendigoadvertiser.com.au/story/3971376/bendigo-mosque-years-in-the-making/.

shouts and interjections. Opponents claimed 'the mosque would bring violence to Bendigo and the city would be overtaken by Sharia law'.[31] At the vote, the plans were approved 7 votes to 2. The meeting was covered live by the *Bendigo Weekly* and the *Bendigo Advertiser*.[32] Protesters taped more black balloons to Councillor Weragoda's house that evening.[33] Weragoda said he had also received 'emails linked to my colour and my race'.[34] A man was later arrested and convicted for making death threats against Weragoda.[35] Queensland-based Mike Holt, head of Restore Australia, commented that the Bendigo mosque issue had united Australian anti-Islam forces: 'We were not united before. But this issue has managed to unite us.'[36]

Following the troubling council debate and black balloon campaign, a 'small army' of people rallied to put up hundreds of multi-coloured balloons 'to send a message that everyone is welcome in Bendigo'.[37] A Change.org petition in support of multiculturalism and diversity in Bendigo was also started. On 21 June, a peaceful protest was held in Hargreaves mall, handing out more coloured balloons with tags saying: 'racism has no place in Bendigo'. Counsellor Weragoda was also presented with a bunch of colourful balloons to replace the black balloons tied up outside his house.[38] Local Christian leaders supported the peaceful demonstration of support for diversity in the community, which included Uniting Church and Anglican ministers and representatives from Amnesty International. About 120 people were at the demonstration at its peak. Later in 2014, an Interfaith Council was established, comprising Anglican, Buddhist, Catholic, Muslim and Sikh representatives.

31 'Bendigo Mosque: Council Approves Construction Despite Fiery Public Meeting,' *ABC News*, June 19, 2014, www.abc.net.au/news/2014-06-19/bendigo-council-approves-mosque-despite-objections/5534634.

32 Lisa Waller, Kristy Hess and Kristin Demetrious, 'Twitter Feeders: An Analysis of Dominant 'Voices' And Patterns in a Local Government Mosque Controversy,' *Australian Journalism Review* 38, no. 2 (2016): 47–60.

33 'Bendigo Mosque: Black Balloons Hung Outside Councillor's House,' *ABC News*, June 20, 2014, www.abc.net.au/news/2014-06-20/backlash-against-bendigo-mosque-plans-includes-black-balloons/5538424; Stephanie Corsetti, 'Objections to Bendigo Mosque Discriminatory and Racist, Council Lawyer Says,' *ABC News*, December 2, 2014, www.abc.net.au/news/2014-12-02/objections-to-bendigo-mosque-discriminatory-council-says/5934442.

34 Hannah Carrodus, 'Rainbow Balloons Fly in Support of Diversity.' *Bendigo Advertiser*, June 21, 2014, www.bendigoadvertiser.com.au/story/2367115/rainbow-balloons-fly-in-support-of-diversity/.

35 Markus, *Division in Bendigo*, 11.

36 Johnson, 'Anti-Islam Lobby Group.'

37 'Coloured Balloons Challenge Bendigo Anti-Mosque Protests,' *SBS News*, June 20, 2014, www.sbs.com.au/news/article/coloured-balloons-challenge-bendigo-anti-mosque-protests/mc54fi1lj.

38 Carrodus, 'Rainbow Balloons.'

Opposition to the mosque continued. A group of 18 objectors to the development appealed to the Victorian Civil and Administrative Tribunal (VCAT). The grounds for appeal were concerns about 'lighting, privacy, visual impact, traffic congestion and noise'.[39] These formal grounds contrast markedly with the fears about domestic abuse, violence against women, terrorism and Islamist violence expressed in protests and public meetings. While the appeal was being heard, local protests and counter actions continued. In February 2015, one of the councillors who had voted against the mosque, Elise Chapman, raised controversy on social media linked to the mosque debate. In response to tweets in favour of the mosque, Chapman posted graphic images of five baby girls with mutilated genitals.[40] Linking Islam with female genital mutilation, sexism and physical violence, she said, 'Every day in the media there are cases of people being raped by Muslims … and there is no doubt a mosque would see more Muslims move to Bendigo'.[41] Twitter suspended her account in response to complaints, and an online petition was established calling for her to be removed from the council.[42] Her actions were referred to a Councillor Conduct Panel, where she was found guilty of misconduct, a conviction which was upheld on appeal to VCAT. Local and state government members and civil society organisations attempted to repair the social divisions that emerged over the mosque proposal. In April, a lunch with political and community leaders was held to celebrate multiculturalism and promote social cohesion. Following the lunch, two federal Labor MPs met with local Muslim leaders at the site of the proposed mosque. Two cars towing A-frame trailers with anti-mosque messages drove past the site repeatedly while the press covered the visit and the protest.[43]

39 Stephanie Corsetti, 'Bendigo Anti-Mosque Protesters Take Battle to Victorian Planning Umpire VCAT,' *ABC News*, December 1, 2014, www.abc.net.au/news/2014-12-01/bendigo-anti-mosque-protesters-take-battle-to-planning-umpire/5930672.

40 'Bendigo Councillor Elise Chapman Tweets Genital Mutilation Image To Mosque Supporter,' *ABC News*, February 27, 2015, www.abc.net.au/news/2015-02-27/bendigo-councillor-tweets-genital-mutilation-image-elise-chapman/6267958. Chapman's views were earlier canvassed in the *Herald Sun*: 'Support and Opposition over Proposed $3m Bendigo Mosque,' *Herald Sun*, July 7, 2014, www.heraldsun.com.au/news/opinion/support-and-opposition-over-proposed-3m-bendigo-mosque/news-story/46c9e11bd05a3f12d186164e08dc96e9.

41 Nico Bucci and Raina Spooner, 'Bendigo Councillor Elise Chapman Tweets Genital Mutilation Image to Mosque Supporter,' *The Age*, February 26, 2015, www.theage.com.au/victoria/bendigo-councillor-elise-chapman-tweets-genital-mutilation-image-to-mosque-supporter-20150226-13ppyf.html.

42 'Bendigo Councillor's Genital Mutilation Tweet Sparks Online Petition,' *ABC Central Victoria*, February 27, 2015, web.archive.org/web/20160907172030/http://www.abc.net.au/local/stories/2015/02/27/4188205.htm.

43 Adam Holmes, 'Drive-by Protest at Mosque Meeting with MPs,' *Bendigo Advertiser*, June 16, 2016, www.bendigoadvertiser.com.au/story/3016560/drive-by-protest-at-mosque-meeting-with-mps/.

VCAT dismissed the planning approval appeal on 6 August 2015. Two weeks after the appeal was dismissed, protests and counter protests were staged in Bendigo. The PDLA had recently been deregistered when its anti-Islam activities were found to be beyond the scope of its incorporated objects (which were to raise awareness of domestic violence).[44] However, another anti-Islam nationalist group, The United Patriots Front (UPF), had formed in May 2015, partly in response to image problems experienced by the earlier similar groups Reclaim Australia and the Australian Defence League.[45] Local objectors to the mosque invited the UPF to Bendigo to join the campaign.[46] The UPF organised a demonstration of about 200 people, described more broadly as an 'anti-Islam demonstration', 'part of a vocal campaign to stop a mosque from being built in Bendigo'.[47] Left-wing groups including Socialist Alternative and No Room for Racism organised a counter protest of a similar size. There was a heavy police presence. The ABC reported that the 'different groups continued to try and circle around police lines to have a head-on confrontation, but were kept apart'.[48] Officers had barricaded the Bendigo Town Hall in preparation for the demonstration and used pepper spray in order to keep the two groups of protesters separated. Lead objector in the appeal to the mosque's planning approval, Julie Hoskin, spoke at the event, claiming that 'the majority of people in Bendigo opposed the mosque'.[49] Anti-mosque counsellor Elise Chapman was seen in the crowd wearing an Australian flag, holding a sign that said, 'Islam oppresses women'. The protests and police action shut down the centre of town for the afternoon.

On the same day in August that these protests were staged, a halal 'Diversity BBQ' was held in the Yi Yuan Garden near the Chinese Museum. It was coordinated by the Bendigo Action Coalition, an informal coalition of local activists who organised in support of multiculturalism, in partnership with the Muslim community.[50] It was held away from where the UPF protests

44 Hall, 'Anti-Islam Group Deregistered.'

45 Jeff Sparrow, 'Members of the Far Right are Threatening Political Violence. Whatever Happened to those Anti-Terror Laws?' *New Matilda*, November 21, 2015, newmatilda.com/2015/11/21/members-of-the-far-right-are-threatening-political-violence-whatever-happened-to-those-anti-terror-laws/.

46 Email correspondence with Timothy W. Jones, 29 March 2022.

47 Tom Cowie, 'Bendigo Mosque Protest: Anti-Mosque and Anti-Racism Protesters Clash,' *The Age*, August 29, 2015, www.theage.com.au/victoria/bendigo-mosque-protest-antimosque-and-antiracism-protesters-clash-20150829-gjaml8.html.

48 'Mosque Controversy Drives Rival Protest Groups to Rally in Bendigo,' *ABC News*, August 29, 2015, www.abc.net.au/news/2015-08-29/rival-protest-groups-rally-in-bendigo-over-mosque/6734702.

49 Cowie, 'Bendigo Mosque Protest.'

50 Email correspondence with Timothy W. Jones, 29 March 2022.

were scheduled and had a family feel with clowns, bands, colouring in and chalk drawing. Without the advertising budget or media-grabbing spectacle of the UPF, it garnered little attention in the press. The council commenced consultations with local stakeholders about how to respond to the situation, which had become disruptive and upsetting to the whole community. Business representatives were concerned about the disruption to commerce and sought protection for their economic interests, and many were concerned to counter the violent expressions of racism and neo-fascism. An 'Eat, Drink, Shop' campaign was launch by local traders to bring people back into the CBD and support local business after the protest shutdowns.[51]

On September 16, protests again erupted at the Bendigo Town Hall over the mosque. In an apparently unplanned protest, a group calling itself 'Rights for Bendigo Residents' disrupted the council meeting, demanding that a referendum be held on whether a mosque should be built.[52] The group of about 150 people heckled the council and chanted 'no mosque'. Unable to contain or curtail the intervention through discussion or normal meeting procedures, the major, Peter Cox, decided to abandon the meeting. Police were called to clear the hall and ended up having to escort the mayor and councillors out of the building for their safety. At the conclusion of the meeting, Julie Hoskin sat in the mayor's chair to shouts of 'Julie for mayor'.[53] Following this incident, public access to council meetings was limited to live telecast for several months.[54]

51 'Buy Local Campaign Lifts Bendigo Traders' Spirits After Mosque Protests Mar Profits,' *ABC News*, September 7, 2015, www.abc.net.au/news/2015-09-07/bendigo-traders-welcome-profits-turnaround-after-protests/6754244.

52 'Bendigo Mosque Protests: Mayor Felt "Numb, Shocked" By Police Escort From Council Meeting,' *ABC News*, September, 17 2015, www.abc.net.au/news/2015-09-17/bendigo-mosque-protests-mayor-felt-numb-and-shocked/6782230; Karen Percy, 'Bendigo Muslim Community Undeterred by Ongoing Protests to Mosque Plans,' *ABC News*, September 17, 2015, www.abc.net.au/news/2015-09-17/bendigo-muslim-community-undeterred-by-ongoing-protests-to-mosq/6784520.

53 'Bendigo Councillors Leave Meeting Under Police Escort After Anti-Mosque Protest Erupts,' *ABC News*, September 16, 2015, www.abc.net.au/news/2015-09-16/police-called-in-to-control-public-at-bendigo-council-meeting/6781712.

54 'Bendigo Council Security Boosted for First Meeting Since September Anti-Mosque Protest,' *ABC News*, October 14, 2015, www.abc.net.au/news/2015-10-14/bendigo-council-boosts-security-for-meeting/6852862; 'Protests and Progress: Four Years That Will Shape Bendigo's Future,' *ABC News*, October 21, 2016, www.abc.net.au/news/2016-10-21/four-years-that-will-shape-bendigos-future/7953536?nw=0&r=HtmlFragment.

In September 2015, Believe in Bendigo was founded by local businesswoman Margot Spalding to demonstrate local support for the Muslim Community and the Islamic Community Centre.[55] On 2 October – the AFL grand final public holiday – the Believe in Bendigo picnic was held to celebrate diversity. Melbourne and local bands played, and Chinese dragon dancers and food stalls entertained participants.[56] Maximising the spectacle, participants were encouraged to wear yellow. Yellow blankets and wrist bands were distributed, funded by local businesses. Oversized iPhone frames were circulated for people to take selfies in with the hashtag #BelieveInBendigo. It was estimated that the event attracted '3000 people in a celebration of compassion and a sea of yellow'.[57] Organisers emphasised that participants were all local, in contrast to the anti-Islam rallies. Russell Jack, director of the Golden Dragon Museum, likened the event to Bendigo's popular Easter Parade as a similar demonstration of diversity and social cohesion.[58]

Conflict came to a head in October. On 3 October 2015, UPF members, including Blair Cottrell, staged a mock beheading outside the Bendigo council offices, spraying fake blood over the steps.[59] The incident was filmed and published on their social media channels, a profitable medium for far-right actors.[60] On 10 October, rival anti-mosque and anti-racism rallies again faced off.[61] In line with similar protests by far-right groups around the world, who had organised a global day against Islam they titled the World Wide Rally for Humanity, the UPF marshalled an estimated 1,000 people to Bendigo.[62] It was prominently reported that many protesters had travelled from New South Wales, South Australia and Queensland. UPF

55 Janine Cohen, 'Believe in Bendigo: Businesswoman Margot Spalding Leads Campaign to Fight Anti-Mosque "Hate",' *ABC News*, November 26, 2015, www.abc.net.au/news/2015-11-23/margot-spalding-fights-hate-in-bendigo-amid-mosque-protests/6956262?nw=0&r=Gallery.

56 Joseph Hinchliffe, 'Sun, Music Make New Believers,' *Bendigo Advertiser*, October 2, 2015, www.bendigoadvertiser.com.au/story/3398144/sun-music-make-new-believers-photos/.

57 'Our Story,' Bendigo Islamic Community Centre, accessed March 20, 2022, bicc.org.au/about/.

58 Hinchliffe, 'Sun, Music Make New Believers.'

59 'Anti-Islamic Group Stage Fake Beheading in Bendigo to Protest Against Mosque Development,' *ABC News*, October 5, 2015, www.abc.net.au/news/2015-10-05/anti-islamic-group-stage-fake-beheading-in-bendigo/6827220; Imogen Richards, 'A Dialectical Approach to Online Propaganda: Australia's United Patriots Front, Right-Wing Politics, and Islamic State,' *Studies in Conflict & Terrorism* 42, no. 1–2 (2019): 43–69, doi.org/10.1080/1057610X.2018.1513691.

60 Alex Hern, 'YouTube Defends Decision to Keep Tommy Robinson on its Site,' *The Guardian*, March 6, 2019, www.theguardian.com/technology/2019/mar/06/youtube-defends-decision-to-keep-tommy-robinson-on-its-site.

61 'Bendigo Mosque: Anti-Mosque Protesters Face Off With Counter Activists,' *ABC News*, October 10, 2015, www.abc.net.au/news/2015-10-10/police-prepare-for-violent-mosque-rallies-in-bendigo/6842862.

62 Vashti Kenway, 'Why its Right to Confront the Fascists,' *Red Flag*, October 12, 2015, redflag.org.au/article/why-its-right-confront-fascists.

spokesman Blair Cottrell addressed the protesters, saying 'In order for Islam to conquer us, we have to be weak … At the end of the day you can't be both a Muslim or an Australian as the two just don't correspond. Ultimately one must conquer the other'.[63] Danny Nalliah, leader of the Rise Up Australia Party, also spoke at the rally.[64] About 300 to 400 anti-racism protesters from the Bendigo Action Coalition and the Melbourne-based Campaign Against Racism and Fascism met at Town Hall and attempted to confront the UPF protesters as they moved into Rosalind Park. More than 420 police were reported to be present and prevented the two camps from physical confrontation. A similar, highly policed UPF protest and Bendigo Action Coalition counter protest was staged in February 2016.[65]

Objectors appealed the VCAT decision to the Victorian Court of Appeal, initially seeking an injunction preventing work on the mosque from commencing pending the substantive appeal hearing in November. At this point, the original 18 objectors had been winnowed down to just two.[66] When their objections were dismissed again, they sought leave for the case to be heard in the High Court, but that was rejected on 15 June 2016. The extensive appeal process bankrupted lead objector Julie Hoskin, who was left unable to pay the legal costs. A City of Greater Bendigo Councillor since October 2016, Hoskin's bankruptcy forced her to resign in September 2018.[67] Hoskin claimed that her lawyer misappropriated funds from the anti-mosque protesters and appealed the bankruptcy determination.[68] At the 2019 federal election, Hoskin ran for the seat of Bendigo with

63 Paul Anderson and Andrew Jefferson, 'Pro- and Anti-Islamic Groups Protest as Bendigo Mosque Rages,' *Sunday Herald Sun*, October 11, 2015, www.heraldsun.com.au/news/victoria/pro-and-antiislamic-groups-protest-as-bendigo-mosque-rages/news-story/d8d629605744a49d45f02256b99d7b9e.

64 Madeleine Morris, 'Bendigo's Anti-Mosque Protest: United Patriots Front Nationalist Group Behind Demonstration,' *ABC News*, October 12, 2015, www.abc.net.au/news/2015-10-12/who-was-behind-bendigos-anti-mosque-protests/6848468.

65 'United Patriots Front Supporters Outnumber Anti-Racism Protesters at Bendigo Rallies,' *ABC News*, February 17, 2016, www.abc.net.au/news/2016-02-27/anti-racism-group-calls-for-peaceful-protest-in-bendigo/7205178.

66 Sarah Farnsworth, 'Bendigo Mosque Injunction Refused as Opponents Attempt to Reverse Planning Approval,' *ABC News*, September 23, 2015, www.abc.net.au/news/2015-09-23/victorian-court-refuses-injunction-to-halt-bendigo-mosque-plans/6799734.

67 Adam Holmes, 'Julie Hoskin Declared Bankrupt One Day Before Sending Councillor Resignation to City of Greater Bendigo,' *Bendigo Advertiser*, September 26, 2018, www.bendigoadvertiser.com.au/story/5667858/hoskin-declared-bankrupt-day-before-council-resignation/; Peter Lenaghan, 'New Look for Bendigo Council as Voters Reject Divided Team,' *ABC News*, October 31, 2016, www.abc.net.au/news/2016-10-31/new-look-after-2016-bendigo-council-results/7979146. The previous councillor, Elise Chapman, notably opposed to the mosque development, lost her seat at the council in the 2016 election.

68 Natalie Croxon, 'Judge Orders Dismissal of Hoskin Bankruptcy Appeal,' *Bendigo Advertiser*, August 23, 2019, www.bendigoadvertiser.com.au/story/6344251/judge-orders-dismissal-of-hoskin-bankruptcy-appeal/.

Fraser Anning's Conservative Australia Party.[69] Hoskin was one of three far-right candidates standing in the marginal Labor seat, along with Rise Up Australia Party and One Nation. Elise Chapman had been nominated as the lead Victorian One Nation candidate in 2016.[70] The UPF's Blair Cottrell, Christopher Shortis and Neil Ericson were convicted of racial vilification in 2017 for their 2015 mock beheading video.[71]

Plans for the Bendigo mosque's design were released late in 2016. Its architecture reflects the design principles of mosques around the world, with significant local inflections. Architect Asher Greenwood had been commissioned by the BIA to design a contemporary mosque. His design responds to both the built heritage of Bendigo and the diverse architectural histories of the multi-ethnic Muslim community that will use it. It features a central courtyard, traditional to Syrian mosques. The courtyard will be lined with laser-cut metal screens, dually referencing Islamic rug patterns and the decorative iron lacework that is the signature of founding Bendigo architect, William Vahland. The prayer hall eschews the domes, common to mosques internationally, instead taking the form of a curved pyramid, inspired by the design of the late nineteenth century Bendigo Law Courts. Its supporting columns will be painted black, referencing the iron bark trees in the surrounding bush setting.[72]

Construction of the mosque began in 2019. Victorian Premier Daniel Andrews took part in a sod-turning ceremony with local councillors and Muslim community leaders.[73] Photographs of the scene depict a semi-circle of dignitaries lofting soil forward with shiny silver shovels.[74] The Victorian government contributed $400,000 to the first stage of the project, which

69 She attracted only 1.64% of first preferences: Croxon, 'Judge Orders Dismissal.'

70 Peter Leneghan, 'Bendigo Anti-Mosque Protester Elise Chapman Named as Lead One Nation Candidate for Victoria,' *ABC News*, January 8, 2016, www.abc.net.au/news/2016-01-08/bendigo-anti-mosque-protester-named-as-one-nation-candidate/7075768.

71 'United Patriots Front Trio Found Guilty of Inciting Serious Contempt of Muslims,' *The Guardian*, September 5, 2017, www.theguardian.com/australia-news/2017/sep/05/united-patriots-front-trio-say-beheading-stunt-during-bendigo-mosque-protest-an-act-of-free-speech; David Lowe, 'Far-Right Extremism: Is it Legitimate Freedom of Expression, Hate Crime, or Terrorism?' *Terrorism and Political Violence* 34 no. 7 (2022): 1433–53, doi.org/10.1080/09546553.2020.1789111.

72 Linda Cheng, 'The Architectural Face Of Bendigo's Embattled Mosque,' *Architecture, AU*, November 26, 2016, architectureau.com/articles/the-architectural-face-of-bendigos-embattled-mosque/.

73 Emma D'Agostino and Elspeth Kernebone, 'Bendigo Mosque Works Begin as First Sod Turned at Site of Islamic Community Centre,' *Bendigo Advertiser*, July 26, 2019, www.bendigoadvertiser.com.au/story/6295558/a-day-of-joy-as-mosque-construction-begins/.

74 Larissa Romensky and Natalie Kerr, 'Bendigo Mosque Construction Begins as Premier Daniel Andrews Turns First Sod,' *ABC News*, July 26, 2019, www.abc.net.au/news/2019-07-26/bendigo-mosque-sod-turned-after-years-of-controversy/11347164.

includes a sports hall and community space.[75] The prayer hall is due to be built in later stages, depending on further fundraising. The staging of the build, its reportage and even the design of the centre that is being pursued foreground the shared community facilities.

Building social cohesion

The protest and social conflict over Muslim inclusion in Bendigo society and its built environment stand out in Australian history as a nadir of religious conflict. Mosques built earlier in Victoria, or even contemporaneous to the Bendigo Islamic Centre, did not receive comparable protest or opposition.[76] In Newport, in the inner west of Melbourne, the Australian Islamic Centre was being constructed at the same time as the protests and appeals against the Bendigo centre took place.[77] There were no reports of far-right public protests, nor were there technical objections to planning permission made by people associated with anti-Islamic political movements. The particular ferocity and scale of the conflict in Bendigo can usefully be understood in reference to three factors: the specificity of social conditions at the site related to a 'boom and bust' in cultural diversity, the history of xenophobia and the far right in Australia, and the way that religious difference was managed by the council and state government, especially the operation of discourses of multiculturalism and social cohesion at the frontline of conflict between the far-right, left-wing and Muslim communities.

The controversy over the mosque arose at a time of rapid social change in Bendigo. After the gold industry collapsed, Bendigo entered a long period as one of the most homogeneous and white regional towns in the country. It was only in the second decade of the twenty-first century that migration of people from minority cultures and religions had begun to grow, and cultural diversity was still less than half the social, religious and cultural mix of Bendigo during the gold rush. The Muslim population of Bendigo was more than doubling

75 Natalie Croxon, 'Bendigo Islamic Community Centre Takes Shape as Construction Continues,' *Bendigo Advertiser*, July 11, 2020, www.bendigoadvertiser.com.au/story/6824891/bendigo-islamic-community-centre-takes-shape/.
76 Yasmeen Vahed and Goolam Vahed, 'The Development Impact of Mosque Location on Land Use in Australia: A Case Study of *Masjid al Farooq* in Brisbane,' *Journal of Muslim Minority Affairs* 34 no.1 (2014): 66–81, doi.org/10.1080/13602004.2014.888284.
77 Julie Rudner, Fatemeh Shahani and Trevor Hogan, 'Islamic Architectures of Self-Inclusion and Assurance in a Multicultural Society,' *Fabrications* 30 no. 2 (2020): 153–75, doi.org/10.1080/10331867.2020.1749220.

at the time of the mosque planning application. As registered in the census between 2011 and 2016, the population rose from 200 to 460. A significant number of this growth (168) was from new migrants to Australia.[78] A century of cultural homogeneity did not equip the Bendigo community with the tools, values or attitudes to adjust easily to this rapidly expanding diversity, small as it was. Close to half of the population had 'negative views or concerns over the prospect of an increase in the Muslim population'.[79] Furthermore, as Andrew Markus observed, municipal organisations in areas with 'historic and currently low levels of cultural diversity have little experience or expertise in the handling of controversial issues within multicultural contexts'.[80] It is notable that the local cultural institutions celebrated for representing religious and cultural diversity – the Stupa and the Chinese Museum – are not linked to influxes of culturally or religiously diverse migrants. The Chinese community memorialised in the museum is historic, and the Stupa, as noted in Popout Six, has strong links to white Western Buddhists.

Opposition to the mosque was grounded in views of Islam as being particularly incompatible with the Australian way of life and an imminent threat. Numerous commentators and scholars have noted how, following the September 11 attacks on the World Trade Center, xenophobic sentiment became narrowly focused on Islam.[81] Earlier waves of right-wing political violence had broader and more distant targets such as 'communism' or 'immigration'. Twenty-first-century anti-Islam rhetoric portrayed the political ideology of Islamist groups such as Al Qaeda and Islamic State as the authentic representatives of the whole religion. Ironically, Australian anti-Muslim political activity increased with the wave of Muslim migrants fleeing conflict and Islamist persecution in Iraq and Afghanistan. The public rallies in opposition to the Bendigo mosque proposal, thus, came at a time of heightened tension around Islam.[82] In addition to the public protests

78 Markus, *Division in Bendigo*, 27.

79 Ibid., vii.

80 Ibid.

81 Amber Hart, 'Right-Wing Waves: Applying the Four Waves Theory to Transnational and Transhistorical Right-Wing Threat Trends,' *Terrorism and Political Violence* 35, no. 1 (2021): 1–16, doi.org/10.1080/09546553.2020.1856818; Linda Briskman, 'The Creeping Blight of Islamophobia in Australia,' *International Journal for Crime, Justice and Social Democracy* 4, no. 3 (2015): 112–21, doi.org/10.5204/ijcjsd.v4i3.244; Adrian Cherney and Kristina Murphy, 'Being a 'Suspect Community' in a Post 9/11 World – The Impact of the War on Terror on Muslim Communities in Australia,' *Australian and New Zealand Journal of Criminology* 49, no. 4 (2016): 480–96, doi.org/10.1177/0004865815585392.

82 Benafsha Askarzai, 'The Burqa Ban, Islamophobia, and the Effects of Racial 'Othering' in Australian Political Discourses,' *Australian Journal of Politics and History* 68, no. 2 (2022): 218–41, doi.org/10.1111/ajph.12790.

and sustained opposition to the Bendigo mosque, street demonstrations against Islam were also held in 2015 and 2016 in the Melbourne CBD and in the suburbs of Coburg and Melton, where there was a perception that the Muslim community was growing.[83] Anti-Islamic street action was legitimated by political inquiries into links between halal certification and terrorism and a proliferation of anti-Islam political parties.[84]

Earlier waves of Muslim migrants experienced racism, social ostracisation and exclusion; however, there is less evidence that 'Islam as a belief system' factored into this discrimination.[85] In early twentieth century discourse and policy invention, Muslims were excluded as people labelled as 'Asiatics', not as Muslims. Further, South Asians were often and inaccurately imagined as 'Hindoos'. A distinctive feature of the twenty-first-century anti-Islam movement is its engagement with the (ostensible) beliefs and principles of Islam and Islamism. Their vision of Islam is one of a violent, colonising political movement with a desire to impose Sharia law on all people.[86] They view Islam as incompatible with Australian values and lifestyles; as one mosque opponent wrote: 'every time a mosque is built in Australia a little bit of this nation dies and is replaced by the Middle East'.[87] Anti-Islam groups mobilise an alternative ideology in their fight, which several commentators have likened to a civic religion combining ANZAC mythology and Christianity.[88] Some mosque opponents in Bendigo saw the conflict over planning permission as a restaging of the iconic World War One campaign, posting on social media: 'Most important place in our history – MUSLIMS WILL NOT WIN!!! The ANZACS must rise again – starting in BENDIGO!!!'[89] The Christchurch mosque shooting in March 2019 led

83 Stephanie Anderson, 'Melbourne Counter Rallies, Bendigo Mosque Protests Cost Taxpayers $2.3 Million, Police Say,' *ABC News*, December 8, 2016, www.abc.net.au/news/2016-12-08/victorian-islam-counter-rallies-cost-2-3-million-police-say/8100294.

84 Fatima Measham, 'Keep Islamophobia on the Fringes Where it Belongs,' *Eureka Street*, October 26, 2015. www.eurekastreet.com.au/article/keep-islamophobia-on-the-fringes-where-it-belongs.

85 Mario Peucker, Peter Lentini, Debra Smith and Muhammad Iqbal, '"Our Diggers Would Turn In Their Graves": Nostalgia and Civil Religion in Australia's Far-Right,' *Australian Journal of Political Science* 56, no. 2 (2021): 189–205, doi.org/10.1080/10361146.2021.1935448.

86 James Stewart, 'Anti-Muslim Hate Speech and Displacement Narratives: Case Studies from Sri Lanka and Australia,' *The Australian Journal of Social Issues* 54, no. 4 (2019): 418–35, doi.org/10.1002/ajs4.83.

87 Measham, 'Keep Islamophobia.'

88 Peucker et al., 'Our diggers.'

89 Ibid.

to a decrease in anti-Islam demonstrations. However, a small number of anti-mosque protesters continued to picket the mosque site weekly at the time of writing.[90]

The Bendigo council has been widely applauded for its handling of the contentious planning application and its support of multiculturalism in the region. In November 2016, the council was awarded the Planning Institute of Australia's President's award for excellence for its handling of the planning permit application for the Bendigo mosque.[91] Planning Institute of Australia Victoria's president, James Larmour-Reid, said that the award was made in recognition of the way the council dealt with the contentious issue, its: 'adherence to planning law, policy and process; its sound governance practices; and its efforts to mitigate the social impact of a highly divisive issue upon its staff and citizens'.[92] Two investigations into the controversy and government and community responses were also conducted.[93] They admired the council for both following the law regarding planning applications and taking a moral stand in support of the Muslim community in the face of intimidation and threats. However, they also identified a number of significant deficiencies in the way authorities responded to those threats.

Perhaps the most serious deficiency was identified by Andrew Markus, who showed that the handling of the application and protests did not acknowledge or address the beliefs and anxieties of mosque opponents.[94] While authorities repeatedly affirmed the social values of multiculturalism and religious diversity, Markus found that authorities did not acknowledge or understand the level of public concern about the growing presence and impact of Muslims in the community. Political leaders affirmed Bendigo as a place that celebrated multicultural diversity and welcomed immigrants. They depicted mosque opponents as a small minority and emphasised the role of non-local anti-mosque campaigners. Judging that reasoned engagement and consultation with opponents was unlikely or impossible,

90 Lisa Martin, 'A Blessing In Disguise? Bendigo at Peace With its Mosque After Years of Far-Right Protest,' *The Guardian*, July 20, 2019, www.theguardian.com/australia-news/2019/jul/30/a-blessing-in-disguise-bendigo-at-peace-with-its-mosque-after-years-of-far-right-protest.

91 '2016 PIA Victorian Awards for Planning Excellence Announced,' Landscape Australia, November 7, 2016, landscapeaustralia.com/articles/2016-pia-victoria-awards-for-planning-excellence-announced/.

92 Ricky Ray Ricardo, 'City of Greater Bendigo Wins Award at Victorian Planning Awards for its Involvement in Mosque Crisis,' Landscape Australia, November 7, 2016, landscapeaustralia.com/articles/city-of-greater-bendigo-wins-award-at-victorian-planning-awards-for-its-involvement-in-mosque-crisis/.

93 Rudner, *Social Cohesion in Bendigo*; Markus, *Division in Bendigo*.

94 Markus, *Division in Bendigo*.

the council did not explore other means of engaging and influencing opponents that may have more effectively worked towards improving social cohesion. Markus identified several strategies that could have been usefully deployed to avoid escalation of conflict, including smaller-scale consultations facilitated by trusted community leaders in the 'middle ground', clear and timely messaging about the council's powers, emphasising the relevant constitutional and human rights considerations, and foregrounding the impact of the anti-mosque campaign on vulnerable fellow citizens. The council's failure to engage substantially with mosque opponents has had asymmetrical impacts on the Muslim community. Islamophobic protest has forced Muslims into roles where they explain and apologise for their faith.[95] New mosques are being built in literally transparent designs to debunk myths of terrorism.[96] However, there has been limited acknowledgment of, or engagement with, the beliefs and politics of anti-Islam social movements.

In many respects, the protests and counter protests were a painful debate between different groups of white settlers about who gets to be 'local' – who will be allowed to feel like they belong. At the heart of the anti-mosque protests was a profound fear that religious outsiders were going to make their hometown 'foreign', literally transforming it into the Middle East. On the other hand, in their attempts to promote multicultural social cohesion, authorities repeatedly described Muslims and their allies as 'local', while the protesters were dismissed as mostly being 'outsiders'. In some ways, the problems with religious diversity and social cohesion represented in the mosque controversy are a testament to the problematic 'success' of the White Australia Policy. Whiteness shaped racial and religious discrimination through and beyond the life of the IRA. Islam's long history in Australia was successfully erased from local memory. The Muslim population of Bendigo only returned to similar proportions to what it was at Federation after a 100 year 'whiteout'. The erasure of Muslim history in Australia – which both predates Christianity and facilitated Christian dominance in the country – means that Muslim communities in the recent past have had to constantly

95 Mario Peucker, '"You are Essentially Forced Into Being An Activist": The Interplay Between Islamophobia and Muslims' Civic Engagement in Australia,' *Religion, State & Society* 49, no.1 (2021): 23–40, doi.org/10.1080/09637494.2021.1900766; Anita Harris and Shakira Hussein, 'Conscripts or Volunteers? Young Muslims as Everyday Explainers,' *Journal of Ethnic and Migration Studies* 46, no. 19 (2020): 3974–991.

96 Glenn Murcutt, *Architecture of Faith* (exhibition), 9 August 2016 to 19 February 2017, National Gallery of Victoria, www.ngv.vic.gov.au/exhibition/glenn-murcutt/; Linda Cheng, 'Murcutt's 'Extraordinary Enlightenment': Australian Islamic Centre,' *Architecture, AU*, August 3, 2016, architectureau.com/articles/murcutts-extraordinary-enlightenment-australian-islamic-centre/.

renegotiate their entry and integration into Australian society. But it also points to the limits of multiculturalism. As Ghassan Hage observed in *White Nation* 25 years ago, public discourses of multiculturalism commonly do not engage with those white people who experience non-white migration as loss. As we saw in Bendigo from 2014, their consequent exclusion from mainstream political discussion contributes to the formation of 'a home-grown Australian neo-fascism'.[97] Thus, the hope for a socially cohesive future in Bendigo, and more widely, needs to be grounded in more than a handsome and historically informed mosque architecture. It requires the difficult work of genuinely engaging with the fears and historical fantasies of disaffected white people, as well as tracing the historical agency of Muslim South Asians, who found ways to continue to practice their faith through and despite discrimination.

The mobilisation of history in Bendigo's built heritage is a celebrated feature of its identity, planning and culture. The Chinese goldfields history is memorialised in the Golden Dragon Museum, located in the historic civic centre of Bendigo adjacent to Rosalind Park, where over 100 years ago, Bendigo's Muslims celebrated Eid and delighted locals with their prayers, feasts and celebrations. Bendigo's first mosque, however, is being built in a quiet, out-of-the-way location in an East Bendigo industrial estate. Its 'non-monumental' design quietly but strenuously asserts Islam's long association with colonial Australia: from the locally mined sandstone walls to an industrial 'chimney stack' style minaret, and founding Bendigo architect William Vahland's signature decorative cast iron.[98] In the face of violent Islamophobic protests, the local community (both Muslim and non-Muslim), government and media rallied to show their support for Bendigo Muslims. The proposed Islamic Community Centre was increasingly represented as not being exclusively Muslim, but a place for the whole community: a 'community centre with a mosque inside'.[99] This proposed building is saturated in references to the past in order to make a community safe in a troubled present, hoping to conjure forth a socially cohesive future.

97 Ghassan Hage, *White Nation: Fantasies of White Supremacy in a Multicultural Society* (Routledge, 2000), 21.

98 Cheng, 'The Architectural Face.'

99 Romensky and Kerr, 'Bendigo Mosque Construction.'

10

Conclusion: Womin-dji-ka (welcome) to Bendigo, a city of flourishing diversity?

By examining histories of cohesion at the local scale, this book has revealed the far-reaching and cumulative effects of modest acts that hold social, religious and spiritual meaning: acts such as donating money, breastfeeding, praying, blessing, wishing, writing letters, supporting neighbours, organising and attending meetings. These acts enable larger groups to gather and identify as one. When economic, material and social conditions permitted a built space of faith or spiritual expression, faith-based and interfaith connections and belonging were often 'scaled up' into congregations and community. Conversely, where economic conditions declined, so too did the struggle to maintain cohesion intensify. This was perhaps no more pertinent than in 2015 to 2016, when dissent over the proposed Bendigo mosque became violent, as discussed in Chapter Nine. Amid the vocal furore, one quiet act of recognition and respect affirmed Bendigo's grassroots commitment to keep struggling for social cohesion.

Since 2016, Bendigo's processional culture has reflected the sovereign right of Djaara people to welcome newcomers to their land through the organisation of the Easter Parade assembly.[1] A photograph of the 2019 parade shows Djaara people leading the parade through Bendigo's streets. They hold a banner on which 'Womin-dji-ka' is boldly painted; below, a translation '(Welcome)', in English and in brackets, asserts Djaara sovereignty.

1 Ralph Beh, Major Events Officer and Parade Co-ordinator, City of Greater Bendigo, personal communication to Jennifer Jones, October 19, 2023.

Traditionally and into current times, the Bendigo parade has moved along Pall Mall, one of Bendigo's principal streets. Wide and tree-lined, Pall Mall extends north from the central junction of Charing Cross, where the large and ornate 'Alexandra Fountain' honours the Princess of Wales and marks the centre of Bendigo city.[2] Opened by Alexandra's sons, Princes Albert and George, in 1881, this monument symbolises imperial relations and displays Bendigo's enormous goldrush wealth. Built of highly polished Harcourt granite, it literally manifests the upturning and transformation of the land in this district. Staging the Easter Parade along Pall Mall, with its references to London landmarks and its grand colonial buildings and impressive monuments, was intended to invoke imperial patriotism and pride in the city's development. The order of assembly reflected and reinforced the gendered, classed and racialised structures of empire and attributed importance to participants relative to this hierarchy. Historian Michael Roper has argued that public rituals, including processions, can bolster existing social hierarchies.[3] The early Easter parades of the 1870s were led by the mayor in full regalia, followed by members of the legislative assembly and councillors of Sandhurst, Eaglehawk and surrounding shire councils, and then by members of various boards and committees.[4] Their rank and distinction were also established by their elevated means of conveyance in horse-drawn carriages. This contrasted the procession of the friendly societies and fire brigades whose members walked behind, each clustered behind their ornate banner of allegiance. While this illustrates how 'imperial locations' have been 'power-saturated sites of cultural conjuncture and contest', they have also been (as this book has revealed) sites of connection, cohesion and repair.[5]

As a collective form of expression, parading makes visible the tight forms of cohesion that are usually created and sustained in the more private spaces, like those of community organisations and religious congregations. The makings of interfaith and multi-religious social cohesion become apparent when these associations are brought into public space: a cohesion

2 'Alexandra Fountain,' National Trust Database, accessed October 27, 2023, vhd.heritage.vic.gov.au/search/nattrust_result_detail/68184.

3 Michael Roper, 'Inventing Traditions in Colonial Society: Bendigo's Easter Fair, 1871–1885,' *Journal of Australian Studies* 9, no. 17 (1985): 31–40, doi.org/10.1080/14443058509386911.

4 Michael Roper, 'Inventing Traditions in Goldfields Society: Public Rituals and Townbuilding in Sandhurst, 1867–1885,' (Master's thesis, Monash University, 1986), 212.

5 Tony Ballantyne and Antoinette Burton, 'Introduction,' in *Moving Subjects: Gender, Mobility, and Intimacy in an Age of Global Empire*, ed. Tony Ballantyne and Antoinette Burton (University of Illinois Press, 2009), 3.

visible to, and extended by, spectators – themselves of diverse faiths and religions – as they rub shoulders on footpaths and move along streets where they also conduct their daily lives. This intimacy of scale fosters a sense of commonality within the crowd; a shared appeal draws upon 'the ease of access, comfort of contact and sharing of affinities, which underpin much of social life'.[6] As celebratory events that bring heterogeneous groups into one space, parades have the capacity to unify and to challenge people just by being together in the same place on the same day.

Therefore, while organisers may have included marginalised groups for one purpose, like the Aboriginal participants that joined the Easter procession in 1891, the intentions of actual performers and the interpretations of the crowd may have differed. Described in 1891 through a European lens as a 'band of aboriginals', their presence was likely designed to cultivate entertainment and exoticism at the tail of the procession.[7] Chinese pageantry, as noted in the introduction, was also included to foster a carnival atmosphere. The long-lasting benefit that resulted from Chinese participation was a negotiated outcome, one that responded to the demands of the Chinese community and met the needs of parade organisers. As the chapters and popouts of this book have shown, the proximate and shared daily practices of spirituality, faith and religion on the gold fields were often at odds with the more divisive or racialised identities asserted through institutions, media or prevailing discourse. The nexus between race and religion has been a complex and shifting one, underscored by the forces of the markedly Christian, self-consciously white-driven project of settler colonialism. The cohesive operations of difference apparent in Bendigo's Easter Parade displayed possibilities for the city's identity despite current assertions of essential racial difference between Europeans and people of Chinese, South and Southeast Asian descent. This public celebration of faith, and multi-faiths, has taken place for over a hundred years.

Through our methodical focus on the history of cohesion, we have developed new understandings of 'the politics of nearness', including how people mix and learn from each other in public and in more concealed meeting spaces.[8] Sometimes in a single ceremony or event, or over years and decades, the spiritualities, religions and faiths of others became familiar

6 Suzanne Hall, *City, Street and Citizen: The Measure of the Ordinary* (Routledge, 2012).

7 'The Easter Fair. Sandhurst,' *The Herald* (Melbourne), March 31, 1891, p. 1, col. 5, nla.gov.au/nla.news-article242124666; Roper, 'Inventing Traditions.'

8 Hall, *City, Street and Citizen.*

through the physical nearness of neighbours.[9] Our interest in nearness has shown how the daily and private intimacies of spirituality and faith – those beliefs and acts of trust and of worship – are inseparable from love, marriage, child-raising and self and familial belonging. It is also evident that these forces have shaped less frequent and more spectacular intimacies – those of congregations, parades, legal proceedings and festivals. Many of the stories presented across the chapters take notice of negotiated and sometimes tenuous forms of connection that might otherwise be elided. The local focus of these histories brings the granularity of this historical diplomacy into view and reveals how faith, spirituality and religion might inform and support fragile but essential efforts to communicate. The change that saw Djaara people lead the Easter Parade's order of assembly exemplifies such quiet but powerful neighbourliness.

Local Djaara and Aboriginal community–controlled organisations invite Indigenous community members to 'help celebrate and represent Mob by leading the parade and welcoming thousands of visitors to Bendigo'.[10] Asserting survival and celebrating identity at this important local event provides local settlers and visitors with 'a starting point, an invitation to meet' their Indigenous neighbours.[11] Local public acts are thus enlisted, as Penny Edmonds argues:

> for powerful and affective processes of social transformation and are testament to the urgent and genuine desire of Indigenous and non-Indigenous peoples alike … to forge different relationships with each other to create new cross-cultural and equitable futures. Such performances are thus crucial to the radical political work of reconstructing history for the purpose of building affective engagement between people … in moves towards new postcolonial socialities.[12]

9 Ibid., 95.

10 Bendigo Reconciliation & Allyship Committee, 'DJAARA will be leading the Bendigo Easter Festival parades once again this year …' Facebook, March 20, 2024, www.facebook.com/bendigoreconciliation/photos/djaara-will-be-leading-the-bendigo-easter-festival-parades-once-again-this-yeara/732834428961434/?_rdr.

11 Megan Davis, 'Speaking Up: The Truth About Truth-telling,' *Griffith Review*, no. 76 (2022): 25, www.griffithreview.com/articles/speaking-up/.

12 Penelope Edmonds, *Settler Colonialism And (Re)conciliation: Frontier Violence, Affective Performances, and Imaginative Refoundings* (Palgrave Macmillan, 2016), 8.

Celebrating and crediting the authority of traditional ownership at the Easter Parade establishes a nuanced dialogue between Indigenous participants, organisers and audiences. While not in itself addressing inequalities in health, education, child removal or incarceration rates, this symbolic act creates a local platform for acknowledging these issues as outcomes of dispossession.[13] This dialogue recognises the centrality of access to land; its resources have facilitated Bendigo's settler diversity at the cost of Djaara wellbeing and opportunity. Now the permanent parade leaders on their birthright Country, Djaara people invite newcomers to participate in relationship-building, an essential first step for fair reparation and repair.

13 Megan Davis, 'Speaking Up,' 28.

Glossary

Bunjil: The creator being in Djaara spirituality, represented as an eaglehawk.

Djaara: The Aboriginal people of the Dja Dja Wurrung language group in central Victoria.

Djandak: The Djaara term for Country, which encompasses spiritual, cultural, and physical connections to the land, including kinship relationships with plants, animals, and ancestral beings.

Eid al-Adha: A principal Islamic holiday, also known as Abraham's Day.

Eid al-Fitr: An Islamic holiday marking the end of Ramadan, the month of fasting.

Guan-Di: a diety worshipped in Chinese mythology and culture.

Haskalah: An intellectual Jewish movement in Central and Eastern Europe that emphasised rationality and intellect, leading to the modernisation of Jewish practices.

Hoi Gong Ceremony: performed to bring new lion statues to life.

Kashrut: Jewish dietary laws that dictate food preparation and consumption.

Laanecoorie: The Dja Dja Wurrung name for the Loddon River.

Mindi: The giant serpent in Djaara spirituality, responsible for enforcing Bunjil's laws and ceremonies.

Mohel: A person trained to perform the Jewish ritual of circumcision.

Ultramontanism: A movement within the Catholic Church that emphasised the authority of the Pope over national or diocesan authority.

White Australia Policy: a racial policy established by the 1901 Immigration Restriction Act, aimed to limit non-European immigration.

Womin-dji-ka: A word meaning 'welcome' in Dja Dja Wurrung language.

Index

Note: Page numbers in **bold** indicate figures and tables.

Aboriginal *see* First Nations people
Aboriginal protectorates 30, 32–33
see also Chief Protector of the Aborigines; Coranderrk Aboriginal Station
Acts *see* legislation
Ah Poo, James *see* Appoo, James
All Saints' Cathedral 75, 184, 190, 192, 195–196
church building 190, 192, 196
demographics **180**, 188, 192, 195–196
St Paul's Cathedral 75, 184, 190, 196
ancestor worship *see* Chinese religious practices
Anglicanism 176–177, 183, 188–190, 192, 195
see also Church of England
anti-Islam sentiment *see* Islam
antisemitism *see* Judaism
Appoo, James 65, 67–68
Argyle, Edward **31**, 35, 48–50, 55
Australian Government *see* government
Australian native animals 47, 58

Backhaus, Father Henry, 131–146, 152, 167, 185, 190, 203
see also Catholicism
Ballarat, Victoria **6**, 15–16, **92**, 217
Judaism in 85–88, 90–93, 98–101, 155–156
Barapa Barapa (First Nations people) 15–16, 34–35, 48, 57–58
Beernmarmin *see* Farmer, Tommy
Bendigo Benevolent Asylum 1, **7**, 73, 76, 138–139, 185
see also charity; health
Bendigo Hospital 1, 73–79, 138–139, 185
Bendigo Mosque 11, 22, 223–242
Bendigo South *see* Golden Square Methodist Church
Bendigo Trust 214, 216
birth *see* childbirth
Booth, Abraham 28, **31**, 35, 37, 41, 43, 45–50, 53
Booth, Hannah (*née* Holloway) 28, 35–36, 41, **55**
Booth, John (child) 41, **54**
British
imperialism displays 1–2, 11, 24, 60–70, 164–165, 244
imported divisive politics 21, 161–165, 171–178
law in Australia 17, 62–65, 90, 164
patriotism for in Australia 18, 82–84, 94–96, 101, 162, 164–165, 172, 189–190, 244
Protestantism assumed as default religion 20, 88–91, 97–98, 162, 164, 178, 224, 245
Brown, James 114, 121–122, 124–125, 127, 129

Brown, Kate 112, 121, 123–124, 127
Brown, Mary Agnes 122, 128
Buddhism 19, 213, 216, 219–222, 230, 238
  see also Great Stupa of Universal Compassion
Bunjil the eaglehawk (First Nations ancestral being) 16, 249
burials *see* death

Calvanism 113-115, 118, 129
  see also Protestantism
Campbell, Alick 35, 40, 57–58
Campbell, Archibald Macarthur **30–31**, 38, 40, 45
Campbell, Emma (*née* Kerr/Curr) 8, 29, 33–35, 40, 56–58
Catholicism
  anti-Catholic sentiment 20, 161–164, 171, 173–174
  Backhaus, Father Henry 131–146, 152, 167, 185, 190, 203
  church building 141, 147, 151–153, 190, 199, 203–209
  demographics 10, 21, 147, 179, **180**, 183, 188, 190–193, 198–200
  Devotional Revolution 134–136, 153
  education 136, 141–143, 145–147, 185–186, 191, 193, 198–199
  employment 145, 147–148, 167, 183, 186, 204, 207
  Irish Catholicism 20, 134–136, 146–147, 152–153
  politics and 146–148, 150, 163, 186
  religious practices of 133, 136–139, 149–151, 193, 198–200
  Sacred Heart Cathedral **7**, 10, 22, 190, 203–209, 224
  as social community 149–153, 199, 203–209
  St Kilian's Parish 75, 137–141, 148–149
  women and 147, 149, 151–152, 185
  see also Cullen, Cardinal Paul
censuses 21, 180–181, 187, 193, 195–196, 198, 200–201, 238
Chapman, Elise 231–232, 235–236
charity 1, 99, 142, 184, 190, 192–193
  Catholicism and 138, 151
  Hospital Sundays 73–79
  Islam and 228–229, 237
  for medical needs 74–79, 170, 173
  as performative 73–74, 77–78
  against racism 234–235
  as social unifier 73–79, 86
  views on 8, 75–78
  see also social justice
Chief Protector of the Aborigines 56
  see also Aboriginal protectorates
childbirth 34–35, 115, **117**, 121–122, 124–128, 158, 192
  see also women—and motherhood
children 41, 61, 74, 91, 113–117, 120–129, 158, 229
  see also education; health
Chinese 3–4, 44, 156
  anti-Chinese sentiment 3, 67, 69–70, 213–214, 216
  Bendigo Chinese Association 214, 216–217
  Emu Point Joss House 10, 211–216, 228
  Hoi Gong ceremony 214–215, 249
  legal system and 8, 59–71
  migrants 18–19, 59–70, 211, 216
  miners 18–19, 108, 213
  religious practices 18–19, 59–61, 63–70, **104**, 108, 211–216, 249
  temples **6**, 19, 211–216, 228
  views on 19, 69–70, 213–214, 216
  violence against 213–214, 216

Christianity 1, 17–20, 90–91, 179
Chinese 19, 213
demographics 17–18, 21, **180**, 182–183, 188, 195, 200
English Reformation and 20, 23, 63
First Nations and 17, 29, 33
interfaith marriage and 138, 145, 155–159, 185, 207–208
Church of England (C of E) 10, 18, 20, 189–190
see also Anglicanism
class system 81–101, 107–108, 123–124, 150, 168–169, 174, 178, 183–188, 244
Collier, Andrew 172–173
Confucianism 61, 66, 77, 213, 216
see also Chinese—religious practices
Copock, Frank 10, 204–205, 207
Copock, Paul 10, 203–209
see also Catholicism
Coranderrk Aboriginal Station 33, 35, 56–58
Cornish miners 165–168, 170, 179, 184–185, 200
Cottrell, Blair 234–236
courts *see* legal system
Crane, Bishop Martin 9, 131–132, 144–149, 152–153, 185
see also Catholicism
crime 61, 86, 136, 163, 175–178, 230, 236
see also legal system; legislation
Cullen, Cardinal Paul 135–136, 142, 144
see also Catholicism
Curr, Emma *see* Campbell, Emma

Daoism *see* Taoism
death 9, 113, 115–116, 140, 152, 186
burials 10, 58, 103–109, **117**, 136–138, 177
cemeteries 4, 10, 103–109, **117**
children 107, 111–113, 115–117, 120
commemoration of 109, 149, 213
funerals 135, 140, 149
from illness 116, 126, 129, 151, 174, 177
mining-related 116–117, 172–174, 177
women 58, 84, 115–117, 151
see also White Hills Cemetery
Devotional Revolution *see* Catholicism
discrimination
anti-Catholic sentiment 161–164, 171, 173–174
anti-Methodist views 173–175, 177
antisemitism 71, 82, 100, **104**, 107, 171
against Chinese 3, 67, 69–70, **104**, 107–109, 213–214, 216
First Nations people and 4–5, 16–17, 30, 32–33, 39–41, 52, 56–58, 62, 247
against Islam 107, 229–233, 235–242
in legal contexts 24, 59–71, 90–91, 224, 241, 249
dispossession *see* Djaara; First Nations people
Djaara (First Nations people) 5, 27–58, 243, 245–247
Christianity and 17, 29, 33
Country (Djandak) and, 5, 15–16, 25–28, 32–33, 38–39, 43–44, 56–58, 247, 249
dispossession of 4–5, 8, 16–17, 24–25, 27–58, 62, 247
employed by whites 32–33, 35–44, 47, 52–53
forced removals from land 29, 32, 35, 56–58, 247
language *see* Dja Dja Wurrung
names given by whites **38–39**

relationships with other First Nations 15–16, 35, 57–58
spirituality and 11, 16–19, 27–29, 33, 66
traditional lifeways of 5, 8, 16, 27–30, 38–40, 48, 51, 66
violence against 5, 16, 29–30, 32, 35, 57–58, 247
women 29, 33–36, 40–41, 56–58
see also language
Dja Dja Wurrung (Djaara language) 5, 17, 66, 243, 249
Djandak (Djaara Country) 5, 15–16, 25–28, 32–33, 38–39, 43–44, 56–58, 247, 249
see also Djaara
donations *see* charity
drought 51, 112–113, 140, 143, 194
see also land management; water management
Duck Swamp Station 31, 35, **42**, 44, 46
Duke of Wellington (First Nations individual) **38**–41

Eaglehawk, Victoria **6**, 125, 194, 244
demographics 181–182, 187–188
employment in 181–182, 188, 192
mining in 182, 187–188
religion in 161–163, 166, 184
schools in 121, 142
Edgars Plains Station 32, 34, **42**
education 53–56, 81, 121, 158
Catholic 136, 141–143, 145–147, 185–186, 191, 193, 199
Jewish 81, 158
Protestant 136, 141–142, 176, 184, 198
state sponsored 141–143, 145–146, 163, 185–186, 194
employment 35, 133, 181–184, 207–208, 227
Catholicism and 145, 147–148, 167, 183, 186, 204, 207
First Nations and 32–33, 35–44, 47, 52–53
government provided 148, 181, 191, 194, 207, 221
Irish and 139, 143, 145, 147–148, 167
Islam and 226–227
Judaism and 89–92
in Melbourne, Victoria 151, 187
Methodism and 170, 178, 183–184
Presbyterianism and 114, 121, 127, 193
professionals 65, 181–182
unemployment and 187, 192, 194
women and 53, 121, 123–124, 127
see also education; mining
Emu Point Joss House 10, 211–216, 228
see also Chinese—religious practices
English Reformation (theological movement) 20, 23, 63
see also Christianity
environment
drought 51, 112–113, 140, 143, 194
land management and 5, 27–30, 41–51
mining impact on 15, 24–25, 115, 140, 195
water management and 48–51, 105–106, 143
European settlement *see* white invasion and settlement

Fahey family 152–153
famine 134–135, 138–139, 145
Farmer, Tommy (First Nations individual) 17
farming and pastoralism 27–32, 43–58, 145–151, 191
by First Nations People 32–33, 35–44, 47, 52–53

by Irish 139, 143, 145, 147–148, 150–151, 182, 199
see also legislation; stations
Federal Government *see* government
Fernyhurst Station *see* Edgar Plains Station
First Nations people
Christianity and 17, 29, 33
Country and 5, 15–16, 25–28, 32–33, 38–39, 43–44, 56–58, 247, 249
dispossession of 4–5, 8, 16–17, 25, 27–58, 62, 247
employed by whites 32–33, 35–44, 47, 52–53
forced removal from land 29, 32, 35, 56–58, 247
languages *see* Dja Dja Wurrung
relationships with white settlers 30, 32–34, **37**, **42**, 47, 52–53
traditional lifeways 5, 8, 16, 27–30, 38–41, 44, 48, 51, 66
views on 39–41, 52–53, 56–57, 245
violence against 5, 16, 29–30, 32, 35, 57–58, 247
women 29, 33–36, 40–41, 56–58
fundraising *see* charity
funerals 135, 140, 149
see also death

Galway, Mick 40, **42**, 56
Gannawarra Station 30–31, 35, 40, 44–47, 52, 56–57
gold; goldfields, gold mining *see* mining
Golden Square Methodist Church 188–189, 195–198
Goold, Bishop James (later Archbishop) 133, 136, 140–142, 145–146
see also Catholicism
government
Commonwealth (including Federal) 20, 150, 186–187, 194–195, 207, 224, 231
Victorian 29, 43, 62, 70–71, 73–74, 79, 142, 191–192, 194
see also legal system; legislation
Great Stupa of Universal Compassion **6**, 11, 22, 217–222
see also Buddhism
Green, Reverend John 33, 56–57
Greene, Molesworth 31, 34, 56
Green family 220, 222–223
Guan-di (Chinese deity) 213
see also Chinese—religious practices
Gunbower Station 40, **42**, 45–50

Hamburger, Isidore *see* Herman, Solomon
Hamilton, Jane (*née* Brown) 111–129
Hamilton family 111–129
health
Bendigo Benevolent Asylum 1, 73, 76, 138–139, 185
Bendigo Hospital 1, 73–79, 138–139, 185
disease 77, 112–113, 115–**117**, 173–174, 178
healthcare facilities 1, 55, 73–79, 138–139, 185
Hospital Sundays (charity event) 73–79
mining and 115–116, 172–174, 178
see also childbirth; death
heritage activism 214–216
heritage tourism 217–220
Herman, Leah see Oxlade, Elizabeth
Herman, Samuel 88, 155–156
Herman, Solomon 9, 155–159
Hinduism 61, 66, 69–71, 107, 239
Hoey family 114–**117**, 121–129

Hoi Gong Ceremony (Chinese) 214–215, 249
see also Chinese—religious practices
Holloway, Edward **31**, 43
Holloway, George **31**, 36–37, 39, 41
Holloway, Hannah *see* Booth, Hannah
Holloway, John 28, **31**, 35–37, 43, 45–50, 53
Holmes, Alice 40, 56
Hoskin, Julie 232–233, 235–236
Hospital Sundays (charity event) 73–79
see also charity; health

illness *see* health
immigration *see* migration
Immigration Restriction Act 1901 (IRA) 224–225, 241
see also White Australia Policy
interfaith interaction
conflict and 8–20, 22, 131, 135–136, 138, 161–178, 185–187, 220–221, 225–242
cooperation and 2–4, 8, 15, 73–79, 139, 207–208, 230
fostering social cohesion 2–4, 73–79, 86–87, 220–221, 232, 243–247
marriage 9–10, 57–58, 138, 145, 155–159, 185, 207–208
personal vs institutional 2, 20, 171–172, 185–187, 207–208, 245
public spaces and 22, 25, 59–79, 150, 223–225, 234, 242, 245
as spectacle 2–4, 11, 60–61, 67, 77–79, 214–216, 219–220, 223, 243–245
support for 2–4, 171, 173–175, 220–221, 230–234, 240
viewed as threat 13, 25, 69–70, 78, 135–136, 161, 185, 225–242
see also social cohesion
Irish
Catholicism 20, 134–136, 146–147, 152–153
demographics 134–135, 138–139, 182
employment and 139, 143, 145, 147–148, 167
famine and 134–135, 138–139
farming and 139, 143, 145, 147–148, 150–151, 182, 199
migrants 123, 131–153, 182
miners 138, 143, 145, 148, 167, 182
women 134, 138–139, 156
Ironbark Chinese Camp 212–213
Islam
anti-Islam sentiment 229–233, 235–242
demographics 225, 227–228, 237–238
employment and 226–227
identity and 239–242
Islamic Community Centre 228, 234, 242
migrants 19, 227, 237–238
mosques 11, 225–242
religious practices of 19, 223–225, 227–228, 239, 242
trade with First Nations people 19, 226
views on 13, 223–224, 229–232, 238
Islamic Community Centre 228, 234, 242
see also Islam
Islamophobia *see* Islam

joss house *see* Chinese—religious practices
Judaism, 8–9, 18, 81–101, 155–159
antisemitism and, 71, 82, 100, **104**, 107, 171
in Ballarat, Victoria, 85–88, 90–93, 98–101, 155–156

migrants, 18, 81–101
Reform Judaism, 82, 95–98
religious practices, 18, 82–85, 88–96, 158, 249
synagogues, 81–88, 93–101, 158
views on, 95–96, 100
women and, 9, 84, 90–91, 93, 155–159

kashrut see Judaism—religious practices
Kerang, Victoria **6**, 38, 40–41, 50, 53–55
Kerr, Emma *see* Campbell, Emma
kosher see Judaism—religious practices

Laanecoorie 8, 15, 27, **48–49**, 51, 132
Lake Boga Station 38, 47, 52–53
land Acts 43–44, 145
see also legislation
land management 5, 27–30, 41–51
see also legislation
language 60–69, 212
First Nations 5, 17, 66, 243, 249
racist and racialised language 36, 39–41, 229–230, 236
Lanuremin (First Nations individual) **39**, 41–42
law and law courts *see* legal system; legislation
Leaghur Station 31, **42**, 48, 50
legal system 59–71, 89, 90–91, 231–232, 235, 247
British influence in 17, 62–65, 90, 164
discrimination in 24, 60–63, 67–71, 90–91, 224, 241, 249
religion under 20–21, 59–71, 90–92, 231–232, 235
as symbol of imperial power 60–61, 63–65, 71
see also crime; legislation; White Australia Policy
legislation 43–44, 51, 67, 89–91, 142–146, 186, 216, 224–225
see also crime; legal system
Lodden River *see* Laanecoorie
Lutherans 75, 179, 184

Marks, Harry 1–4
marriage 9–10, 53–**54**, 57–58, 137–139, 155–159, 184–185, 207–208
McCarthy, Bishop John 186, 190–191
see also Catholicism
medicine *see* health
Melbourne, Victoria **6**, 175, 181
Anglicans in 189–190
Catholicism in 133–134, 143, 150–152, 193
Chinese in 234
courts 65, 70
employment 151, 187
Islam in 227–228, 237, 239
Judaism in 74, 81, 83, 85, 88, 94–95
migration to 83, 187, 189
Methodism 165–169, 183, 188, 195
anti-Methodist views 173–175, 177
Cornish Methodists 165–168, 170, 179, 184, 200
demographics 169, 172, **180**, 188, 192, 195, 200–201
employment 170, 178, 183–184
miners 163–166, 168, 179, 183–184
politics and 150, 161–165, 171–176, 178
Primitive Methodists 166–169, 179, 183, 188
as social community 166, 168–173, 176, 195–196
Wesleyans 53–55, 75, 166–169, 175, 183–184, 188

migration
Chinese 18–19, 67, 211, 216
Cornish 165–168, 170, 179, 184–185, 200
demographics 180, 185, 225, 227, 238
Irish 123, 131–153, 182
Islamic 19, 227–228, 237–238
Jewish 18, 81–101
outmigration 99, 124, 128, 167, 187–190
schemes to assist 134, 138, 185
viewed as threat 207, 224–225, 241–242
women 111–129, 138, 155–159, 182, 185
see also White Australia Policy
Mindi, the giant serpent (First Nations ancestral being) 16–17
mining 23, 165–166, 174–175, 179–184, 187, 213
Chinese miners 18–19, 108, 213
Cornish miners 165–168, 170, 179, 184–185, 200
decline in 24, 126, 143, 167, 180–184, 187–191, 200
effect on Aboriginal people 4–5, 24–25
environmental impact of 15, 24–25, 115, 140, 164, 195
health and 111–116, 172–174, 178
Irish miners 138, 143, 145, 148, 167, 182
Jewish 89–91
quartz reef mining 5, 126, 140, 143, 166, 187
wealth and 136–137, 168, 174, 181–183, 187, 244
see also employment
Moore, Mary *see* Watson, Mary
Morepin *see* Duke of Wellington
mosques, 11, 225–242
see also Islam
Mount Hope Station 31, 35, 40, **42**, 44–46, 48, 56–57
Moy, Ah 59–60, 64–65, 67, 69
Muslims *see* Islam

native animals 47, 58
native plants 58, 236

O'Hoy, Dennis 214– 216
see also Emu Point Joss House
O'Hoy, Louey 214
Old Sandhurst Town (former tourist site) 11, 217–222
Oxlade, Elizabeth 9, 155–159

pastoralism and farming 27–32, 43–58, 145–151, 191
by First Nations People 32–33, 35–44, 47, 52–53
by Irish 139, 143, 145, 147–148, 150–151, 182, 199
see also legislation; stations (pastoral)
patriotism
for Britain 18, 82–84, 94–96, 101, 162, 164–165, 172, 189–190, 244
racism and 229, 232–236, 239
Patterson, John (son of Emma Kerr/Curr) 34–35
Pental Island Station 38, **42**, 44, 46
Pericoota Station 38, **42**, 45, 48, 52
philanthropy *see* charity
politics 14, 141–142, 162, 192, 207, 231, 235–236
Catholicism and 146–148, 150, 163, 186
Protestants and 161–162, 164–165, 168, 176–177, 186
see also legal system; legislation
Port Phillip District, Victoria 29–30, 33, 103
Presbyterianism
church building 184, 193

demographics 17, **180**, 183, 188, 192–193, 195, 197
education 114, 121, 123, 193
employment and 114, 121, 127, 193
migrants 111–129
religious practices of 18, 113, **117**–121, 124–127, 129, 165
St Andrew's Church 75, 193
protectorates *see* Aboriginal protectorates
Protestantism 20–23, 85, 90–91, 161–178, 186, 188, 199–201
as assumed default British religion 20, 88–91, 97–98, 162, 164, 178, 224, 245
British identity and 82, 162, 164–165, 189, 190

racism 2, 41, 207
antisemitism 71, 82, 100, **104**, 107, 171
in cemeteries **104**, 107–109
against Chinese 3, 67, 69–70, **104**, 107–109, 213–214, 216
against First Nations people 4–5, 16–17, 30, 32–33, 39–41, 52, 56–58, 62, 247
identity and 239–242
against Islam 107, 229–233, 235–242
in legal system 24, 59–71, 90–91, 224, 241, 249
protests against 230, 232–235
racist and racialised language 36, 39–41, 229–230, 236
violence and 30, 32, 213, 231, 238
see also discrimination
Reformation (theological movement) *see* English Reformation
Reform Judaism 82, 95–98
see also Judaism
religious decline *see* secularisation
Reville, Father Stephen (later Bishop) 132, 144–150, 152–153, 186
see also Catholicism
Robinson *see* Lanuremin
Rosalind Park **7**, 24–25, 64, 75, 224, 235, 242

Sacred Heart Cathedral (Roman Catholic) **7**, 10, 22, 190, 203–209, 224
see also Catholicism
sanitation *see* health
Scotland 111–114, 120–121, 123–124, 126, 128
secularisation 21–22, 70, 161–201, 208–209
selection *see* pastoralism and farming
Serpentine Station **31–32**, **38–39**, 41–42, **47**, **48–49**, **50**
settlers *see* white invasion and settlement
Sharia law *see* Islam
social cohesion 13–25, 90, 186, 237–238, 243
fostered through celebration 2–4, 73–79, 86–87, 220–221, 232, 243–247
viewed as threat 13, 25, 69–70, 78, 135–136, 161, 185, 225–242
see also interfaith interaction
social justice 74, 150, 163, 167–178, 197–198, 203–206, 208–209
see also charity
squatters *see* pastoralism and farming
St Andrew's Church (Presbyterian) 75, 193
stations (pastoral) 28–53, 56–58
St Kilian's Parish (Catholic) 75, 137–141, 148–149
see also Catholicism
St Paul's Cathedral (Anglican) 75, 184, 190, 196
synagogues **7**, 81–88, 93–101, 158
see also Judaism

Tandarra Station 40, **42**, 45–46
Tanne baluk (First Nations people) 32
Taoism 66, 213
see also Chinese—religious practices
tourism 11, 214, 216–222
Tragowel Station 28–29, 31, 35–51, **54–56**, 58
United Patriots Front (UPF) 232–236
Uniting Church 10, **180**, 197–198, 201, 230
see also Protestantism

Victorian Civil and Administrative Tribunal (VCAT) 231–232, 235
see also legal system
Victorian State Government
see government
violence 213–214, 216, 229, 231–232, 238
against First Nations people 5, 16, 29–30, 32, 35, 57–58, 247
see also crime

Wadawurrung (First Nations people) 15–16
water management 48–51, 105–106, 143
see also drought; legislation
Watson, Mary (*née* Moore) 52–53
Watson, Samuel 52–53
White Australia Policy 24, 71, 216, 224–225, 241, 249
see also *Immigration Restriction Act*
White Hills Cemetery **6**, 10, 103–109, **117**
see also death
white invasion and settlement
British patriotism and 18, 82–84, 94–96, 101, 162, 164–165, 172, 189–190, 244
employment of First Nations people 32–33, 35–44, 47, 52–53
imperialism displays 1–2, 11, 24, 60–70, 164–165, 244
land management 5, 27, 29–30, 41–51
relationships with First Nations people 30, 32–44, 47, 52–53
views on First Nations people 30, 36, 39–41, 56–57, 245
water management 48–51, 105–106, 143
see also Britain; drought; legislation; pastoralism; violence
women 41, 52–53, 84, 111–129, 134–135, 138–139, 151, 155–159, 185
and motherhood 9, 111–112, 116, 119, 121, 123–125, 129
as breadwinners 121, 123, 127, 129
death and 58, 84, 114–**117**, 121, 151
employment and 53, 121, 123–124, 127
First Nations 33–36, 40–41, 52, 56–57
see also childbirth
World War I 9, 180, 182, 186–187, 189, 191
World War II 100, 194, 198, 200
Worrall, Reverend Henry 161–162, 165, 175–176
see also Methodism

Young Christian Workers (YCW) 203–206, 209
Yung baluk (First Nations people) 32

www.ingramcontent.com/pod-product-compliance
Lightning Source LLC
LaVergne TN
LVHW020507100826
845148LV00003B/720

* 9 7 8 1 7 6 0 4 6 7 2 7 2 *